A Year of Days

with the Book of Common Prayer

A Year of Days

with the Book of Common Prayer

Bishop Edmond Lee Browning

The Ballantine Publishing Group ❖ New York

A Ballantine Book
Published by The Ballantine Publishing Group

http:\\www.randomhouse.com

LIBRARY OF CONGRESS CATALOGING-IN-PUBLICATION DATA
Browning, Edmond Lee.
   A year of days with the Book of common prayer / Edmond
Lee Browning. — 1st Ballantine Books ed.
      p.   cm.
   ISBN 0-345-41682-1 (paper)
   1. Devotional calendars. I. Episcopal Church. Book of
common prayer (1979)   II. Title.
BV4811.B756   1997
242'.2—dc21
                                                           97-21593
                                                              CIP

Text design by Holly Johnson

Cover design by Cathy Colbert

Cover art © Pearl Beach/Stockworks Stock Illustration

Manufactured in the United States of America

First Edition: November 1997

10   9   8   7   6   5

To Patti
You have put gladness in my heart. . . .
—*PSALM 4:7*

Some of these pieces have appeared in Forward Day by Day, a publication of Forward Movement. I am grateful for their permission to reprint them here.

January 1

They will climb from height to height. . . . —PSALM 84:6, p. 708

The Cathedral of St. John the Divine in New York City boasts the tallest crossing of any cathedral in the world. At a youth retreat one year, Philip Petit, the famous French aerialist, invited a volunteer to cross it on the tightwire with him. A young girl volunteered, and back and forth they went, his sure feet making their way out over the empty air, the girl clinging to his back, terrified but exhilarated.

Afterward, she said she never would have believed that she could do such a thing. She said that she had had to trust the tightrope walker completely, to trust her life to him. She said that she had learned something about trusting in God from that experience that she would never forget.

I'll bet she did. Perhaps you and I will never have such a graphic lesson in trust—I'm all but certain I will not!—as that young girl had. But that kind of trust is exactly what we need if we are to live our lives in any degree of spiritual freedom. God does not keep us from danger; there is plenty of that in our lives. But trust in God lets us walk in those dangerous places with confidence. We are not alone in danger. High above a thousand-foot drop on a thin wire, God is carrying us. Terrified sometimes, but exhilarated, we are learning how to trust.

January 2

. . . let the whole world see and know that things which were cast down are being raised up. . . . —COLLECT FOR THE ORDINATION OF A PRIEST, p. 528

The presence of God in my life, once I acknowledge it, is not something I can later decide not to know. Once I begin my walk in company with Christ—whether I walk it well or not—I am never again without him. And the walk I walk with Christ is not along a road with no rocks in it. When Jesus healed people, we are not told that he healed them and that thenceforth they never got sick again or never had any problems in their lives or never died. They must have died—or they'd still be here!

They were not restored to a magical life outside the realities of mortal existence. They were returned to their lives, their frustrating, exhausting lives, to lives studded with joys and sorrows—like our lives are. The hand of God that touched them didn't yank them out of this reality and into another. They went on to live and die in the world of history in which we live and in which we will die.

The presence of sorrows and ambiguities in human life is not a sign of the absence of God. Life *is* hard. Life is terribly uncertain. But we know that we are not alone. That our lives don't hang, unprotected, tossed to and fro by the anonymous winds of indifferent space. That God contains our lives.

January 3

Dear Friends: The birth of a child is a joyous and solemn occasion in the life of a family. —THANKSGIVING FOR THE BIRTH OR ADOPTION OF A CHILD, p. 440

I have the good fortune to be a grandfather. Twelve times. Oh, sure, I loved being a father. There were so many of us Brownings—Patti and I have five children—so much to keep track of with the comings and goings of all of them through the years, that I never really thought much about becoming a grandfather until the reality of it was almost upon me. I was unprepared for the emotional power of seeing that first tiny member of our next generation. I often wonder exactly what it is about the grandchildren that moves me so. Part of the power is that I myself have changed since the early days of fatherhood. I know more than I did then—more of the good and more of the bad of life. And part of the power is that there are things about my grandchildren that put me in mind of my children's youth—a look, a way of walking, some little habit that reminds me suddenly of a long-ago child. A grandchild permits a certain amount of going back in time.

But most of all, my grandchildren bring me face-to-face with the future. They will inherit a world that will little resemble the one I live in. They will inherit the earth from my generation. I didn't think about this as much when their parents were small as I do now. Too busy, I guess—too busy worrying about their day-to-day concerns. But I think of it now.

January 4

In all that you do, you are to nourish Christ's people. . . . —THE *ORDINATION OF A PRIEST,* p. 531

If ever there were a time when the world needed our attention, it is now. If ever there were a time when the harvest was ready and the window of opportunity very brief, now is the time. Now is the time when American culture, sick to death of its crass and bloated materialism, cries very loudly for spiritual nourishment. Look at the best-selling books about secret, magic prophecies. Look at the desperation with which people follow each new spiritual fad: the crystal readings, the New Age gurus. Look at how people long for values, and how efficiently an astute politician can exploit that longing. People long for news of a reality that imparts spiritual meaning to the discouraging reality in which we live. People long for news of God.

And then look at the Church: We, the custodians of this good news, are too busy arguing with one another over our internal arrangements to answer this longing with the only thing that can satisfy it. We are almost completely self-absorbed. It will not be long before the world concludes we are uninterested in the spiritual life to which they are beginning to feel the stirrings of a call. We will leave them to their crystals and their gurus if we abdicate our God-given responsibility to reach out to them. We haven't much time.

January 5

Grant that we may not so much seek to be consoled as to console. . . . —A PRAYER ATTRIBUTED TO ST. FRANCIS, p. 833

Sometimes, I will look back at an especially rocky stretch in my journey and wonder how on earth I made it through. Life sure can be hard. And cruel. Will I stand here today and tell you that it doesn't hurt? I would be lying. But will I stand here and tell you that we have no health left, no strength? That, too, would be a lie, for we have one another in Christ, and nothing that can happen to us can defeat the power of God working through the community of love.

What I know is this: It is precisely in the places in which we have known pain that we have known strength. Scar tissue is tougher than other tissue. By God's grace, we grow together in hard times—because we have to. Necessity impels us. And we are shaped by this growth. We are shaped and strengthened much more by surviving the hard times than we ever are by the genteel kinds of education we might prefer. For an individual or for an institution, it is the same: adversity shapes and strengthens us. We might wish with all our hearts that things were otherwise, but we cannot deny what we have learned and how we have grown from what we have endured. We shrink when we hide ourselves away with our sorrows. We grow when we share them with others.

January 6

For only in you can we live in safety. —SUFFRAGES FOR
MORNING PRAYER, p. 97

"Bring me word, that I may also go and pay him homage."
When I was a boy, this remark of King Herod always sent
chills up my spine. It was so false, so evil. It was like the radio
dramas I never missed on Saturday afternoon: the unsus-
pecting hero might walk right into an ambush. "Don't go in
that house," I would say out loud, "the bad guys are in there!"

The stories of Jesus' life were told for years before they
were written down. People loved stories and honored story-
tellers in a way that I imagine was very like the way we used to
hang on every word of those old radio shows. We saw
nothing with our eyes, but our imaginations were hard at
work, and we saw with our minds.

In this story, as in the radio shows, the hero was saved in
the nick of time. We hear the villainous Herod laying his terrible plot, we hear the wise—but maybe a little gullible?—old
kings falling for his line. Don't do it! And they don't. They are
warned.

There is a dramatic imagination in us that thrills to these
close calls. We never tire of hearing them. They are preserved
for us so that we will remember what a wonder our redemption is, how clearly it shows the hand of God at work in the
world.

January 7

O God, whose mercies cannot be numbered . . . —COLLECT AT
THE BURIAL OF AN ADULT, p. 493

God does not cheapen himself or us by offering us easy answers
to the anguished *Why?* that we who are human cannot help
but ask. The mystery of life and death and suffering remains a
mystery in all human generations, and it is no less a mystery
for us. We don't get a quick fix from our faith.

But we do encounter a God who sits patiently beside us in
grief—silently, usually, like an orthodox Jew sitting shivah
with his bereaved friend, offering no words to explain away a
mystery that is beyond words. God sits with us in our sorrow.
In the days and weeks after a loss, as we sit together in the
silence, something new begins to creep into our consciousness. The faith that has sustained our whole lives will begin to
knit our sorrow over this death together with what we believe
about the life to come. Faith and experience will knit together
like a broken bone knits together as time passes. We begin to
be able to see for ourselves what is already a reality for those
who have gone on ahead of us, something the tears of early
bereavement make it hard for us to see at first. They begin to
appear in our vision of heaven, taking their place in the communion of the saints. We begin to feel their presence, not just
their absence. Once again, the resurrection faith to which we
cling gently bathes our hearts, and our hearts are healed.

January 8

Let us with gladness present the offerings and oblations of our life and labor to the Lord. —OFFERTORY SENTENCE FOR THE HOLY EUCHARIST, p. 377

It sounds crazy, to someone accustomed to the cynicism which surrounds us, to assert that wealth and security is to be found in giving money away. "That's just crazy," he responds, clasping what he has closer to his chest. "I have to prepare, take care of myself; you just never know. Best to be careful, you can never be sure." Clasping his treasure to his chest like that, though, his arms are not free to embrace his life. He can embrace nothing. He cannot enjoy the fruits of his labor, however wealthy he may have become: joy will elude him until he comes to know the God of life as someone worthy of his trust. All the money in the world will not bring him peace.

Self-fulfilling prophecy: spiritual attitudes are always self-fulfilling. Suspect the world and you will find abundant reasons to suspect. Greet the world with open arms and an open heart, though, and you will never cease to find reasons to rejoice. The degree of a person's wealth has almost nothing to do with a person's sense of security and joy. That is a spiritual matter, not a fiscal one.

January 9

Let your way be known upon earth; your saving health among all nations. —SUFFRAGES FOR EVENING PRAYER, p. 122

Anybody can be saved. God's love is universal. Believing is not first and foremost a matter of who you are and where you're from.

This matters to us a lot these days, as we struggle with the relationship between our faith and our culture. Some of what we accepted as essential to the faith for many, many years was in reality nothing more than good manners for Western society. Some of our givens are really aesthetic choices, not theological judgments. We have, on occasion, taken local practice within a European context and dressed it up in the clothing of absolute and normative truth for all time and all places. Facing this can be a painful and divisive thing for people of faith, but the pain of it is a growing, athletic pain, the pain of muscles and sinews stretching and growing larger and stronger. We are now in the process of discerning one from the other, of learning again, as the lovers of tradition have often had to learn, what must remain and what can change. In this age of lightning communication, we are helped in this process by the witness of people from other cultures which confronts us at every turn. We are only at the beginning of a process which will revise our understanding of ourselves, add lenses to our self-examination other than the European one to which we have become so accustomed.

January 10

Deliver us from the presumption of coming to this table for solace only, and not for strength. . . . —*EUCHARISTIC PRAYER C,* p. 372

I travel a good deal. I just returned from a visit to the Church in Burma. Before that, I was in Central America. Many of these churches are in countries where there has been tremendous suffering in recent years: civil wars, repressive governments, crippling economic conditions. Terrible problems we do not have here. The people cling together and support one another. They take serious risks for their faith. These churches feel to me like what I imagine the early Church to have been, that community of people who worked tirelessly to bring in the harvest of God because they didn't think they had much time. The Church is energized and growing where that sense of urgency prevails. And where it does not, where people think we've got all the time in the world, where the government does not send soldiers to close our doors and close our mouths? Strangely passive, almost bored, self-absorbed.

I want us to remember the urgency our forebears felt, that sense that there isn't much time, that we must make every minute count. There really *isn't* much time. Every minute *does* count. A hungry world waits for the nourishment of God, and we are called to bear fruit for its nurture.

January 11

. . . so that we who are wearied by the changes and chances of this life may rest in your eternal changelessness . . . —*COLLECT AT COMPLINE,* p. 133

God is present in the midst of change. Change can be painful sometimes, as growth is always painful some of the time. The Church itself changes. Already it hears voices it did not let itself hear before: the voices of women, of children; the voices of poverty; the voices of Asian and African and Caribbean Christians who struggle to hold onto a lively faith distinct from the ethos of the colonized; the voices of African American Christians whose forebears first heard the gospel as enslaved people, and who know that they must be vigilant against its perversion ever again in the service of oppression; the voices of gay and lesbian Christians whose work and money has always been welcome in the Church while their experience has always been ignored. There will be more voices as the years unfold.

Because this process of listening is so difficult, the wider culture tires of it quickly. People of faith are charged *not* to tire of it, to persevere in listening to the voices of those yet unheard, with guiding a response to them that is loving and brave enough to receive truth as well as impart it. It has felt natural to us for a long time to bring Christ to the world. We know and like the feeling of our own largesse. It will be more difficult, sometimes, to receive Christ from the world.

January 12

Grant that all married persons who have witnessed these vows may find their lives strengthened and their loyalties confirmed.
—CELEBRATION AND BLESSING OF A MARRIAGE, p. 430

The person in my life who has taught me the most about God is my wife.

There are so many things about the way Patti has lived her life that has shown God to me. Those of us who speak of God in public a lot can slip dangerously into thinking of ourselves and our careers as centerpieces. We can forget that, although we do represent God to others, they also represent God to us.

I remember very clearly that time in our marriage—it was when we were overseas—when I was very full of my work and the building of the Church in that difficult place. I was becoming uninvolved in our family and in our relationship. And Patti called me to account. She insisted that I see that I wasn't God for the Church, and that both the Church and our family would suffer terribly if I went on living as if I were.

That was a crossroads for us. If she had allowed me to hide piously behind my important work, I really don't know where we would be today as a family. She was Christlike in that moment, prophetic: holding up God's truth to someone who didn't want to see it. Kind of like Jesus overturning the moneychangers in the temple. By no means was she meek. And in her fierceness about this uncomfortable truth, she made me much more than I had been before.

January 13

From all oppression, conspiracy, and rebellion . . . Good Lord, deliver us. —THE GREAT LITANY, p. 149

We live in an age that finds it hard to trust. Cynical and unsure, suspicious and pessimistic, unable to enjoy the gifts we have when they are right before our eyes, we vote lethargically or not at all, despair of our political choices, assume the moral bankruptcy of every institution in our society. Weird conspiracy theories attract a following: that the government is spying on us, that supermarket bar codes are really sophisticated mind-control devices, that AIDS is the product of germ warfare— crazy things. We live in an age that finds it easy to suspect.

This is too bad. The spiritual life is all about trust. We grow spiritually by learning to trust in God, not by covering our flank and greeting every new occurrence with suspicion and mistrust. No one ever grew that way. Cynicism does not make us grow; it makes us shrink. The healing love of Christ flows abundantly over all of us, but only the open-hearted can avail themselves of it. They know how trust is rewarded, how possible life seems when one dares to believe and acts on that faith. They know the sweetness of living a confident life: the joy of such a life is self-fulfilling prophecy. The more I trust in God's goodness at work in my world, the more evidences of it I will see and the more opportunities for its exercise I will create. Blessing begets blessing in the economy of God.

January 14

Be our light in the darkness. . . . —COLLECT FOR AID AGAINST PERILS AT EVENING PRAYER, p. 123

It can be disconcerting to be changed by one another. When we encounter another in any kind of depth at all, we're venturing into the unknown, and most of us are reluctant to do that. But think for a moment: there are occasions in life in which we do volunteer to be changed by community. When we marry we do that; when people get married, they do so with some understanding that their lives will not be the same as they were when they were single. They may not grasp just how different their lives will be, and their deepening awareness of the extent of it may be something of a jolt, but brides and grooms do know when they begin that they are starting out on a new life, a new way of being themselves. And when a child is expected, we know that life will be forever changed. Again, we may not grasp until later just how total that change will be, but we know that we will be different people because we are moms and dads than we were before. I can go further: Patti and I have five children, and I can honestly say that each one of them made me different from what I was before his or her arrival in our family. Made all of us into different people. Every time, the culture of our family became more complex, richer. Every time, something precious and unique was added to the mix. And all of us were changed.

January 15

MARTIN LUTHER KING, JR.

*Set us free, O God. . . . —COLLECT FOR THE FIFTH SUNDAY
AFTER THE EPIPHANY,* p. 164

Most people you meet don't think the poor in spirit are blessed, don't think that the meek will inherit the earth.

I am reminded of exactly why it is that the poor in spirit are blessed: they are the ones who know they need blessing. Those who think they're rich don't feel a need. Those who think they're free never ask to be released.

I have several friends who are in recovery from addiction. They have all told me the same thing: it was not until they realized the totality of their bondage that they could begin to take the first halting steps toward freedom. "When I was drinking," one man told me, "I thought I was completely in control of my behavior. I told myself I could stop anytime I wanted to, and I believed that. I believed it even after I had lost my wife and the respect of my children because of my drinking. It was only when I admitted that this was a lie that I could begin to get better."

His insistence on his own freedom kept him in chains. We are not free just because we think we're free. Sometimes that belief enslaves a person as totally as any system of institutional slavery ever could. It is not always our weakness that throws up obstacles in our path toward God; sometimes it is our consciousness of our own strength.

January 16

Keep us, O Lord, as the apple of your eye. . . . —COMPLINE,
p. 132

I love to watch my grandchildren play together. They live in different parts of the country, but every once in a while we manage to get the whole tribe in one place. It's amazing; they go for months and months without laying eyes on each other, and in five minutes they're tearing around the yard whooping and yelping and laughing so you can hardly hear yourself think. They are related. They are instant companions. Their parents sit in lawn chairs with us while they run around, and we talk about nothing much. From time to time one of them runs up and asks a question, or demands that we all look at a cartwheel or settle an argument, and then they run away again. God was good enough to us to allow us to sit among these generations, good enough to them to give them the memory of it to carry throughout their lives. God is on their side, and in their lives it is easy to see it. How amazing the process of growth is! And how good at it they are—give them half a chance and they blossom and bear fruit so abundantly, learn so quickly, love so easily, play so hard. And how good it makes us feel to see it.

But God is on the side of all children. Bless them all: I have lived more of my life than I have yet to live. They are just at the beginning of theirs. Life can be hard, but it is a beautiful, beautiful thing. It hurts us all when it is anything short of beautiful for a child.

January 17

. . . you hate nothing you have made. . . . —COLLECT FOR ASH WEDNESDAY, p. 264

Now, at the close of the second two thousand years of Christian faith, we are experiencing the life-changing power of history at every turn. My church, which has reflexively interpreted its world from a position safely within the categories of European experience—specifically, English experience, as if God himself were English—confronts the fact that an increasing number of its members do not claim that experience as their heritage. A church that has been so identified with the world view of white people that for years it didn't know there *was* another worldview now notices that a majority of its members worldwide are people of color. A church that has emphasized the experience and interpretation of males now confronts the experience and interpretation of women, and it notices that they are sometimes quite different. No wonder we find life together difficult sometimes.

I know that there are those who wish that we could return to a time when we all agreed. But I think we look backwards at the remembered unanimity of those days and forget that their unanimity arose in large measure from the fact that there were large segments of God's children with whom we were not living in community. Of course you all agree when you surround yourself only with people who resemble you! But when the diversity of the infinitely varied family of God is honored, there are going to be bumps in the road.

January 18

. . . so that in unity and peace we may proclaim the one truth . . .
—COLLECT FOR THE CONFESSION OF ST. PETER, p. 238

We look back at earlier periods in history, and they look simpler, better, more moral. People often say they wish we were more like people used to be then. But it is all right that we are not like them. The project of Christian faith is not to find a golden age of the past and live in it, but to live the authentic life of Christ in the age we're in. God alone is eternal and unchanging; we who live on the earth experience change, and our institutions change with us. Even the church of antiquity, which we sometimes imagine to have been a place of sweet consensus and certainty, was anything but that. It was wracked with controversies every bit as hard to handle as ours. Each age has its own agenda: the issues were different, but passions ran as high then as they do among us today. We must not forget, when we long for the imagined consensus of another age, that people killed each other in those days over whether or not the Father and the Son were coeternal. And that in every age—perhaps not with actual bloodshed, but certainly with vehemence and passion—issues that mattered to the Church have been divisive and often painful.

Of course feelings run high when we discuss important things. We care passionately about them, which is exactly as it should be. And has always been.

January 19

By everlasting life, we mean a new existence. . . . —CATECHISM,
p. 862

You probably know that there are stories in other religions
about people being raised from the dead. Osiris, for instance,
one of the gods of the ancient Egyptians, is killed and cut into
little pieces, and then the pieces all come back together and
he lives again. Persephone, daughter of the Greek goddess
Demeter, comes back from the land of the dead every spring,
and the flowers and trees celebrate. Ours is not the only faith
that has stories about a god who rises from the dead.

But ours is the only one whose rising God takes death
upon himself *for our sake*. The other gods of the ancient world
are in it for themselves. Their story is just that: their story. If
something good happens out of their rising—like the coming
of spring—it is a by-product. It is not expressly purposed for
our good. It is not for us. It is for them. The ancient world
believed that the gods created humankind to serve them, to
amuse them, to take part in their drama. Our belief is different. We believe that God created us in order to love us. We
are made for the purpose of love. It is this act of love which
defines us.

So we do not lose heart. We are not playthings in the
hand of a powerful and indifferent God. We are sons and
daughters, brothers and sisters. We are a new creation.

January 20

Why do we pray for the dead? —CATECHISM, p. 862

Because we still love them and they still love us.

It's not because they need something from us. They are part of a reality we are also part of; the difference between them and us is that they know what it is and we don't. We make up things about it, of course—pave its streets with gold, imagine its beauty—but we don't know a thing about it.

But we do know them. Human beings are created from love: the love of God, the love of parents. The love that we feel for one another is what hurts us when someone dies. If we had no love, we wouldn't miss them as we do.

Sometimes I think about people who have gone on before—my dad, my brother, Patti's parents. I still love them all. I wonder what their existence is like, and I haven't a clue. But I do know that this energy between us, the energy we call love, is eternal. The soul is made of it, and it is set free from all the compromises and disappointments we experience when the soul leaves the body. Do they still love us? Do they miss us as we miss them? They don't have to miss us, for we are present in their hearts with much greater power than we ever were when they were alive. They are now perfected, made entirely of the love we shared on earth and continue to share.

January 21

. . . you have created us male and female. . . . —*CELEBRATION AND BLESSING OF A MARRIAGE,* p. 425

Why do we have weddings in churches? Why do our brothers and sisters who are gay or lesbian long for rites which recognize their loves, their ways of being family, and why does this discussion touch all of us at so deep a level of our theological and emotional being? The family is a human institution, all right, but we know from a place deep within us that it is much, much more. Why do we know this?

The Holy Family, which we remember with such sweetness, the young mother with her baby, the older father looking on, the angels and the shepherds and the animals all adoring—that family's life was hard. It was a family that represented something other than the norm in the society in which Mary and Joseph lived, and in that small town there was some scandal attached to their situation. There had been talk of divorce before the baby came, remember? And there would be conflict in that family. Life together can be hard. But life is also holy—all of it. Our life is not divided into the religious and the nonreligious. It is all sacred, not in the false pastels of sentimental memory and nostalgia, but in the brisk, bold brush strokes of the truth. Jesus came into the world to save the world, the whole of the world. There was nothing outside God's intention in that act, and there is nothing outside it now. Life is hard. Life will always be hard. But it is holy.

January 22

I believe in God. . . . —*THE APOSTLES' CREED,* p. 120

The term *believer* is not a very busy one in the Old Testament. In fact, it's not there at all that I can see. People in the Old Testament do, on occasion, fail to believe something God has told them—which always turns out to be a big mistake—but the people of those days don't seem very often to have envisioned a moment in which one moved from unbelief to belief. Life in God's community was a given for the people of Israel. The issue they faced was not whether or not to be a member of the community, but how righteously or unrighteously they would live that communal life.

Community is in short supply these days. We long for it—invent small towns that never existed, put them in television shows, and wish with all our hearts that we lived in them. We want fellowship. Where I live, most of the bookstores are now also coffee bars, and people actually go there with each other on dates. We are aware of our own aloneness. Modern people cannot describe themselves as "unfaithful" exactly—it is more a case of being unaware there is anything larger than ourselves to which to *be* faithful.

But there is, and we approach it together. I do not learn, all by myself, what it is to be a child of God. It is not a solitary activity. I learn from my membership in the family of God.

January 23

That this evening may be holy, good, and peaceful . . .
—SUFFRAGES FOR EVENING PRAYER, p. 122

We don't bring our holiness *to* God: we get it *from* God. Holiness is not a category of the world; from the beginning holiness has been a category of the spirit. And, from the beginning, the hallmark of behavior people have recognized as holy has been that it summons recognition of the reality of the spirit among us. That is what the intricacies of Hebrew laws concerning cultic purity were about. That is what the layer upon layer of custom in our liturgy is about. Holy behavior in the household of God is that behavior which demonstrates our right relationship as creature to our loving creator. Holiness is about the spirit.

But it happens for us in the world.

We are so profoundly mixed: flesh and spirit, animals with immortal souls, so tethered to the earth and straining so to gain heaven. The idea of the holy, the sanctification of matter by spirit—a bush that burns and is not consumed, the prosaic elements of bread and wine becoming sacred body, sacred blood—is a profoundly mixed idea. We are not gone to heaven, disembodied, divorced from the earth. And neither are we doomed to a crass and materialistic determinism. We are called, instead, to be holy, unwavering in our honesty about the way things really are in a broken world, and equally firm about the very different realities of the kingdom of heaven.

January 24

Let your people sing with joy. —SUFFRAGES FOR EVENING
PRAYER, p. 121

What does it take to be happy? I think we are happiest when
we know ourselves to be in the service of God, focussed on a
reality larger than ourselves. This is true even when that service is hard, as it often is. No amount of inconvenience or
effort can take that joy from us; it is why we are here. Some
saints of the past were inconvenienced to the point of death,
and they did not count it too high a price for the sake of this
treasure. People of faith in some parts of the world still face
this threat today. Martyrdom happens now, not just in the
early centuries of our common life: more people have died for
the faith in this bloody century than in all the famous centuries of Roman persecution combined.

I think often of the saints of the past and the present. In
accounts of their deaths, we often read of their joy in giving
their lives to God, even in the midst of great suffering; they
died singing hymns, some of them, or reciting psalms. I pray
for that unconquerable joy for myself, especially when life is
hard, and I pray for it for you, too. It is likely that you and I
will not be called upon to sacrifice our lives, although we can
never know the end of life until it is here. Perhaps we will not
be asked to die for Christ, but we can choose to live for him,
joyful in the knowledge that we are offering ourselves fully,
free in a way that no amount of power could give us.

January 25

. . . for darkness has been vanquished . . . —THE EXULTET AT THE EASTER VIGIL, p. 286

This is the cold, dark time of the year, the time of early evening darkness, the time of ice and snow. The time of year when everyone seems to have a bad cold or to be just getting over one. The warm glow of the Christmas holidays seems like it was a good while back. We are tired of cold and dark.

The seed companies know we feel this way. Is your mailbox full of their catalogs, as ours is? It has always made me smile: opening up my mailbox in the dark of winter and seeing the glorious color pictures of daffodils, of lovely pink blossoming plum trees, of rosy apples, pears, strawberries. They know we need a lift right about now, the seed companies, and they send us one. I, for one, appreciate it.

Those of us who love to garden have a vivid mental picture of the pruning process. If you take growth off the end of a branch, it will concentrate its energy down below where you cut, and it will send out more growth down there.

That's true for people, too. If we are to be productive with the energy God has given us, we have to focus it. I think of times in my life when I have been pruned, when God has shown me that I must abandon a certain direction if I am to grow in the areas of life in which I am intended to grow.

More than once, I have had to cut something out of my life in order to bear fruit somewhere else. This pruning does not happen without pain. But it always bears fruit.

January 26

Do you renounce all sinful desires that draw you from the love of God? . . . . —HOLY BAPTISM, p. 302

In some of the oldest Christian churches, the baptistery is an octagonal pool in the back of the church, set down into the floor, so that one must descend a few steps to enter it. Often it is separated architecturally from the rest of the church, or you can see signs that it was separated at one time. And often there were two doors to the baptistery, a little, narrow one through which people entered and then a wide one through which they streamed into the nave of the church. In through the narrow door and out through the wide. With these two doors, the nameless architects of ancient times perfectly expressed what is going on in the sacrament of initiation by which one becomes a Christian. In through the narrow door: the life of faith is not always an easy one to choose. Choosing it involves *not* choosing some other things, primary among them the self-centeredness that life in the world encourages. To the world outside—in those days and in our day as well—choosing life in Christ looks like a radical loss of freedom and autonomy, a narrowing of one's options. We say things like "It is not I who live, but Christ who lives in me," and the world does not understand such talk. Especially our world, so remarkably pre-occupied with the pursuit of power and its maintenance. But we show Christ most truly when we care for the ones with whom he chose to surround himself.

January 27

. . . you give to some the word of wisdom. . . . —COLLECT FOR THE FEAST OF A THEOLOGIAN AND TEACHER, p. 248

Knowledge and wisdom are not the same thing. I have known more than one person with very little in the way of formal schooling who was very wise.

Experience teaches us better than anything else if we let it. It's interesting, though, that its instruction is not automatic. I have also known many people who had all manner of experiences and appear not to have learned from any of them. Something in them will not allow them to turn loose of their preconceived rules for the way the world works. They go to their graves insisting on them, regardless of what evidence to the contrary they may have seen.

Once we were in Paris and stopped to have a cup of coffee in a café. At the next table was another group of Americans. One of them was holding forth at great length about how terrible the restrooms were in France, about how hard it was to find a hotel with a proper bathroom. On and on—about plumbing! There we were, in one of the world's most beautiful cities, Notre-Dame Cathedral across the street, the city of the Louvre, of La Sainte-Chapelle—and the subject was bathrooms. Patti and I could barely contain our laughter until we were safely out of earshot.

We can refuse to be taught by the wonders the world has for us. Nobody will make us become wise. We don't have to grow if we don't want to. But we shrink if we don't.

January 28

. . . special gifts of grace to understand . . . —*COLLECT FOR
THE FEAST OF A THEOLOGIAN AND TEACHER,* p. 249

It is easy to miss the hand of God in the events of our lives.
We all know people who see absolutely no evidence of God's
presence in their lives or in the world. Risking a further honesty, we admit that there have been times when we have *been*
those people, when the hand of God was hidden from us. We
all know what a bitter thing it is to think oneself alone in the
face of the difficulties of life.

Modern people of faith often think of doubt as a new disease. It seems to us that faith was easy and universal in former
times, that everybody believed, that the people of the past
lived unanimously in a world without doubt. We wish we had
lived back then, for if we did, surely the discouragements and
cynical nibblings at the corner of our faith would not assail us
as they do now. But scepticism is not something new. They
were not so different from us—even Jesus' closest friends
often didn't get it, even with Jesus standing right there beside
them, as sometimes we don't get it.

And that's okay. Doubt is essential to human understanding.
God gave us reason so that we would use it, and doubt is the
engine reason uses to approach belief. We focus our quizzical
minds on the things that *don't* make sense to us, not on the
ones that do.

January 29

The peace of God, which passeth all understanding . . .
—*BLESSING AFTER THE EUCHARIST,* p. 339

I used to think that eventually I would reach a place in my life where I wasn't wrestling with problems. That was when I was very young. I'm not sure when it began to dawn on me that life *is* a series of problems, but I know it now: we never get to a place where there aren't problems to be overcome. Solve one and you've got two or three more waiting in the wings, and that's not a sign that something is wrong. It's just the way life is.

So the peace of God is not the state of nirvana. It is cluttered, at least while we walk the earth. The peace of God enters a decidedly messy world, and the world is going to stay messy for as long as we're in it. Try as we might to impose order.

The peace of God: the soul that can view the messiness of the world and still feel the love of God. Still feel it, and still show it. The soul that can find within itself the willingness to walk into the messy world and minister to a small corner of its chaos. The soul that understands its own limitations and accepts them, but knows God to be much, much larger. We are in good hands, whatever befalls.

January 30

Remember that thou keep holy the Sabbath day. —*THE THIRD COMMANDMENT,* p. 318

Of course, Sunday is a work day for me. It has been for more than forty years now. I can't imagine what it would be like just to stay home and read the paper. In a thousand ways—the gleam of polished silver and polished wood, the purity of the flat white disks of communion bread, the purple well of wine in a deep chalice, the smell of candle wax, the starched smoothness of carefully folded altar linens—I experience the peace of God through my senses on Sunday morning.

All of these things are the work of human hands. The things that happen in houses of worship only happen because people care enough to see that they do. Church is as beautiful as the people care to make it. Everyone involved in the enterprise depends on everyone else. In this, it is exactly like life: we make it work by working on it, and we do this together. No life is lived all by itself. Life is lived and thrives only in community.

After all the services are over and the last hand has been shaken, it is time to go home. Sunday night supper at our house is usually something very simple. Patti and I are tired after the day, content just to enjoy the quiet and one another—and, finally, the newspaper. We read each other snatches of it until we get too sleepy to pay much attention, and then we go to sleep. Not much rest on our Sundays, but they are holy nonetheless.

. . . you have caused a new light to shine in our hearts. . . .
—PREFACE FOR EPIPHANY, p. 378

Often, when we were on Okinawa, the lights would go out—the power supply was somewhat unsteady in those days. The kids were little, and supper time was always a circus anyway, but when the lights went out suddenly in the middle of it, everything came to an abrupt halt for a second. Then we'd get out the candles and get some light on the subject, finishing our supper by candlelight.

The children just loved this. Sometimes they'd beg to have candles at supper time even when the electricity was working. It seemed exciting to them. And to tell you the truth, it was oddly wonderful for us, too. Somehow the conversation was different when the lights went out, quieter. I think we all felt safe inside, in our little pool of candlelight. After supper, we'd put the children to bed by the candles and make sure they could hear us from their beds in the dark. And we would sit at the table and talk quietly, marooned in the dark. We were always a little sorry when the lights flickered back on later in the evening.

We were young then, Patti and I. Now those children have children of their own, and Patti and I look toward retirement. She still lights candles just about every night we're home together for dinner, though, and we always remember those nights long ago. Safe and surrounded by a pool of light, like the love of God.

February 1

. . . that our divisions may cease . . . —PRAYERS OF THE PEOPLE, p. 390

We uphold the vision of God's kingdom, in which every barrier humankind has erected to the unity of the human family comes crashing down. One day our divisions will cease; regretfully, that day is certain to come in another world, better than this one.

But we hold up the vision of that better world's oneness to this world's brokenness, and it is essential that we do. Do we disagree passionately? Do we differ? Do we frighten each other, sometimes, with our differences? Yes, we do. But are those reasons to abandon one another, to live apart in little clumps of similarity, surrounded only by people who resemble us?

Absolutely not. Cumbersome as it can be, institutional unity—in the nation, in the Church, anywhere—is a powerful symbol of spiritual unity. It is a worthy investment of the money, energy, and talent it takes to maintain it. It is worthy, too, of our best effort as we seek to transform it. Let us fix what is broken in our society. Let us be serious about political reform. But let us make that effort with sincerity and mutual trust, turning our backs on the partisan spirit of fragmentation so pervasive in our land. It is shortsighted and dangerous, for a nation or for a church. Now is no time for the people of God to grow farther apart. Now is a time when we need to be closer together.

February 2

In the temple cult of Jesus' time, a child was presented at the temple shortly after birth. With the sacrifice of an unblemished lamb for a rich child or an inexpensive pair of doves for a poor one—I imagine Mary and Joseph came with doves—the child was consecrated to God. For protection. For sanctification. As a beginning of the lifelong process of being an observant Jew.

Now this sanctification was something Jesus didn't need. Nor did he need protection. He didn't need to have his sins washed away, either, years later when he presented himself for John's baptism. Yet all these emblems of incompleteness, all these signs of need and weakness that included the bodily weakness that ends in death, he embraced every one of them. When the all-powerful sinless One takes our weakness upon himself, do we dare to deny its existence? If we do, we blaspheme. And if we do not, if we accept the fact of our great need of God, we are given the strength we need by the one from whom all strength comes.

February 3

You are sealed by the Holy Spirit in Baptism and marked as Christ's own forever. —HOLY BAPTISM, p. 308

Dead of winter. Blizzard. Patti and I were looking forward to being marooned together for an evening at home when the phone rang. It was the daughter of a good friend. She had just given birth, and it was way too early. Her baby weighed a little under a pound. The doctors were preparing these first-time parents to lose him. And she wanted to know if we would come up to Connecticut and baptize the baby. We went.

I didn't know a human being could be that small. A man's hand would have held him easily. I could see through his fingers. The nurse brought me a little paper medicine cup with water in it. "I baptize you in the name of the Father, and of the Son, and of the Holy Spirit," I told him as I made a cross on his tiny forehead.

I looked at that tiny human being, and I knew I saw Jesus. That was what Patti and I had come out in a blizzard to see. Like the shepherds on that long-ago night in David's city, we saw the hope of the entire human race in a little tiny child, the human being as God intends it: a perfect, pure thing— weak, endangered, but perfect and magnificent. I've done baptisms in some pretty magnificent places, but I have never felt the presence of Jesus Christ more clearly than I felt it that night.

You'll be glad to know that he did live, and that today he is a bright and busy toddler. He does not know that he was Jesus to me when he was born.

February 4

May Almighty God in mercy receive your confession of sorrow and faith. . . . —*SACRAMENT OF RECONCILIATION*, p. 451

Repentance is a complex thing. It aims for one thing only: to restore us to the loving God in whose image we are made and from whom we have fallen so profoundly away. Christian repentance has nothing to do with punishment and nothing to do with shame. It has nothing to do with perpetuating the barriers of prejudice and ancient hatred human beings keep so stubbornly in place against one another. We repent in order that we might once again live in the harmony with God and neighbor for which we were created.

This fact leads us to something odd: My repentance may not be about a sin I myself have committed. I may need to be in a state of repentance about something somebody else has done to me. Not that I will take the blame for it, but that I will find the strength to set aside the hurt that it has caused me. Perhaps the one who has hurt me regrets his deed; perhaps he does not. I can exercise little control over one or the other. My own actions are the only ones I control. I alone decide whether I will live with anger over my injuries or allow God to transform them into gracious pockets of compassion within my soul. For it is the one who has suffered who knows best what it is to suffer. Those

who have known pain are best equipped to see it in others. And those are the ones God can use in the mighty work of reconciliation.

February 5

Grant that we may always be ready to give a reason for the hope that is in us. . . . —COLLECT FOR THE FEAST OF A MARTYR, p. 247

One of the controversies of the early Church was called the Donatist controversy. Should priests and bishops who had fled persecution be allowed back into the Church? The Church venerated her martyrs. Many early bishops were martyrs. The stories of their faith and bravery were legendary.

But some of the leaders of the Church fled and hid, and when it was finally safe to be the Church openly, there began a powerful movement to deny them their offices. Emotions ran high about this. Blood was shed over it.

The rare courage to be a martyr, like all human virtues, is a gift from God. Not everyone had it. Eventually, the Church decided to welcome the leadership of those who had fled. The rightness of one moral choice over another is usually a pretty complex thing, and it is all too easy, from a safe distance, to criticize the courses others take.

Were the leaders who escaped cowards? Ultimately, that question is between God and their immortal souls. Could God still work through them, even if they were? Unquestionably. As God can work through us, warts and all.

February 6

Deliver them, O Lord, from the way of sin and death.
—*PRAYER AT HOLY BAPTISM,* p. 305

In ancient Christian baptism, powerful signs of the new creation were everywhere: a symbolic rebirth in physical nakedness, special clean clothes afterward, the family meal shared for the first time with the baptized, the family story told and retold. Those baptized into Christ unmistakably died to the old life and joined the new, and this new reality would be the deciding one in their lives ever after, beyond profession, beyond ethnicity or race, beyond lineage, beyond station in life. They were in a new place; they were "in Christ." That which had been promised to the new Jerusalem would become the birthright of the believer. The righteousness that had been transgressed again and again would be alive in their hearts, sealed there by the power of the Holy Spirit.

We read in the Book of Acts how difficult it was for those first Christians when they began to experience the continuing reality of sin in their community, how painful a thing it was when they discovered that their charismata did not transport them magically into heaven right here on earth. We know the feeling of that loss of innocence, we who have admitted in the secrecy of our hearts just how and just where we ourselves have fallen short. We are the body of the risen Christ, but this is manifestly not heaven. We've got a long way to go before we're there.

February 7

Share the Gifts of God. —*AN ORDER FOR CELEBRATING THE HOLY EUCHARIST*, p. 401

Yet another story in the paper today about an elected official skimming money off the top of funds entrusted to him. "Everybody's in it for himself today, right, Father?" the taxi driver says, catching sight of my collar in his rearview mirror, as we creep through the traffic on Second Avenue. "Oh, I don't know about that," I say. "I know lots of people who aren't."

But it is true that to do work of righteousness and mercy demands a strength we do not possess on our own. We are not unselfish by nature. We struggle not only against the world's self-aggrandizement, but also against our own. I know that I carry within myself the capacity for evil; I am not naive enough to believe that only those who disagree with me are capable of it. All of my righteousness comes, not from me, but from God. God supplies us with this power, and gives it as it is needed. The desire to be truly good, to live an unselfish life is our clearest sign that the power to see it through will be given us as well. So be of good cheer. Take courage. The world can be better than it is, and so can we. We are not doomed to act only on our most selfish impulses—with God's help, we can transcend them and act otherwise. Don't be discouraged by your own faults—God can overcome them, even if you cannot.

February 8 ❧❧❧❧❧❧❧❧❧❧❧❧❧❧

. . . that we, being delivered from the fear of all enemies, may live in peace and quietness . . . —COLLECT FOR PEACE AT EVENING PRAYER, p. 123

At a time in our national history when, the Dow-Jones tell us, the American economy is booming, when unemployment is down and new businesses are beginning, why on earth do you suppose it is that so many people still feel so precarious? Downsized people are finding real jobs again. Companies are hiring. The economic cycle is clearly on an upswing. Isn't it odd that we seem not to trust it, we who have a history of doing the opposite; it has been much more typical of Americans in this century to trust our prosperity too much than to trust it too little. But we are suspicious now. We pass laws denying compassionate service to immigrants because we think they drain our economy, even as study after study shows beyond doubt that they enlarge it. We assert that crime is a more and more threatening social problem in our country, even as city after city reports statistics demonstrating double-digit shrinkage in violent crime for the past several years. We are more safe, yet we cannot seem to stop feeling less safe.

I wonder if we have not become addicted to fear. I wonder if we would recognize ourselves without it. But it is not our natural state; we were not born full of fear. We learned it. And we can, if we will, learn otherwise.

February 9

O God, from whom all good proceeds. . . . —COLLECT, p. 229

What on earth is the same today as it was at the end of the last century? Hardly anything. In the 1890s, the Wright brothers were still dreaming of a flying machine that had not yet taken its first short flight; the other day, the crew of the space shuttle laughed and joked with Mission Control about having a pizza party on board. In the 1890s, doctors could ease pain, sometimes, but rarely could they cure. Today, human knowledge has destroyed many diseases, intervened in the genetic destiny of the unborn to heal disease in bodies not yet fully formed in the womb. At the turn of the century, women could not vote; today, a woman president appears likely in the not-too-distant future. Things that then seemed certain about marriage and the family, about the education of children, about warfare—all these things have changed dramatically.

You just never know. Many things of which we are now quite certain will one day be revealed as quite mistaken. We smile at the ideas and machinery of another age, but we and our artifacts will seem quaint one of these days. We are repulsed by the idea of chattel slavery as practiced in America not two hundred years ago, yet we ourselves are content to live in a world in which millions of children go to bed hungry. One day, that will seem every bit as perverse as slaveholding now seems. God's judgment is eternal. Ours is very temporary.

February 10

. . . a comfort in sorrow, and a companion in joy. —PRAYER
FOR THE PARENTS, p. 444

Another terrible newspaper story of a child, starved to death
by her own mother. At her death at the age of four, she weighed
fourteen pounds. I put the paper down for a moment—I just
cannot bear to read any more.

I pick up the paper again. The mother has a history of
mental illness. I don't know if she is capable of understanding
what she has done—I almost hope not. I search within myself
for the power to forgive this woman I do not know, and I do
not yet find it. And so I just pray for her: for her, for her child,
for her illness, for her guilt. And for the world's loss.

There are many things in life we cannot seem to find it in
our hearts to forgive. Forgiveness does not always come easily.
I don't think God needs us to pretend something we don't
feel, or to deny the existence of injustice or cruelty where it
occurs. I think God only requires that we tell the truth about
ourselves, and calls everyone to do just that—including the
perpetrators of terrible things such as this. We cannot manu-
facture forgiveness. It is a gift from God. All we can do is tell the
truth, strive for justice and mercy, ask for the gift of forgiveness when we cannot find it in our own hearts, and wait.

February 11

This is another day, O Lord. —PRAYERS FOR USE BY A SICK
PERSON IN THE MORNING, *p. 461*

I have a friend who is a priest in a church in a poor neighborhood. Life is hard there, and the congregation is poor.

One of the volunteers there came to the church from a long period of incarceration. The crime for which he had been imprisoned was a violent one; he himself says that his sentence was fair. Shut away from society for many years, he came face-to-face with his own weakness and sin and turned his life around. He began to work closely with the prison chaplain. He began to feel valued, for the first time in many years. The chaplain saw that he was intelligent and talked to him about his future as if he had one. And the man began to believe that he did. He signed up for a college course that was offered at the prison. He did well. He earned a college degree, one course at a time. And then he earned a master's degree. All as an inmate.

Finally, he was released. He had nowhere to go, so he was referred to the church. He spends his days at the church, volunteering. He does whatever is needed. He is my friend's right hand.

He sends out resumes for jobs he finds listed in the paper. He is honest, in his cover letters, about where he got his education and why. They are good letters, but no prospective employer calls him for an interview. He is not stupid. He knows that nobody will. "I know it's not personal," he tells

my friend, and it breaks her heart. Over and over again, he is not given the chance to show the world that he has grown from his own experience, that he has learned life's lessons the hard way. Over and over again, the world tells him that there is no forgiveness.

I heard about this man, who faces a hard world every day. Who repents of his own hardness. Who knows what it is to be in chains. I think of his determination not to be discouraged, and I think of what that must cost him every day. In his story, we see longing for forgiveness, longing to join the human family as a valued member. Longing to live.

February 12

Help us to eliminate our cruelty to these our neighbors.
—*PRAYER FOR THE OPPRESSED,* p. 826

When I was in seminary, we had a controversy that tore our community in two. During my first year, the seminary admitted an African American man into the incoming first-year class. When the seminary trustees found out about the admission they demanded that the seminary rescind it—this sounds crazy now, but those of us who were around in the 1940s remember many more egregious things than that. You can imagine the turmoil in our community when this happened.

A number of faculty members and many of the students left. I left. But during the summer came word that the seminary and the trustees had reached an agreement. The man was admitted again, and—with extraordinary grace—he agreed to come. Of all the students who had left, though, only one returned. It was me.

I know that some of my classmates thought I was wrong to go back, to reward a concession that must, in some cases, have been only a grudging one. But I wanted to be there to help it work. I wanted to be there for our new colleague as he began what could only be a stressful period in his life's journey. I had been part of the protest, and now I wanted to be part of the reconciliation. And I knew I could not be part of a reconciliation if I were not around.

Controversies end. They come to some resolution. And then our common life has to go on.

The wicked arrogantly persecute the poor. . . . —PSALM 10:2,
p. 594

The world operates according to its time-honored principle of divide and rule. It continues to experience the need to sort human beings into groups based upon power inequalities. It finds many ways to do this, some overt, some so subtle as to be all but invisible. There continue to be in-groups and out-groups. It tries to enlist the Church in this effort, seeking our reassuring baptism of its prejudices. How does the household of God respond?

By demonstrating that these divisions are false ones, that they are not only unfair, they are ungodly. By affirming within its walls the radical equality of all God's people, the Church can model the household of God in which there are no outcasts. We show the world what it looks like for the poor to be blessed. For the mourners to be comforted. For the weak to be strong. Within our society we can live this way, and by doing this we can point the way for the larger society to follow. The struggle for justice is not just for the sake of the Church, it is for the sake of the world.

February 14

FEAST OF CYRIL AND METHODIUS

. . . to confront one another without hatred or bitterness . . .
—*PRAYER IN TIMES OF CONFLICT*, p. 824

One of the most important things a person can learn is how to respond with an open heart to someone who has caused her injury. To be honest about one's own pain and also mindful about what good *does* abide in the one who has caused it, about what potential there is for mending a relationship damaged by the injury is no easy thing. This kind of open-heartedness has nothing to do with a masochistic enduring of aggression. To value ourselves as God values us is to know that we are deserving of the fair treatment we are duty-bound to give others. Asserting that right makes you strong.

Many times in my life, I've found it necessary to work, over an extended period of time, with someone who has done something very hurtful to me. Each time, a decision has been required of me: do I linger over the insults of the past, or do I attempt to forge a better future? Sometimes, it's true, a further relationship is not possible. More often, though, it is. When I have been able to open myself to the possibilities of that future, I have been rewarded much more often than I have been disappointed.

"But it's human nature to be wary when someone has hurt you," someone might say. Yes, it certainly is. But it is part of the divine nature, that nature that includes not only the sorrows of the past but the potential of the future, to forgive.

February 15

Do you renounce Satan and all the spiritual forces of wickedness that rebel against God? —*HOLY BAPTISM*, p. 302

The early Christians had a very vivid understanding of evil. Their world was full of demons roaming the world in search of opportunities to inflict pain. It may be that most of us do not share that particular vision of how evil works, but I think we all agree that it exists. That it still clings to us. That it is stronger than we are. We remember the people in the Bible who were possessed by demons, how helpless they were against their tormentors. But we also remember that the demons themselves were powerless against the power of Jesus. Sternly, he commanded them to depart, and they had no choice but to obey. Evil may be stronger than we are, but Jesus whose signal attribute is self-giving love is stronger than both of us.

It is key, for me, that this power of which I speak is to be found in self-giving. It is the opposite of aggressive power. It is intent upon the emptying of the self rather than upon the self's inflation. It is not neutral; it is biased toward the poor and weak, unlike the world's power, which hastens to the feet of the great. We partake in that power when we behave like it. When we try to ape the power arrangements of the world, we become just another player—and a minor one, at that—on the world's stage. Our only true power is in the truth we speak. We have no other power.

February 16

O God, you have bound us together in a common l
—PRAYER IN TIMES OF CONFLICT, p. 824

I know that there are those who believe that the Church should not speak on political issues. It is not our business. Others simply sneer at our statements on political issues. "Fat lot of good you're doing," they say. But I think again of the prophets of old; power usually did not listen to them, either. The success of our witness is not measured in the polls; its measure is its fidelity to the spirit.

There is no more powerful witness than the inclusiveness of the faith community. A safe haven for the one who has no home, a welcome for the outcast and the sinner: these ancient images of the church are exactly what the modern world needs. We must stand shoulder to shoulder with those whom the world would forget, show forth the wide embrace that knows no enemies, only sisters and brothers. We must trust those who are different from us, respect their ability to understand their own situation in life.

Let the voices of love be strong, and the voices of hate will not prevail. I want to be one of those strong voices. I want to be part of God's reconciling power. Wherever the demon of bigotry shows himself, I want to reject his savage counsel and speak the strong, loving words of Jesus to the world. The powers of hatred will not prevail against that love.

O God, the fountain of wisdom. . . . —PRAYER FOR CONGRESS
OR A STATE LEGISLATURE, p. 821

Human wisdom is deficient if it fails to take human experience into account. I cannot assume that I understand another person's reality if I have not lived his life. There is a sense in which we cannot know one another fully.

Because we cannot, we must listen carefully. My wife and I have the custom of writing letters to each other about things. Sometimes I find myself better able to express exactly what I mean that way and better able to understand exactly what she means. I'm often struck by how differently we perceive something; we bring ourselves to whatever we see. True in a marriage, true in society as well: I remember how the O. J. Simpson trial revealed this about Americans. People were angered by it. But there's little to be gained by bemoaning it. There's only one way to deal with the perceptual gulf that exists between the races in our country: really hearing one another. Only you can tell me what your life is like; until you speak, I will not know. When I assert what I know about the way life is, I must do so with humility. I only really know how it is for me. And so we must go slowly as we talk to one another, respecting the indisputable fact that two people can look at the very same event and see it quite differently.

February 18

You were lost, and are found; you were dead, and are now alive in Christ Jesus our Lord. —CONFESSION OF SIN AT THE HOLY EUCHARIST, p. 331

No Christian concept puts people on the defensive as quickly as the concept of repentance. But the most important thing to remember about repentance is that it is much more about accepting responsibility than it is about blame. In the ecology of human relations, it is always possible to find reasons for the things we do. You know people, I am sure, who have an elaborate list, always at the ready, of reasons why every mistake they've ever made was someone else's fault. Their company can wear thin pretty quickly.

But my repentance is about my acts, not someone else's. We did not create in their entirety the situations in which we find ourselves. We inherited some of them. But we are the ones who are here, now. We may not have caused all our ills, but only we can end them. Repentance is as much about the future as about the past; it is a turning from present failure to a new beginning. When I repent, I do not just recant the actions of my past: I choose to act differently in the future.

February 19

Eternal God, the heaven of heavens cannot contain you, much less the walls of temples made with hands. —*A LITANY OF THANKSGIVING FOR A CHURCH,* p. 578

Churches sometimes burn down. Old ones, architectural treasures of their communities, full of precious memorials to the beloved dead. All those hopes, all that generosity, all that beauty. The people stand by helplessly and watch. Oh, no. No. This can't be. This can't be happening.

Poking around in the rubble, they know the emotion of everyone who has ever seen the dream of years dissolve before his eyes. What do you need when you have lost everything? More than anything else, you need to know that the defeat which lies before you, ashes and cold embers of all your hopes, does not mean the end of God's plan. It's easy to see the place of good things in our journeys. What we need is the grace to see the bad things as having a place, too. To trust in God when you are discouraged beyond discouragement, when your heart is broken by bitter disappointment, that is no easy thing. And that is what we need.

But when a church burns, the people don't just wander off into the discouraging night. They rebuild. In the process, they usually find reservoirs of spiritual energy they didn't know they had, and they usually find it in the gift of their own community and common purpose. The church, built again, is a sign of the promise: Do not be discouraged. God is with you and you are with one another.

February 20

. . . in quietness and in confidence shall be our strength. . . .
—PRAYER FOR QUIET CONFIDENCE, p. 832

People sometimes ask me why faith is at such a low ebb in modern people's lives. I think I know: isn't the lack of faith which has caused this era to describe itself, often, as "post-Christian," at bottom, the bitter fruit of too many disappointments? Haven't we seen too many stunning examples of human cruelty, too efficiently brought into our living rooms on the evening news? Isn't that what has sapped the strength of belief, turned us to desperate self-medication with compulsive consumerism, compulsive abuse of our own sexuality and that of others, compulsive substance abuse? Isn't the world just brokenhearted, trying to comfort itself with things that do not comfort, like an abandoned child trying to rock herself to sleep, weeping and weeping for her parents? Isn't the world like that little child? And doesn't a child who lives through that grow up like the world is now: bitter, expecting nothing good, abidingly angry at the betrayal of all her hope? That is what is wrong with the world. Her hope has all been drained away.

But we are not abandoned. Whatever we have lost, we can never lose the presence of God. God accompanied our birth and accompanies our life. God will accompany our death, and we will live in eternity in the loving embrace of God. On earth, we show this embrace in our relations with one another—or we can choose not to show it. That part is up to us.

February 21

. . . I do believe the Holy Scriptures of the Old and New Testaments to be the Word of God. . . . —THE ORDINATION OF A PRIEST, p. 526

I imagine you feel the same reluctance I do to force Christian concepts back onto the Hebrew Scriptures. There is plenty of glory in the Incarnation for Christians—more than enough to go around—without robbing the Jewish people of their integrity by projecting its explicit expectation backward onto their sacred texts. These texts are sacred in themselves to the Jewish people today: in themselves, not for the sake of later Christian ones. To view Jesus as the fulfillment of Scripture, as he seems to have viewed himself, need not compromise the power of the Hebrew Scriptures on their own. I don't have to establish word-for-word correspondence between Jesus' words and deeds and the Old Testament record in order to believe that he was the expected Messiah of Israel. Did Isaiah think he was talking about Jesus of Nazareth when he wrote his famous prophecies: "For to us a child is born"? I don't think he did. Exactly which Scripture was Jesus quoting when he said, "Out of the believer's heart shall flow rivers of living water"? I surely don't know. But I know what he meant. He meant that we are bearers of life and regeneration to other people, that new life can flow through us and from us in a wide, merciful stream.

February 22

. . . take away the arrogance and hatred which infect our hearts. . . . —*PRAYER FOR THE HUMAN FAMILY,* p. 815

My mother sometimes talked to me about the suffering of the Armenian people—usually when I complained about something I didn't want to eat. She thought of those children and their mothers, uprooted from their homes, marched, starving, to their execution sites miles away. I don't know how much attention I paid to her back then. I was just a little boy, and there was a lot I didn't know.

One of the things I didn't know was how intimately connected my own beloved free country was to the reality of genocide. The story of the Native Americans who met the European visitors to America was distorted in those days. And the story of the people brought here in chains from Africa was also gone, the language, the history, the memory of African places, all silent, all gone. I did not know, in those days, what we had done here in this free land.

There is anger when the innocent dead are mourned. But there must also be the sanctification of anger. We will be controlled by vengeance if we are left to our own devices. Upon the altar of God, we lay everything: all our sorrow, all anger, all fear. In God's hands, our strong emotions, even the frightening emotion of terrible anger, can do us or others no harm.

February 23

Give us grace to continue steadfast in the confession of this faith. . . . —COLLECT OF THE HOLY TRINITY, p. 251

The waning years of this remarkable century have confronted people of faith with what amounts to a revolution in just about every facet of human life that matters at all. Nothing is as it was: not human sexuality; not the politics of poverty; not relationships between men and women; not the culture's understanding of the rights of children and those of racial and ethnic minorities; not our understanding of war and peace, of disease, of hunger; not the level of violence we can tolerate in our media, in our corporate boardrooms, in our homes, in our streets.

The loudest voices one hears these days from the community of faith are those voices decrying the moral and political changes and uncertainties in our society; they call for their rejection in the name of religious values. It is as if there were no Christian reality save that of the Christian Right. But there is—it is a reality based on open-mindedness, a commitment to unwavering honesty about history and contemporary life, and a healthy respect for human common sense. Millions of people live compassionately in it. For millions of people, human reason and experience are not suspect but are instead embraced as the means by which truth may be apprehended.

After all, all I know about God is what my life has taught me. That's all anybody knows.

February 24

. . . set him free from every bond. . . . —COLLECT AT THE TIME
OF DEATH, p. 464

My father was an alcoholic. I cannot recall a time when he was
not afflicted. He was quiet and very kind. He was intelligent,
and he was a genius of a businessman. He had a sweet dignity
about him. But his addiction would reduce him to staying
alone in his room for days at a time. At those times, I would
see him briefly in the upstairs hall, making his way to the
bathroom, and he would be unable to speak to me. Or I would
hear his door open from my room, hear his uncertain foot-
steps down the stairs. I would hold my breath until I heard
him reach the bottom without falling. I remember how hard
it was on my mother.

The sorrow of this resided permanently in our house. We
were never without it. He would go to the hospital and dry
out. When he returned, we would all feel so hopeful. I think
he did, too. I remember sitting at the dinner table once when
he came home from the hospital, enjoying a wonderful, special chicken dinner my mother had made. Seeing him in his
chair, right where he belonged, I thought, *Dad's going to be
all right now.* I thought that every time he went. But it was
never true.

I don't remember a time when I did not feel profoundly
sorry for him, because I know he hated being the way he was.
He's been dead for thirty years now. To think that in the
larger life he has been healed gives me immense comfort.

February 25

When I hear about a massacre in a mosque or a car bomb exploding in a bustling marketplace, I think about the huge gulf between these actions and the great systems of faith from within which, from time to time, they appear. There is no justification in any of the world's great religions for the snuffing out of innocent life. The majestic tradition of the law in Judaism, the self-giving of Christ, the lofty vision of God that Islam holds out to the weak and the poor, assuring them that station in life is no barrier to life in the way of righteousness: these make no recommendation that would support the taking of innocent life as a means of protecting the glory of God. These abuses of the great traditions do not spring from within them. They are from somewhere else.

The transformation of good things into bad things is the way the devil works. That is how evil works best: it worms its way into the precincts of holiness, knowing that human passion and commitment live there, and that it is possible to turn them just a bit, bringing bigotry out of belief.

No godly program involves violence. One that claims to do this is simply not godly, and it doesn't matter whose program it is. Death is our ancient enemy; it can never become our friend and ally in righteousness. That is a lie. And we are not supposed to be in the business of lies. We are supposed to live in the truth.

February 26

I have been lucky enough to travel to many parts of the world in my life. Patti and I were missionaries early in our marriage, and so we lived in a number of out-of-the-way places during those years. And then in the years that I've been a bishop, the support of world mission has been a large part of my ministry, so there was traveling involved in that. And now, in this ministry, I do a lot of traveling in support of all our dioceses here in the United States and in the Church beyond our shores as well. So my bag doesn't stay unpacked for very long.

"Don't you get tired of it sometimes?" people ask me. I can honestly say that I don't. I may get physically tired, but spiritually I always feel excited about the newness of wherever it is that I'm going. And I am never disappointed. The welcome I receive always warms my heart. There is always much to love in every place I go—loving people I would not have met had I stayed home, beauty I would not have seen. Each place is a family, a community of love. I visit a church and see that they're having a strawberry festival week after next—I mentally check my calendar, even though I know I'll be three thousand miles away by then. More often than not, I find myself wishing I could stay longer when it is time to leave.

We're not meant to live alone. We're unhappy when we try. We're meant to band together and love one another.

February 27

. . . make this a temple of your presence and a house of prayer.
—*CONSECRATION OF A CHURCH*, p. 568

In my line of work, I visit lots and lots of churches. Sometimes I'm involved in the consecration of a new one, and that is a wonderful experience. The community that has worked for years to bring it about is gathered in thanksgiving for the completion of their task. Usually the architect is in attendance at this event, so I get to meet him or her and express in person my admiration of an artistry I can hardly even imagine. The architect's art is a mystery to me; I can't imagine having the kind of understanding of light and space and materials that can take the faith and tradition of a worshiping community and express it in steel and concrete and glass and wood. I am in awe of such an artistry.

New churches are not the only ones I visit, of course. I have also been lucky enough, in my travels, to worship in churches almost as old as our faith itself. I don't meet the architects there; they are unknown, their names lost in the passing of the centuries, forgotten for hundreds and hundreds of years. Only their work lives on, bearing the imprint of their imagination and their genius. I stand in their churches and feel the generations of the faithful still alive in them. To me they do not seem dead; they whisper in those sacred spaces in which they worshiped, gathered there in silent prayer with those of us who came long after them.

February 28

. . . whose service is perfect freedom . . . —COLLECT FOR PEACE
AT MORNING PRAYER, p. 57

How can a world like ours, so remarkably preoccupied with the self and its needs and desires, know about the freedom that comes with self-sacrifice? The surrender of the self-centered freedom that people clasp so tightly and compulsively to themselves is the only way to true and joyous freedom. We are not free just because we think we rule ourselves. A world in which I were the only one whose desires mattered would be a lonely place. A world without limits thinks it is free, but it is really in bondage to itself.

On the outside wall of the Episcopal Church Center back in New York are these words from one of our beloved prayers: "Whose service is perfect freedom." I take the time to read it every time I pass by, as a sort of prayer upon entering or leaving the building. I do that because it is true. We are truly free, fully and radically free, only in a community defined not by power and competition but by love. We move out of the narrowness of self-absorbed isolation into the wider fellowship of joy, the company of those who have found a spiritual freedom in serving others that they could never have known had they remained anxiously focussed on their own desires and fears.

February 29

O God, who wonderfully created and yet more wonderfully restored the dignity of human nature. . . . —COLLECT FOR *THE SECOND SUNDAY AFTER CHRISTMAS DAY,* p. 214

We know that the good news was not good news to many people when it first was shared. By the latter decades of the first century, the Church was already seeing the beginning of official persecution. There were already martyrs. There was no question any longer of an imminent return of Christ, such as many people had expected in the early days; it looked like the Church was in this for the long haul and that difficult days were ahead. And they were. The world was a hard place then. It's a hard place now. Sometimes we find it hard to believe that God wants us to have life and to have it abundantly. We look around, and our hearts sink at what we see.

The loving spirit people had come to know in those first Christian communities was not something they saw very often when they looked around them. It's not something we see every day, either. We see hard things, and some of us are tempted to give up.

I can understand the impulse to turn away from a world in which terrible things can happen. But withdrawal from the world cannot be our way. The Spirit is among us for the world. The Spirit is here to transform it. We may be weak, our hearts may grow faint within us, but the Spirit is strong. We may stumble and fall, but the Spirit moves on and on.

March 1

Lord Jesus Christ, who didst stretch out thine arms of love on the hard wood of the cross . . . —COLLECT AT MORNING PRAYER, p. 58

Can we act in love even when we don't feel loving? I think so. Remember how Americans were glued to the television when the Alex Haley novel *Roots* was televised? Remember how terrible it was to see the inhumanity of slavery night after night in our own living rooms—how everybody talked about it? Yet it was only a little more than a hundred years ago that that's how things were. Many pulpits of my own Episcopal Church rang with defenses of slavery as a part of God's plan for humankind. We are horrified now to think that it could have been so in America. Our children today can't believe it when we tell them that we went to segregated schools as children, but most of us did. But that has changed now, and the change did not come about as a result of a universal outpouring of good feeling. It came about as a result of certain people deciding to act in love and justice, despite the opinions of others who did not think it just or loving or appropriate to free the slaves.

It's true that many hearts have still not changed. But society has grown on the issue of race. Society can move in the direction of love if it is led by people who think it should, and this shepherding of the world by the spirit of Christ will not be stopped. We can trust the Shepherd even when we can't even trust ourselves.

March 2

. . . pour out your Spirit upon all flesh. . . . —COLLECT AT MORNING PRAYER, p. 100

Human beings are strange creatures. They are animals with immortal souls, unable to live fully in either the material or the spiritual world alone. We hang suspended between flesh and spirit, with one foot on either side. That's how we're built. We are beings who tend to be separate called to oneness, people who dream of heaven, hip-deep in the earth. People who want to love and don't know how. But if it were impossible for us to learn how, God would not have called us to do it. And to do it together. If our limitations were the only reality we had, there would be no reason for any communal life at all.

But we are more than our limitations. The Spirit is among us to give us the strength and wisdom we need to be more than we are, to help this old world become more than it is. It is enough for us that the Spirit is among us, more than enough. It is abundant life, even in the face of the sufferings we see around us, even in the face of those we mourn within our own hearts. Life in the Spirit is abundant life: not heaven on earth, but earth in sure and certain hope of heaven.

March 3

. . . incline our hearts to keep this law. . . . —THE DECALOGUE, p. 318

God knows that our culture, which uses sex to sell everything from toothpaste to auto parts, a culture that celebrates violence in its movie theaters, in its popular music, in its sporting events, in the competitiveness of its business arrangements, has not disseminated a message of peace and the dignity of all human beings. It has disseminated another message, and here is what it is: My gratification is my God. My desire is my only morality. Other people are objects, and we are not joined in any kind of covenant that in the least cramps my style. We have become a culture in which the common weal is all but irrelevant, one that considers the question "what's in it for me?" as the ultimate—perhaps the only—moral question. And until we can regain a moral dimension beyond the self that can inform and guide our individual and common life, we will find no lasting joy.

"I just want to be happy," you sometimes hear someone say. But it is a curious truth that the one who is seeking happiness never finds it. Happiness always comes as a by-product of something else—it does not exist as a separate entity. It is those who know what it is to give themselves to something larger than they are who know joy.

March 4

Acknowledge, we humbly beseech thee, a sheep of thine own fold, a lamb of thine own flock. . . . —COMMENDATION AT THE BURIAL OF THE DEAD, p. 483

You often see pictures of Jesus with sheep—carrying the lost sheep on his shoulders, separating the sheep from the goats at the Last Judgment. The sheep are always fluffy and white—nice, fat, contented sheep with mild faces. Maybe not too bright, but certainly innocent. The goats are easy to spot—skinny and brown, with a sly, conniving look about them. It's a cinch to separate the sheep from the goats.

But a friend of mine was visiting a Caribbean island. A friend who lived on the island asked if she had seen any sheep yet.

"No," she said. Her host smiled. "Do you know the difference between a sheep and a goat?" he asked her.

"Well, sure," she said in surprise. "Sheep are fluffy and white, and goats are skinny and brown." Then her host told her that on that island, sheep aren't fluffy and white. They're skinny and brown, just like the goats. It's not easy to tell them apart when they're together in a flock.

We think we know the judgment of God, but we do not. You think you know the difference between a sheep and a goat, but sometimes you don't. So be careful when you make a moral judgment about someone else, or even about yourself. Sometimes a sheep and a goat can look a lot alike.

March 5

If we say that we have no sin, we deceive ourselves. . . .
—*PENITENTIAL ORDER FOR THE HOLY EUCHARIST*, p. 320

A clear and simple choice between obvious good and obvious evil: there are those who believe that this is what Christian moral thinking is. But I am not one of them. Anglicans understand moral choice to be a struggle, one that is often carried out publicly in our church, through arguments that can be bitter indeed. And we understand moral choice to be a private struggle also, a careful and sometimes painful examination of the soul with rigorous honesty about what we find there. We all want to be included among the righteous, but it is no easy thing to know what it is to be among the righteous. There is little black and white, many, many shades of gray. If only the Christian moral life could be like a recipe book: a cup of this and a teaspoon of that and you're guaranteed a perfect cake every time without having to think about it all that much. But people who cook know that even if you go by the book, your cake may just work out differently. A recipe is no guarantee of success in cooking or in anything else.

We are men and women, not cartoon caricatures. So much of a decision is dependent on who is making it. So much more than we would like it to be. But that is the way it is.

March 6

O God, whose Son Jesus is the good shepherd of your people . . .
—COLLECT FOR THE FOURTH SUNDAY OF EASTER, p. 225

I've been a priest for more than forty years, and I have never known God to withhold the truth from people willing to strive for it. And I have never known the struggle to be easy, either in my personal life or in the lives of the communities I have served, large or small. God does not bring us together in order that we should not grow in wisdom and moral stature. God doesn't bring the Church together in order that the joy of life in harmony with God's gracious will should elude us. That's what the Church is for: to sustain the people of God in their journey together toward union with God. God is not interested in our going backward or remaining where we are. We want a closer walk with God, not a more distant one. And that is what God wants, too.

Uncertain of exactly where the good lies in a given situation? So am I, often. The theologian Paul Tillich once said that the most painful thing about being human is that we do not know and yet must choose. I know what he meant. So do you.

But I also know that we can trust God to guide us through whatever we must pass through on that walk. We can trust God never to abandon us. And, although we sometimes have a hard time telling the sheep from the goats, we can trust the Good Shepherd to do for both of them what they need.

March 7

O God of unchangeable power and eternal light . . .
—COLLECT FOR THE ORDINATION OF A BISHOP, p. 515

A famous series of Giotto frescoes adorns the walls of the Basilica of St. Francis in Assisi, the saint's hometown—depictions of famous moments in his life. I think of one of them especially, the one in which the pope has a dream of Francis holding up the church of St. John Lateran. We see the pope lying in bed—he's wearing his tiara so we'll know who it is—looking at Francis, who calmly supports one end of the great church. The pope was reassured by this dream; the spiritual renewal Francis represented would strengthen the Church, give it the wherewithal to be faithful to God's call, from which it had sagged dangerously away.

Franciscanism recharged the human faith journey. From time to time, new things appear to do that. Eventually the new thing becomes part of the landscape of faith. It strengthens and instructs. It even strengthens and instructs those who oppose it.

I look again at that fresco. There is Francis, supporting the Lateran church. But he's not holding it straight up over his head, so that it will remain level. He's just holding one end up—the thing is tipping sharply, disconcertingly, to one side. It's not falling down. But it's not the way it was, either.

While there is, ultimately, nothing to fear in God's purpose for us, it isn't because nothing will change. We don't trust God not to change things. We just trust God.

March 8

. . . read, mark, learn and inwardly digest . . . —COLLECT FOR *PROPER 28*, p. 236

The Bible is alive. I am more and more sure of that with every passing year. A lifetime of reading Holy Scriptures is very much like a long marriage: the two of you sit down to breakfast across from each other for thirty or forty years, and you think you know each other completely, and then one of you says something so surprising, so unexpected, and you realize you haven't scratched the surface of this human being to whom you are closer than you are to anyone else in the world. Reading the Bible is just like that: you get to thinking you know what's in there, but then one day you open the book and there is something you've just never seen before. And suddenly a piece of the Bible has a whole new significance it did not have before. And you may have read that passage a thousand times. It happens to me almost every time I sit down to begin work on a sermon.

Sometimes it is time for a moment of insight. They just don't come until their time arrives, so we'd better be on the alert for them. You can see something for decades without really seeing its importance in your life, and then one day you look at it and suddenly there it is.

March 9

Do you, then, forgive those who have sinned against you?
—*RECONCILIATION OF A PENITENT*, p. 451

The idea of Christian forgiveness is one of our teachings that has often been perverted to the ends of the powerful. I've talked to victims of domestic abuse who feel guilty because they are having a hard time forgiving their abuser. But forgiveness does not mean that history has not occurred or that the abuse has somehow not happened, or that a psychological "oh, what the heck, that's okay" state has somehow been achieved. Whatever it means in an individual case, it is certainly something that takes time. For someone accustomed to punishment, premature emphasis on forgiveness will be difficult to hear as anything but a counsel to acquiesce in her own abuse, and that's not what she needs. She needs to be empowered to focus on God's saving might and how it can show in her life.

In the fundamental story of the Jewish people—the Exodus—we do not see them struggling to forgive Pharaoh. They had other things on their minds—they needed to get out of Egypt! But we also do not see the Israelites dreaming of revenge against Egypt; we see them getting on with their lives.

That's the way it has to be with us. When someone is chronically abusing you, you need to do what you must to make it stop. That may mean ending the relationship. You

may be too angry and hurt to summon any forgiveness. Let it lie. God can and will work in you to heal your wounds until a forgiveness that fits can grow.

March 10

We commend this nation to thy merciful care. . . . —*PRAYER FOR THE PRESIDENT OF THE UNITED STATES AND ALL IN CIVIL AUTHORITY*, p. 820

"One nation under God," we say when we pledge allegiance to the American flag. We've been saying the pledge that way for so long that we forget that it didn't originally have the words "under God" in it. They weren't added until the 1950s.

When we look back to the august figures of our past, we often impute to them all the virtues we wish we had. But do you know what the largest religious group in our population was back during the colonial period? Presbyterian? Anglican, maybe? Congregationalist? It was none of these. The largest percentage group of Americans in those days was the un-churched. People with no religious affiliation at all.

It's a mistake to try to make the people of the past over in the image of the way we wish we were. Scepticism and doubt are not twentieth-century ailments; they are old. As old as humankind itself. We tend to associate unbelief with modernity and to think that everybody was religious and observant in the old days. But, apparently, that wasn't the case.

Of course, I do believe we are a nation "under God." I do believe God loves us and longs for our good—as God longs for the good of the entire human race, those who believe and those who do not.

March 11

. . . a spirit to know and to love you . . . —HOLY BAPTISM,
p. 308

How can you believe, if you don't know anything about God?
For we know so very little about God.

We can do what we can. We learn what we can. You
explore the spirit of God the same way you explore the spirit
of another person: You spend time in God's presence. You
examine your own heart and mind with respect to God. You
watch the world for signs of the Spirit. You read what people
in the past have felt and thought about it, and talk to people in
the present who are also seeking. You sit quietly in meditation
and see what comes up. Being able physically to see or hear
God wouldn't actually help all that much, anyway; a person's
spirit is largely hidden from others. We do not know one
another well except after long acquaintance and shared history. The disciples, who ate and talked and walked with Jesus
every day, were forever getting it wrong about who he was,
but they all ended up thinking he was the Messiah eventually.
It wasn't something they learned, the way you learn multipli-
cation tables. It was something into which they allowed themselves to grow.

March 12

. . . many times he held back his anger and did not permit his wrath to be roused. For he remembered that they were but flesh, a breath that goes forth and does not return. —PSALM 78:38-39, p. 698

We do meet those impossible people sometimes: so self-destructive, and yet so appealing. Perhaps you have loved one of them—if you have, you know something of the roller-coaster ride they travel between hope and despair. Appallingly deluded and yet capable, sometimes, of terrible honesty. Ridiculously self-absorbed and then unexpectedly generous. Awash in self-hatred and then, suddenly, the purveyors of what can only be called grace. Whatever else they may be, they are not dull.

I wonder if we all are similarly endearing and infuriating to God. Do our mercurial ups and downs, our times of selfishness and our moments of compassion, tug at the divine heart the way we tug at one another's? Scripture suggests that it is so—the psalmist here, for instance, imagines God's patience with human waywardness.

Just a breath. That's about all we are. The older you get, the more true this seems. Human life is short—there's not much time for it to acquire meaning. That is why love matters so much to us. It makes us feel eternal. And so we are—not in the way we think when we are young and strong and someone adores us, but in another Heart, eternally alive in a love we can never lose.

March 13

Grant that those who live alone may not be lonely in their solitude, but that, following in his steps, they may find fulfillment in loving you and their neighbors. . . . —PRAYER FOR THOSE WHO LIVE ALONE, p. 829

Even if you haven't a living soul in the world who loves you, you carry love in your soul. You were created by it, and your life is sustained by it. It breathes with each of your breaths. Most importantly, it plants in you the longing for the love of other human beings, and it is on that longing that we all must act. If we've been living the false life that destructive behavior brings in its wake for a long time, we may not be very good company. That may well account for our loneliness. But there is nobody who cannot learn to change that.

It may be that your path will not be in the company of one person who is intimately joined to you in love. Not everybody is called to the married state. It may be that you are called to a love more general: a life lived in a community of people gathered around a common system of belief. That's what a church is, of course—and many single people have found there the love they did not have in an intimate relationship.

The important thing for our souls is not so much that we all find Ms. or Mr. Right, but that each of us finds a way to give ourselves to something beyond our own narrow concerns. I never knew anyone who found happiness by seeking it. It always comes as a result of giving oneself to the service of something greater than oneself.

March 14

Offer to God a sacrifice of thanksgiving. . . . —OFFERTORY
SENTENCE AT THE HOLY EUCHARIST, p. 376

Growing spiritually is not just a personal affair, or a baptism
of the self-absorption that has characterized American culture
for the past twenty years. Of course, the spiritual life is about
the self, it always begins there. But it is doomed if it remains
there. The Judeo-Christian tradition has from the beginning
been corporate and ethical; "it's good for me" has never been,
by itself, a sufficient rule for living one's life. Neither, however, is an uncritical "Holy Mother Church says so" approach
realistic as a governing principle for most of us in the ethical
choices we must make.

Related to this discussion is the equation between religion
and self-sufficiency currently posited by the Religious Right:
Applying the same rules of survival that function well in the
business world to one's moral life can lead to trouble. "The
Lord helps those who help themselves" is *not* in the Bible, as
so many people think it is. It's something we made up to
excuse our callous treatment of the poor and to insulate ourselves against having to depend on God and one another.

In Scripture, the Lord helps those who need help, and
instructs us pretty clearly that we should do the same for the
widow and the orphan, the stranger, the prisoner, the hungry.

March 15

. . . that we may at length fall asleep peacefully in you and wake up in your likeness . . . —A COLLECT FOR FRIDAYS AT EVENING PRAYER, p. 123

Almost everybody I know is much too busy, yours truly included. Finding quiet time alone is hard. "I'm just too busy to pray," people often say. It makes busy people feel guilty, at first, to sit in silence when they could be doing something. It is important, then, to remind yourself that when you sit in contemplative silence you *are* doing something. You're tending your soul. You're working on the matrix in which you live your life. You need some time to listen to the Spirit. In my experience, the time I have taken to do this has never ruined my schedule. God will provide, I always tell myself when I am worried about time. And God always does.

Perhaps you will not be sitting, motionless, in a quiet room. It may be that the time God provides will be time formerly used in another way: staring into the middle distance on the evening train, for instance, or during exercise, or in the airport waiting room. Washing dishes. Taking a shower. It is often true that the mind and soul are quite available while the body is doing something repetitive. This elegant economy should gratify even the most driven among us: You can put hitherto-unused spiritual energy into focussed use while performing mindless tasks. So even the most mundane activity can become holy, if it is accompanied by prayer.

March 16

He descended into hell. —*THE APOSTLES' CREED*, p. 53

Countless thousands of people in recovery from addictions have been to hell and back. They have lost homes, marriages, careers, the respect of children and friends, almost life itself. There is only one way to begin the process of achieving serenity: by abandoning the fiction that they are in control of behavior that actually controls them. Many, many people have come to understand that only a higher power can save them. And many of these people have gone on to understand that their higher power turns out to be the God of their own religious heritage. Up they come from the AA meeting in the church basement to the eleven o'clock service in the sanctuary, often after a prolonged absence from religious observance of any kind. This has often meant a process of healing connected with very old and deep anger at organized religion.

So much of the religious teaching people absorb as children is intricately interwoven with the stresses and sorrows of their own families. Like everything else we receive as children, religious imagination needs to grow and deepen. You don't do most of the things now that you did when you were twelve; it stands to reason that your faith and those things that support it will change, too. The knowledge of having been raised from the living death of addiction is as good a place as any to start.

March 17

. . . who settest the solitary in families . . . —PRAYER FOR
FAMILIES, p. 828

If we do not take the time for ourselves and our families, here
is what will happen: We will stop wanting to. If we do not
take the time to feel the things we are feeling, we will stop
feeling them. It will be more convenient not to. We will be
more efficient. And inside, we will be almost dead. We will
become addicted to the busyness of our lives, unable to feel at
home unless we are running at top speed. And our families
will make their lives without us, find their comforts elsewhere.
And we will be in our offices, at our meetings, and we won't
even know that it happened.

You must assert your need to gather strength from the
right places, or you may try to gather it from the wrong ones.
So many things are related to this: alcoholism, substance
abuse, sexual abuse. These tragedies have touched some of our
best and brightest. Take care of yourself appropriately, or you
may find a way to care for yourself inappropriately.

God did not call you into family life and working life in
order that you might become angry and sick and dead inside.
God called you to abundant life. Not every day is a wonderful
day. But every day belongs to you, a gift to you from a gracious God. Reclaim your days. Find and savor their sweetness, even if you must do so through tears. Don't let a single
one pass in a blur of responsibility and work. A day is too precious a thing to waste. You never get it back.

March 18

Will you be responsible for seeing that the child you present is brought up in the Christian faith and life? —*HOLY BAPTISM*, p. 302

The newspapers tell us that we are in the midst of a religious awakening in America. They say that church schools are growing again, that young families are returning to church on Sunday, that the baby boomers, in their embrace of the new traditionalism, have made religion part of their program. *Life Magazine*, venerable barometer of the national spirit, has featured religion in more of its covers over the past year than it has anything else—more than sex, more than violence, more than war.

Of course, just because people want to have an ageless body and a timeless mind and be embraced by the light doesn't mean that they know what being a member of a faith community really means. For the first time, we are welcoming adults who have had no model for church life in their upbringing. Their parents, feeling oppressed by a religion they viewed as a punitive collection of rules, vowed that their children would be free of that, and so they have been—free, and almost completely clueless about what life together in faith entails.

You don't really free your children by keeping them in ignorance about their religious heritage. They may—and probably will—reject some or all of what we pass on to them. It's their choice. But it should be an informed one.

March 19

Therefore marriage is not to be entered into unadvisedly or lightly, but reverently, deliberately, and in accordance with the purposes for which it was instituted by God. —CELEBRATION *AND BLESSING OF A MARRIAGE*, p. 423

A couple had gone through the required premarital counseling. They had gone through the rehearsal. The church was full. Everything was going along normally until the priest got to the part about how if anybody knew any reason why this couple should not be married, he or she should speak now or else forever hold his or her peace.

Suddenly the groom spoke. He couldn't go through with it. After a stunned silence, the priest ushered the trembling young couple into the sacristy. The father of the bride turned a deep red. Her mother folded her hands and stared straight ahead.

After a time, the priest came out. He announced that the wedding would not be taking place today after all. The father of the bride invited everybody to go on back to the parish hall; there was no reason why all that food should go to waste just because some people don't have the sense God gave a mosquito.

If that couple ever did finally tie the knot, you can bet they went into it with their eyes open. That young man brought embarrassment on a lot of people, but it was better to do what he did than to enter into marriage with anything other than a whole and willing heart.

March 20

Help us, O Lord, to finish the good work here begun.
—*THANKSGIVING FOR NATIONAL LIFE*, p. 839

Who among us would ever have thought we would see the end of the Cold War? For so many decades, we defined America in relation to our Soviet enemy, locating in the former USSR everything that was evil, tolerating and supporting terrible injustices and corruption in other nations if only they would ally themselves with us. We invested our free-market economy with a moral value that was almost religious in nature, primarily because it was different from theirs.

A Darwinian approach to those who could not prosper in our economy was invested with chilling moral authority: their inability to keep up was framed as voluntary. "If they can't keep up," we said smugly to one another, "it's because they don't want to work." We talked of our grandparents who came here with nothing, about how nobody gave *them* a handout, and an entire nation learned to feel good about turning its backs on the poor. Some of us became ridiculously wealthy selling investments in what turned out to be literally nothing at all. And at the end of the decade, the wall that divided a world we called Free from the monolith we imagined behind the Iron Curtain tumbled to the ground.

True to our entrepreneurial selves, some of us picked up as many pieces of the wall as we could to carry out of Berlin. Up where I live, they sold them at Bloomingdale's.

March 21

. . . look with compassion on us and all who turn to you for help. . . . —COLLECT AT THE PRAYERS OF THE PEOPLE, p. 395

The word "compassion" comes from the Latin. It means, literally, "feeling with," feeling the pain of another. It is something you cannot have if you cannot see yourself in the other. The more different I think you are from me, the less I am able to feel your pain. Put enough distance between us and I don't even have to know you have any. Your pain can become like something on TV to me, an abstract piece of news. Suffering without a face cannot touch us. We just change the channel.

If we cannot summon compassion for our brothers and sisters, is it any wonder that our talk of civil peace and social responsibility falls on cynical ears? We shake our heads about the danger in our streets, about how we don't feel safe walking out at night, but we do not talk as much about the African Americans who are stopped on the street routinely every day because they happen to be driving through the wrong neighborhood, the black accountant who is pulled over and questioned for two hours because his sunglasses fit a profile. There is probably not an African American among us who has not experienced something like this.

Until we understand our common ground and common interests to be more important than those things that make us different from one another, we cannot act from compassion. We will act from suspicion. And we will beget more suspicion. And the only way to stop is to stop.

March 22

. . . those good things which we dare not, or in our blindness
cannot ask . . . —COLLECT AT THE PRAYERS OF THE PEOPLE,
p. 395

We expect failure. We expect it everywhere: in Bosnia, in
Israel, in Ireland, in Africa, in our cities. We expect the defoli-
ation and spoiling of the earth. We are cynical about the
chances for halting it. When we expect failure, we are in a
state of despair.

And we are also in a state of sin, for despair, like violence,
is sin. Both of them ignore the dominion of Christ. Despair
and violence both take matters into our own hands, as if we
were our own God. But we are not God. Only God is God.

We are right about one thing: we do fail when we try to
manage things on our own. Every time. But we are not on
our own. God does not leave us comfortless. Even in the
midst of the bereavement that is our daily portion here on
earth, the hundred sins and sorrows that cause us to lose those
things that we love the most, hope comes from God. We lose
everything, but in Christ nothing is lost. One day we will be
lost to the world, gone from its midst, we and our whole intri-
cate culture buried in the rubble of time, but the world will
still be in Christ. And one day the world itself will cease from
created existence. It is not eternal. It had a beginning, and it
will have an end. But even when it has ended, it will still be in
Christ.

March 23

Mercifully grant that we, walking in the way of the cross, may find it none other than the way of life and peace. . . .
—COLLECT FOR MONDAY IN HOLY WEEK, p. 168

For a number of years, the Dutch priest and theologian Henri Nouwen pastored the residents and staff of the Daybreak community in Toronto, a residential facility for the mentally disabled. Their disabilities are many, and they are terrible: savage inner voices, physical paralysis, epileptic seizures, disordered speech and thinking. Frightening conditions, conditions that repel us.

Nouwen knew about that revulsion. But he also came to know something else: those whose illness is visible teach us about our own illness. They are visibly limited, but all of us are also limited, bound by our secrets every bit as firmly as they are bound by their obvious weaknesses. "After years of living with people with mental disabilities, I have become deeply aware of my own sorrow-filled heart," he wrote.

Suffering can do one of two things: It can cause us to close down, or it can help us to open up. We close down in a vain attempt to protect ourselves from further pain, but it is a vain attempt. The way of human life is not the avoidance of pain. The way of human life is to move through pain into love, to see ourselves in the suffering of others and others in our own suffering.

March 24

O God, whose beloved Son did take little children into his arms and bless them . . . —PRAYER AT THE BURIAL OF A CHILD,
p. 470

Sometimes a news story just gets under my skin and stays there for a bit. The siege of the Branch Davidian compound in Waco, Texas, was like that. Patti and I were horrified by these deaths. The greatest happiness we have in our lives right now is the pure pleasure of being grandparents. We feel a renewed love for all children, as if Patti and I were somehow grandma and grandad to all children, everywhere, as if we knew and loved them all.

So we were haunted by the deaths of those little ones, by the thought of their knowing with certainty that something terrible was going to happen to them and that their mothers and fathers were not going to save them from it. We are haunted by their lives, as well, by the denial to this old world of the gift those lives could have been.

The temptation to isolation has been present in the Church from the beginning, the temptation to withdraw from society into a little knot of self-consciously holy people, turned in on itself, more and more suspicious of the world outside. In Waco, this withdrawal brought about the deaths of dozens of human beings. Withdrawal from the world cannot be our way. Jesus came for the world, to redeem and save it, to transform the world, not to take us out of it.

March 25

Enrich our lives by ever-widening circles of fellowship. . . .
—*THANKSGIVING FOR THE SOCIAL ORDER*, p. 840

There is nothing more important than community. We are in community from the moment of conception, dependent upon our mother, our bodies sustained by her heartbeat.

The mysterious doctrine of the Trinity is really all about this fact: Even God has never been alone. The Father, the Son, and the Holy Spirit, that incomprehensible three-in-one that has always been and will always be—God is a relationship. There is really no such thing as a person alone.

One of the hallmarks of mental illness is the loss of this knowledge. Visit a new psychiatric patient and you are struck by the profound isolation mental disease causes. There may be talk, but it is soliloquy, talk without communication. There may be laughter, but it is laughter without joy. The spirit loses the connectedness upon which it subsists.

And when mental illness is lifted, it is lifted in this way: Community is restored. Isolation is overcome. Disability may remain, but it was never really disability that broke the hearts of those who suffered in this way; it was the terrible feeling of being alone. When, at last, there is healing, talk acquires meaning again. Laughter becomes real again. Love is born again.

I am the resurrection and the life, saith the Lord. . . .
—ANTHEM AT THE BURIAL OF THE DEAD, p. 469

I know a good number of thoughtful, moral people who reject faith in God. It seems to them that the people of faith do not take seriously the pain of a suffering world. That our eyes are so fixed on heaven that we minimize the sorrows of the earth. That our Easter faith is, in reality, a naive denial of a tragic reality. I can see how it might look that way from the outside. A man dies a slow, miserable death, and his friends spread abroad the unlikely story of his resurrection. I can understand why that looks like a denial of reality from the outside.

We can't force people to see us the way we wish to be seen. All we can do to answer the charge that we are unconcerned about this world is to behave in a way that demonstrates our concern. And in a world that cries out for comfort, there is no shortage of ways in which we can be loving. It may be that Christ will always be recrucified, again and again, as long as the world endures. But we need not collude in his crucifixion, like the religious authorities of Jesus' day did, or stand by and watch it happen, like Pontius Pilate. We have choices about who we will be in this drama, and the choices are ours alone. If we do not actively choose the good, we are very likely passively to choose evil.

March 27

Grant that as we joyfully receive him for our Redeemer, so we may with sure confidence behold him when he shall come to be our Judge. . . . —COLLECT FOR THE NATIVITY OF OUR LORD, p. 160

Ours is the most litigious society the world has ever seen. Everybody sues everybody else; people sue manufacturers, doctors, teachers, their own parents. I have read that by A.D. 2000 there will be a million lawyers in the United States. So I guess we can expect to go on suing one another into the new century.

All the jokes about lawyers and lawsuits aside, litigation is one mechanism human society has established to assure that justice will be done. We want people to be compensated when they suffer wrongly. We want life to be fair, and it is not. We erect structures, like our legal system, to make it more fair.

Many people have envisioned the economy of the Kingdom of God as if it were like our legal system, as if it were a court and God were the judge. Everybody will get what everybody deserves. And yes, we do have an ancient tradition of God as our judge. But the judge in our legal system is supposed to be dispassionate; justice, we recall, is often depicted wearing a blindfold. God is not like that; God is the opposite of dispassionate. God is not neutral; the divine justice is anything but blind. God has chosen involvement with us. Unlike the dispassionate judge, God yearns for our release from bondage, our eventual joy in heaven, free at last from the yoke of injustice we wear on the earth.

March 28

There is one hope in God's call to us. . . . —CONFIRMATION,
p. 413

We remember when we were young. We remember all the
hopes we had for ourselves—grand hopes, some of them: we
would be famous movie stars, famous baseball players. We
remember that it seemed that nothing could get in the way of
our hopes. We just wouldn't let it. Oh, we knew that people
sometimes didn't see their dreams come true, but that was
other people. That wouldn't happen to us.

By now, most of us have found out that human hope
requires continual adjustment. Most of us have experienced
things in our lives that we would never have chosen. We used
to think we could do just about anything we wanted to do;
now we know that there are many things beyond our control. We used to feel outraged if something didn't go our way.
Now, we are not surprised.

And yet, we have also come to understand something else:
It has been in those times when things decidedly did not go
our way that we grew the most. We get strong from trouble—
not from the trouble itself, but from surviving it. We learn
and grow from being challenged. The losses we sustain, the
wrong turns; these things form us powerfully. We might
never have chosen some of the things that have happened to
us, but we cannot deny the growth we have known because
of them.

March 29

Mercifully accept the prayers of your people. . . . —COLLECT AT
THE PRAYERS OF THE PEOPLE, p. 394

You may have had the experience of praying mightily for
something you wanted very much. "Guess it's just not God's
will," you may have said to yourself when things didn't work
out as you had hoped, and you set about remaking your plans
and dreams to accommodate the new reality. But what if God
were not far off, deciding whether or not to grant your
request? What if God were right beside you instead, watching
your life grow, helping you to respond with growth instead of
bitterness to the setback you have had? Then your prayer
would be different, wouldn't it? It would be less desperate,
more watchful, quieter; a prayer of willingness to be shown
what pathway opens when another closes. We would not have
unanswered prayer; we would see that there is no such thing.

God—close to us, not far away, and full of hope for our
good. Sharing our experience of pain, yes, and of death.
But—most of all, and always—our experience of hope.

March 30

... the knowledge of your glory ... —PREFACE FOR EPIPHANY, p. 378

Sometimes I stand at the window of our apartment in New York City. We are way up in the air, on the top floor of a tall building. All around me are the lights of the city, apartment buildings and office buildings. I look at the windows of the buildings, squares of yellow light in the black night, and I think of the people in the buildings, eating their dinners, reading their papers, laughing and crying, listening to music, paying their bills, falling in love. For a moment, I see them as God must see them, and I am filled with love for them, for these thousands and thousands of people whom I will never know. I love them for their humanness.

The moment passes. I go and read my paper, pay my bills. But I do not forget that moment of relatedness I felt. I do not forget how real it was, how it heightened my sense of being alive. Those moments are rare for us. But that's the way it is in the household of God all the time: keen awareness of what is, keen love of everything that is, keen and piercing and infinite. Like the impossible beauty of a spring day, the intense smell of the grass, the ache of the evening sun, the flash of light as a fish leaps from the water. That is the way it is in God's reality. That is God's intensity, all the time.

March 31

. . . this fragile earth, our island home. —EUCHARISTIC
PRAYER C, p. 370

The advertising agencies have gotten on board with the environmental movement: They know that we are worried about the earth, so now when they try to sell us something they seek to tie it in some way to ecology. They'll talk about how they've changed their packaging to be biodegradable, or how they've started using recycled material in their product. They'll shoot a car ad in front of a backdrop of some scene of incredible natural beauty, and the ad copy will discuss the oneness with nature you will have if you buy the car. The oil companies, who know that they have a hard sell, take out businesslike ads on the editorial page in which they earnestly discuss the marine environment and the success of their efforts to eliminate oil spills. A clothing company will include, in small print, a line which tells us that the wooden buttons on its sweaters don't come from trees in the endangered rainforests.

But consumption will not save us. We need restraint. This gracious creation was given into our care, and our self-love plunged us into estrangement from it. Human sin is not confined to cruelty between human beings. We have forgotten that we are brothers and sisters of one another, and we have forgotten that we are brothers and sisters of the earth. We have forgotten that we are children of a loving God.

April 1

I pronounce that they are husband and wife. —CELEBRATION
AND BLESSING OF A MARRIAGE, p. 429

Patti and I celebrated our fortieth wedding anniversary a few
years back. We had a ceremony in which we reaffirmed the
vows which made us husband and wife all those years ago.
And, after the ancient custom of Hawaii, where we used
to serve, we wore garlands of beautiful flowers around our
necks. Somebody took a picture of us, and I saw it in the
newspaper: Patti and me standing there wearing lovely ropes
of blossoms, so full of color and life, so fresh and young—
unlike the bride and groom! I looked at the picture in the
paper and remembered our wedding pictures. A few more
lines in our faces now—more in mine than in hers, for some
reason. And my hair could no longer be called red; I guess
you could say I'm a platinum blond now, maybe.

Society is better because people choose to live in community. In fact, society is only possible if they do. We all know
this, and that is why we observe the turning points of all our
communities: the weddings, the baptisms, the ordinations,
the retirements, the funerals, people coming of age in all kinds
of ways, passing from one stage to another in their lives. We
know we cannot exist without one another, and so we go to
the parties, buy the presents, sign the cards, propose the toasts,
sing the songs.

April 2

Make us, we beseech thee, deeply sensible of the shortness and uncertainty of life. . . . —BURIAL OF THE DEAD, p. 489

You can't tell we are Christians by the things that do or do not happen to us. Immunity from trouble is not what our treasure is. We get sick and die, we grow old alone, we fall victim to natural disasters, just the same as those who do not believe. You can't tell we are Christians by what happens to us. But you can tell by what we do with it. Everyone suffers. But we recognize the cross of Christ in the suffering that comes our way. It doesn't make it go away, and it doesn't make bad things good. They're still bad. Pain still hurts. But we follow one who also knew that pain hurts, follow him through his death—which is our death, too—into his life, which will be our life in every way. The ups and downs of this world do not sum up reality for us; there is a treasure that we have.

It is hard to talk about this treasure to those who do not yet believe. Would it be an easier sell if we promised prosperity and freedom from illness, the absence of personal problems, that marriages would never fail, people would never disagree, deals would never go sour? Our lie would be found out pretty quickly. But we can offer a life that has eternal meaning, a life that knows itself to be in Christ in good times and bad, a life that can depend on that presence with us, even in our darkest hour. And we can offer a community centered around this life, a fellowship of people committed to Christ and to one another in love.

April 3

. . . to give to all nations unity, peace, and concord . . . —*THE GREAT LITANY,* p. 151

A large corporate entity—like a church, for instance, or a nation—looks pretty unwieldy from the outside, I guess. It feels pretty unwieldy on the inside, too, sometimes. Every morning I pray that the things we do will contribute to making the church that God wants, and every evening I think through the long day's work and try to measure how well we did. I think about this all the time. It is not just the individual's treasure that is hidden. The church's treasure is hidden, too. The nation's treasure is hidden. Where is our glory? We argue with one another; we disagree passionately about things that matter. Where is our glory when we disagree so much? We thought part of being in Christ was peace, harmony. What is all this noise?

But God can lead us, and God can lead us through bad times as well as good times. Just as God leads the individual, giving her courage to endure things she thought she could never endure, God can do that with society. We can endure our disagreements; we can live through them in a way that sanctifies the pain they cause us.

So we shouldn't think we've been deserted by God because it's often hard to get along with one another. Or that this always means we're being unfaithful. Life together is hard. But that doesn't mean God is absent.

Give to the people of our country a zeal for justice and the strength of forbearance. . . . —COLLECT FOR THE NATION, p. 258

The fastest way to destroy a people is to destroy its memory. That has been understood by despots and dictators throughout the history of humankind, and so the eradication of memories has always been an enterprise of tyrants: stamp out the indigenous language, stamp out the indigenous names, educate the children in the traditions of the conqueror and not in their own traditions, and resistance to our rule will die out in one generation.

We must not let our discomfort at separatist rhetoric blind us to the need for a people who arrived in this country in chains to assess their memories for themselves and to create a community based on them from which to draw strength. That is not "special treatment" or "reverse discrimination." It is the sharing of a story which can only be fully known by those who have lived it. The majority culture in America shares its story easily, through a multiplicity of official and unofficial channels. Minority stories have fewer forums available for their telling. They are harder to hear. But we have nothing to fear as a nation, and everything to gain, from the sharing of history from father to son, mother to daughter: the children of such sharing will be the self-confident adults who know where they come from and what their responsibility is to where they are going.

April 5

Thanks be to God, who gives us the victory through our Lord Jesus Christ. —*OPENING SENTENCE AT MORNING PRAYER [I CORINTHIANS 15:57]*, p. 77

The people of Corinth thought that they were just about in heaven when they found Christ. Many of them thought that the rules of normal life didn't apply to them anymore, that nothing was the same in Christ as it was before. We see St. Paul working with them in the letters he left us, hear him telling them what the Christian life holds—and doesn't hold—for us. Yes, you are in Christ. No, you are not in heaven, not yet. Yes, you are a new creation. No, you are not free of restraints. Bad things still happen. There are still rules. But we shall all be changed.

It sounds to me like the process of discernment was hard in those days too, just as it is for us. And it sounds like people then longed for the rightness and harmony of the kingdom to come fully into their lives, just as we do, and it sounds like they must often have wondered what on earth happened to that rightness and harmony, just as we do.

But our life in Christ soaks into all the goods and bads of our lives. We can fall down, we can make mistakes, we can be cruel, but we do these things as God's beloved children. We have a remedy for them. We can ask God to lead us all into truth together, and we can trust God to do that.

April 6

Blessed Lord, who hast caused all Holy Scriptures to be written for our learning . . . —COLLECT FOR PROPER 28, p. 184

Modern people have a different idea of themselves than the people who wrote the Scriptures had. The primary difference between us, I suppose, is a philosophical one: modern people understand the human experience of the individual to be the deciding factor in the conduct of our affairs and in our process of determining what is true. They didn't do that. The modern human being is self-contained and portable; we don't live in the same place all our lives, or do the same thing, as almost all of them did. We ask ourselves what is authentic for us now, and we listen carefully to ourselves as we answer, with an analytical ear unknown to the human beings who developed these liturgies or wrote these ancient books.

There are those who bewail this. But, we cannot become first-century people. Or tenth-century people. Or even people from the 1950s. Our history has happened and is happening. And it doesn't move backward. It moves forward.

So what we need to do is this: Not opt out of history—for we cannot—but find the ways in our era in which human history is sacred history. What is God saying to us? What are the signs? Knowing the story of what has gone before can help us respond to what is going on now. We are not faced with a simple task of imitating other historical eras. We are faced with the awesome charge of transforming our own.

April 7

The bond and covenant of marriage was established by God in creation. —CELEBRATION AND BLESSING OF A MARRIAGE, p. 423

The people who were alive at the end of the last century felt much the same way we do about family. At the turn of the century, many people of faith were convinced that the family was going down the tubes. Their worry focussed on the prevalence of divorce. There was a movement in the Episcopal Church to introduce a constitutional amendment which would prohibit divorce, a movement much like the Temperance movement which would, a few years later, successfully usher in the era of Prohibition. To my knowledge, the fight against divorce was the Church's first lobbying effort.

Those people were not successful in getting their constitutional amendment prohibiting divorce. Their successors in the Temperance movement did better, but we all know how that experiment turned out. But still, a hundred years ago, a good many people of faith thought that society was literally coming to an end—and it didn't. We are still here. The human family is tough and wiry. It's not going to die. It's just going to change. The family is a human institution, and change is part of what it is to be human.

April 8

O God of peace, who hast taught us that in returning and rest we shall be saved . . . —PRAYER FOR QUIET CONFIDENCE, p. 832

Not too long ago, my mother-in-law died. She was elderly and had been very frail for quite a while. I was smack in the middle of a visit to South Africa when we got the news. Patti wasn't with me—she was en route to Hawaii to help out with our newest grandchild. So we were back and forth on the phone. I rearranged some things, she rearranged some things. We finally got everybody together, and we had a simple but beautiful service. We would like to have been able to spend more time with her. We just did the best we could.

Familiar? This is our lifestyle: morning to night and on into the night, so busy that our own needs and those of our families are squeezed in around the edges, coming in at eleven at night, too tired to do more than say hello and go to bed, longing for a life of our own—or even just an afternoon of our own.

Do we realize the toll this lifestyle takes on us? Do we have time to stop and feel what we are feeling? I know that we do not have the time, but we must take the time. Sometimes we must stop, admit that if we work all day and all night every day and every night we will still not do it all. We must learn to be still and know that God is God.

April 9

When the priest sees that there is hatred between members of the congregation . . . —DISCIPLINARY RUBRICS, p. 409

Anger can be addictive. Righteous anger, especially, anger about something important, something moral. The energy that anger produces in us is exciting. We can grow dependent on that excitement, get so we look forward to feeling it. Aiming and launching a well-placed zinger comes to feel very good indeed, better than the painful, halting process of dialogue could ever feel. A direct hit. A bull's-eye. A victory over the enemy.

But our brothers and sisters are not our enemies. We do not grow from warfare. The internecine fighting—whether in government or in churches—in which we have increasingly become engaged uses energy we need for better things. Let me be clear: Prayerful, honest seeking after answers to the moral dilemmas we face—attitudes toward gay people, the changing roles of women, the life of the family—God will guide us through this prayerful seeking in these judgments we must make. Fighting it out over them will not illumine our hearts. We will not find the truth of God through fighting. Nobody ever has.

April 10

In all time of our tribulation . . . —THE GREAT LITANY, p. 149

Adversity strengthens us. We might prefer to be strengthened in another way, but the fact remains: we get stronger when we face resistance. And the converse is also true: we get weaker when we are unchallenged. I read an article in which is said that the greatest threat to Americans' physical health is lack of exercise. When our bodies are unchallenged, they grow weak and flaccid; eventually, they sicken and die. And the same is true for the fiber of our social fabric and for our communities of faith. It is not good for us to go unchallenged.

As hard on us as it is, one of the things that strengthens the human family most is arguing among ourselves about things that matter. It is how we move forward in history, how we find truth. How much would you really care about someone with whom you never disagreed? That sounds a lot more like apathy than love to me. Love is muscular and tough, and it gets that way the same way a muscle does—by working out. Against resistance.

April 11

. . . out of sin into righteousness and out of death into life . . .
—*EASTER VIGIL,* p. 291

In the observance of the Great Vigil of Easter in Anglican churches throughout the world, we read the famous passage in which the prophet Ezekiel is shown a valley of dry bones. It is very graphically described, so that it is an easy thing to form a mental picture: the dusty white bones, then a great rattling noise in the valley, then the bones coming together as they had been in life, each bone joining to its companion, the muscles building upon them more and more. In Ezekiel's vision, the dead are resconstructed at last, but they are without life. "Can these bones live?" the prophet asks, and in answer, God breathes life into the bodies of the dead, and they live again.

God breathes life into the dry bones of our fractured lives, and we live and grow again. I do not know your sorrow—the loss of a loved one, a sorrowful divorce, a professional setback, a heartache with a child—but I do know that God is in the midst of it, doing what God always does: bringing life from death, planting joy in the place of sorrow, saving the memory of love and loss for the building up of those for whom the life of his own Son was not too high a price to pay. However great a sorrow, however permanent its scars, life goes on and life can again be sweet, not as it was before, but as it can be in the future.

April 12

Savior of the World, by your cross and precious blood you have redeemed us. —MINISTRATION TO THE SICK, p. 455

I have had the profound experience of spending Holy Week in Israel. Even the stones speak there, ancient stories of God's saving action in the lives of those who first embraced the faith we share. We see the faithful and the unfaithful, the frightened disciples who scatter and hide, the brave women who walk out toward the tomb on that first Easter morning. We see Pontius Pilate and his frightened wife. We see rough Roman soldiers struck to the heart by something they could not explain. We see Judas, feel his false kiss. And then we see him again, insane with grief and remorse, and we see him take his own life. We see Peter, and we feel our cheeks grow hot with his shame as he denies Jesus three times.

And now we see Jesus' victory over death. Our pictures of these other events are so vivid, but here my imagination fails me. I do not know what the resurrection means. It is a mystery.

A mystery to us now. But we believe that we will one day live wholly within this mystery ourselves. The categories of human history do not contain our God; our God encompasses them. And so we take heart, in a world that can be a very sad place at times. Christ is risen. This is not business as usual. And for us, as for the whole of creation, those who know it as well as those who don't, nothing will ever be the same again.

April 13

. . . maker of all things, judge of all men . . . CONFESSION OF *SIN AT THE HOLY EUCHARIST,* p. 331

It never occurred to me, growing up, that there was anything odd about this sentence.

But the time is now past when we can say "men" when we really mean "men and women." Many are angered over the exclusiveness of the old usage. Others say, "What's all the fuss? I understand 'men' to mean everybody, and I don't see why other people have to make an issue of it." Whose anger should win the day?

I prefer not to think of the thorny question of inclusive language in terms of anger. I would rather understand it in terms of courtesy and kindness. Once I know that a term is offensive to you, the regard in which I hold you as a brother or sister in Christ will make me forebear to use it. I'll find another way of speaking that will not cause you pain. I'll stretch my imagination to do it, if I have to. You are worth that to me.

I also love language that is beautiful; and I am not willing to sacrifice beauty and dignity and clarity for political correctness. But I don't think I have to. I can use such wisdom as God gave me to find a way to express God's praise in language that is both beautiful and just, and I can count it a privilege and a challenge to do so.

April 14

. . . the new life of grace. —HOLY BAPTISM, p. 308

There is no doubt that the world needs transformation. Our society is gripped by fear of one another. We see a discouraging survival of racism, decade after decade, a discouraging refusal to hear the words of the prophets for our own time when they tell us that the cost of refusal to change our hearts is death. We see a generation of young people who don't think they have a future, who know dozens of people who have died of gunshot wounds, who respond with a look of bitter boredom when someone asks them what they want to be when they grow up. We vote to spend millions for new jails and nothing for drug treatment, in the incredible expectation that punishment will change lives, that those who are contemptuous of authority will go to jail and somehow emerge less so. Like the man a couple of years ago who broke away from a line of antiabortion protestors and pumped bullets into the chest of a doctor at a women's clinic, understanding his own action to be a way of preserving life, we just don't seem to get it yet.

You don't get peace by making war. You just get more war.

April 15

Let everything that has breath praise the Lord. —PSALM 150:6,
p. 808

When the psalmist wrote this, he was thinking of a liturgical setting: harps, drums, timbrels, singers, everyone in his or her own way offering the best there was to the glory of God. The best—every artist knows what that is. The feeling of having stretched as far as you can stretch. The happy exhaustion of having given it all. The arts sprang from religion, a theological and pastoral gift, not an extra little frill for those who happen to enjoy that sort of thing, but central to the human response to God.

Theological? Yes. When the human being stretches as far as possible, tests the limits of training and skill, she is fulfilling God's command: Be fruitful and multiply. Did you think that was just about having babies? The world is filled and nurtured in all kinds of ways besides the obvious one of procreation. The writer. The singer. The actor. The painter. The dancer. God gives us gifts, and we husband them carefully.

Pastoral? Absolutely. The arts enoble both artist and patron. To create is to join in the work of the creator. Through the arts, the people of God come to know one another more fully, more as God knows each of us. They acquire the authoritative voice of interpreters of God's action in the world. They sing and dance and paint one small piece of the sacred story.

April 16

But thou art the same Lord whose property is always to have mercy. —*PRAYER OF HUMBLE ACCESS*, p. 337

One of the hallmarks of mental illness is the inability to enter into the reality of other people. The sufferer is so wrapped up in his own pain that there is no emotional energy left for anyone else's. Often, he cannot even perceive it.

A psychotherapist ministers to this radical shrinking of the sufferer's world by entering into his reality. She does not try to talk him out of his perceptions; she listens to him as he tells her what his world is like for him. With patience and gentleness, she wins the right to show him possibilities besides the bleak ones he knows about; he knows that she has heard and understood him, and he looks at the new possibilities. It can take a long time. But thousands of people who for many years saw nothing before their eyes but their own pain can now see the experience of other people and react to it. In the group therapy that is frequently an important part of treatment, they become agents of healing for their fellow patients.

They can show mercy. Because they have been shown mercy.

It is part of who we are to be merciful; it is God's image in us. Compassion is part of the human being, like fingernails. It is not natural for us not to be merciful; it is a sign of illness when we are not. We show mercy and receive mercy in a gracious cycle, as natural as that of the rain.

April 17

. . . kindle, we pray, in every heart the true love of peace. . . .
—*LITURGY FOR GOOD FRIDAY,* p. 278

America thought, a few years ago, that we were on the brink of world peace. Our enemy of forty years had become our eager friend. We would not blow each other up in a nuclear holocaust after all. Whew.

But now we know that it's not that simple. Tensions that were dwarfed by that long feud have erupted into bloodshed and murder, as the people of Eastern Europe take up causes that go back for centuries, killing and dying for them as if they'd happened yesterday. Our confusion mounts everywhere we turn: Africa, Israel, Bosnia. Bigotry gets an ample hearing in our own country as well: the great racial divide in America yawns so wide we are afraid we will not be able to leap across it. We face a society that is prepared to write off whole populations of the poor, to arm itself against them, to circle the wagons of our dwindling prosperity and keep them out.

These and many other terrible instances of human hatred are what the loving people of God face. We are not strong enough to prevail against them. Only God is strong enough. We cannot rise from the dead on our own. In your own individual life, you know it is true; you cannot survive the valley of the shadow on your own. I know that I really have no strength at all; God has the strength. God gives it to me in answer to my need. God gives us strength to do the things God gives us to do, for we are not brought here to do nothing.

April 18

O God, you declare your almighty power chiefly in showing mercy and pity. . . . —COLLECT FOR THE PROPER 21, p. 234

All of us have had periods in our lives when it has seemed to us that this assertion was not true. "What's going on here?" we angrily ask ourselves or someone close to us. "Why am I being singled out for suffering and pain? What kind of a God permits this?"

You don't have to ask this question for very long at all before you realize that it doesn't take you anywhere. It demands a sensible answer to human suffering, and human suffering is not sensible. A compassionate God doesn't make human suffering into a good thing; it's still bad. Our choice is not between suffering and not suffering; it is between meaning and not meaning. When we lose everything, we still do not lose God; it is this in which God's compassion is shown us.

It takes some time for most people to encompass this truth. I know that it sounds anything but comforting to those who suffer and have not encompassed it. "I don't want Compassionate Presence," they wail. "I just want to stop hurting!" Everyone hurts at one time or another; some seem to get rather more than their share of sorrow. God's own Son was no exception to this human reality.

When something lays me low, I am not comforted by repeatedly asking Why me? I can begin to be comforted only when I begin to ask Where is God in the midst of this?

April 19

Almighty and everlasting God, from whom cometh every good and perfect gift . . . —PRAYER FOR CLERGY AND PEOPLE,
p. 817

My late mother-in-law was a wonderful lady. She was also a poet. Patti remembers sometimes explaining to other children who came to play that her mother was busy writing a poem and so they ought to play outside. This was a real puzzler; nobody else's mother was in the house writing poems! It is sometimes difficult, in a small town, to do something other than what everyone else does.

But Patti and her sister loved to read the poems. Sometimes they were even in them, and that was a thrill. The way their mother wrote about her world gave them a powerful sense of the significance of things which seem on the surface to be ordinary. They would not have known of these things if their mother had not been a little "different."

On occasion, we punish unusual people. We ought instead to give thanks for them. The good gifts we are given come from God. They do not produce a cookie-cutter family of God, in which everybody resembles everybody else. When we seek to discern the gifts God has given us, we need not be content simply to look at what other people are doing and do it, too. We can ask the God who created us in all our uniqueness how we are to use it.

April 20

For it is in giving that we receive; it is in pardoning that we are pardoned. —*A PRAYER ATTRIBUTED TO ST. FRANCIS,* p. 833

There are some people who seem full of love. You know the ones I mean: they make you feel treasured, accepted, heard, understood. They are happy, and their joy fills them and spills over the sides of their hearts, bathing everything it touches with grace. When trouble comes for a visit, your thoughts turn to a friend like that, and the very thought comforts.

Who comforts your friend, though? Where do these gracious souls, brimming over with love, go when they need to be filled? Sometimes we become so accustomed to receiving what we need from a generous and loving friend that we forget to ask ourselves that question.

Some rain must fall into every life. Those rich in love have hard times, too, just like the rest of us. The ones I have been blessed in knowing have gone to God with their emptiness, honestly reaching for the fullness of comfort and joy only God provides. And they receive it. For God does not intend for us to be empty. We ask to be full, and God fills us.

Often God does that for them through another person. That person might be you. It might be this very day. Today you might be the minister of God's comfort and love to the one who usually ministers it to you.

April 21

Enable us to eliminate poverty, prejudice, and oppression. . . .
—PRAYER FOR CITIES, p. 825

The world acknowledges all manner of distinctions among groups of people. Our common life is arranged by ranking them. We always want to know who is powerful and important and who is not, and we treat those two categories of persons in very different ways. Most of the armed conflicts we are reading anxiously about in the newspapers right now arise from some version of this ancient human sin: using the diversity with which God has blessed the human family as a means of exercising unrighteous domination over someone else.

It's not that there is no such thing as differences among people, or that the kingdom of God ought to be a homogeneous one. There are still Jews and Greeks, still men and women; it's just that these differences do not occasion hierarchical relationships of domination in the household of God.

It is often hard for those who find themselves in positions of power to see this. In the last century, many people who considered themselves good Christians ardently defended the American system of chattel slavery. Passages like this one may have made them uncomfortable, but it was in their interest not to grasp their full implications, and so they just didn't. People don't always see what they don't want to see.

It's part of the Church's job to help them.

April 22

Open our eyes to behold thy gracious hand in all thy works. . . .
—*A PRAYER FOR JOY IN GOD'S CREATION,* p. 814

A world in which nature was unrelated to human behavior was a foreign concept to the ancient writers. So vulnerable to the forces of life and death arising from nature were they that they readily saw God's hand in famines, in floods. They were people who understood the economy of the natural order, who knew that it was wasteful to kill a calf for food instead of letting it grow to a productive maturity, who mandated the gleaning of fields by the poor, who understood that the land needed a rest every few years.

In caring for the earth we need not leave the Judeo-Christian tradition. For us, the care of the earth is not just a matter of the right of middle-class people in expensive hiking clothes to commune with nature. We have the integrity of the worker constantly before us in our sacred texts, and we cannot ignore it. We have the widow and orphan before us there, and so we are not silent about incinerator location in poor communities. We have Jesus weeping over the city of Jerusalem, loving the city and its thousands of souls, and so we do not tolerate an environmental policy that punishes urban waste and winks at the manicured excesses of the suburbs. We have the gospel charge to carry good news to all, and so we cannot counsel restraint in the use of rainforests if we are not willing to curtail the lifestyle which consumes most of them: our own.

April 23

. . . that we may be enlightened and strengthened for thy service . . . —COLLECT OF THE HOLY SPIRIT, p. 200

A friend of mine is recovering from a serious injury. She spent months in physical therapy, learning first to stand and sit again, to walk with a walker and then with a cane, to walk up steps. She does exercises which are designed to strengthen her muscles; the therapists tell her that her pain will diminish as her muscles strengthen. And she finds that this is true; slowly but surely, she is getting better. She can now walk long distances, and she has just begun riding a bicycle again.

At first, she could not ride the bike up the gentle slope of her driveway. She would have to dismount and walk it up. It was discouraging, not being able to go up such a little hill. She kept trying; she'd go a few yards up before her strength failed. Then a few yards more. Then halfway. Finally one day, she sailed up the drive, ringing her little bicycle bell in triumph.

Nothing comes to us overnight. God calls us to a life of faith, not a life of magic. When we grow in patience and perseverance, we grow spiritually stronger. That which seemed impossible to us at first grows possible as we endure in hopeful fidelity to God's plan. God does not test us hoping we will fail. God strengthens and encourages us so that we can grow.

April 24

. . . even now, while we are placed among things that are passing away . . . —COLLECT FOR PROPER 20, p. 182

I come across a picture in a magazine advertising a cream that's supposed to make you look younger. A young woman is smoothing it on her face; she looks about my daughter's age. I shouldn't think she'd be worrying about looking old just yet.

The passing of time is our great enemy. We rail against it, trying with all our might to hang onto our youth. We spend billions of dollars every year in the pursuit of an appearance that will contradict the birth dates on our driver's licenses. We jog and golf and pedal, hoping to prolong our lives. Aging brings us closer to the end of this life that we love so much, and so we try to make ourselves believe it isn't happening. We love it here. We don't want to leave.

Sometimes I catch sight of my reflection in a mirror or a shop window. I'm always a little surprised to see that my hair is white, although it has been so for many years. I still feel like the young man I once was. Did that young guy ever think about getting old? I don't recall that he did.

Will we be trim and youthful-looking in heaven? My guess is that we'll stop worrying about things like that. Time will no longer be our enemy, for time is a material reality, not a spiritual one. Our awakening into that reality, incomprehensible to us from here, will be a time of such great joy that our fear of death will be forgotten.

April 25

Turn the hearts of the parents to the children, and the hearts of the children to the parents. . . . —PRAYER FOR FAMILIES, p. 829

I know a young woman whose mother is very ill. The doctors say she hasn't long to live. They live in cities several hundred miles apart, and so she cannot visit her every day. She calls on the telephone, straining to hear something in her mother's voice that will give her a clue about how things are going. She talks to the doctor. She takes Friday off and goes to visit for a long weekend.

The most difficult part of this for her is that she cannot know for sure when her mother will die. She feels terrible when she must leave her mother on Sunday night to return to work, guilty at the thought that her mother might die when she is not there to say good-bye. She feels sad at her mother's pain and weakness, and panic-stricken at the thought that soon her mother will be leaving the world forever. Although it has been years since she "needed" her mom, in the sense of being cared for like a child, she feels a great need for her ongoing presence and love.

What a remarkable relationship that is: the one whose body first nourished us remains intimately connected to us all our lives long. She gives us our earliest lesson in love, and all the rest of our loves are colored by what her love was for us.

April 26

He has filled the hungry with good things. . . . —MAGNIFICAT,
p. 119

Our grandson is trying a lot of new foods these days. I get a kick out of watching him. Enthusiastic and diligent in his efforts with spoon, bowl, and cup, he is not always very skillful yet; he often ends up wearing as much of his food as he consumes. We have serious discussions about what part of his body is growing stronger because of which food; I tell him that drinking all his milk will make him get strong, and he drinks deeply, then flexes a skinny little bicep for me to feel, so that I can marvel at how hard it is.

When our grandchildren visit us, Patti and I love to watch them eat. We feel happy when we see them eating well and growing. I often think of what it must be like to be a mother or father who cannot provide enough food for a child. It would be a deep sorrow. The vulnerability of children provides the human race with an opportunity to show forth the extent of our compassion; when a society allows its weakest citizens to be in want, it cannot claim wholeness for any of its members. We are all in this life together, whether we like it or not, children of a God whom we have often pictured as a loving parent, someone who is delighted to watch as we grow strong. Not just some of us—all of us.

April 27

O God, whose blessed Son became poor that we through his poverty might be rich . . . —COLLECT FOR THE FEAST OF A MONASTIC, p. 198

I heard a story once in which Jesus returned to live among us as one of the poor, without fanfare or even notice. He ministered quietly amid their misery, and the lives of the people he touched were transformed in quiet ways: one man was reunited with his estranged son; a woman found a home. Another person died in Jesus' arms, aware for the first time in years of being loved and cared for. In the end, Jesus himself died, killed by a car as he pushed a child out of its path. The story was open-ended about resurrection; you didn't know at the end whether that would happen or not. It even suggested that he might someday return again. Its point was that Christ's aim is not to take us from this world but to transform it.

This was a very modern story, about as far from the transcendent glory of the ancient Christians' hope as you could get. It was beautiful and moving, so modest in its expectation of transcendence that it literally had none at all, and yet so gripping in its retelling of our foundation story.

What happened in the resurrection? What did the people who beheld the risen Christ see? It is a permanent puzzle. But we do know what it meant: even beyond death, love remains. Death cannot kill it. And we know it when we see it.

April 28

. . . we pray you to set your passion, cross, and death between your judgment and our souls, now and in the hour of our death. —LITURGY FOR GOOD FRIDAY, p. 282

The fullest understanding of human action belongs to God, who alone can locate it in the total picture of history. But that doesn't mean that we bear no responsibility for measuring our actions and those of others against God's law of love as best we can. It just means that our judgment, like everything else about us, will be flawed. Only God's judgment is perfect.

Christians who ponder the morality of another must do so from a position of true humility. I may find myself in a position in which it is necessary that I take a stand that judges another's action, but I must remain aware of my own sinfulness and limitations when I do so. God's judgment is absolute; mine is not. Human judgment has often been shown to be mistaken, and the norms of one age are not those of another.

I cannot avoid ethical choice and moral evaluation, but I can avoid absolutizing the contingencies that make up the parade of human life. They are not the eternal truth of God. They are but the arrangements by which we manage our walk through life on the way to that eternal truth. One day we will know it for what it is, and our minds and the mind of God will be one.

April 29

Deliver us from an inordinate love of this world. . . .
—COLLECT FOR THE FEAST OF A MONASTIC, p. 249

Christians have often been called "otherworldly." When somebody uses that description, it's usually not intended as a compliment; it means that we are so focussed on heaven that we are of little practical use here on earth. Sometimes clergy in particular are embarrassed by this appellation and expend considerable energy demonstrating what regular folk they are, able to toss footballs and talk about the stock market and go to cocktail parties just like anybody else, but afraid to talk anywhere but in the pulpit about the faith that is the center of their lives!

But the truth is that being people of faith, ordained or lay, does make us different from other people in a way that has nothing to do with being better than other people. It has everything to do with being called by God. The life of faith bestrides both worlds, the "regular" one and the other one, the one human beings know so little about. That other world draws us to itself, challenges us to look beyond the prosaic and to find God at work in this earthly world about which we all consider ourselves so knowledgeable.

April 30

O God, the protector of all that trust in thee . . . —COLLECT
FOR PROPER 12, p. 180

My predecessor in this ministry, Bishop John Allin, used to tell a funny story about an airplane trip with Mrs. Allin on a diocesan visitation. As the plane was descending to land, she asked him a question. "Don't talk to me now," he said to her. "I've got to land this plane!"

The bishop was not the pilot, of course; he and his wife were passengers. He was poking fun at his own nervousness; although he logged thousands and thousands of airplane miles as Presiding Bishop, he was not immune to worry at takeoff and landing. I'm not, either; I buckle my seat belt and pray for a safe journey every time. I am aware that my life is in the hands of another, dependent upon the skill of the pilot and of the air traffic control team. It is completely out of my hands.

An airplane takeoff is a dramatic reminder of something that is really true all the time: there are many things in our lives that are beyond our control. After we have exercised whatever common sense and good judgment we possess, after we have done our best, we have to turn it over.

Worry wears us out and accomplishes nothing. By focussing our energy on a future over which we are powerless, it robs us of a present we might actually be able to influence. That's not a good deal. Prayer is a better one. It locates power where power actually resides: not in our morbid imaginations, but in God's loving reality.

May 1

. . . you once delivered by the power of your mighty arm your chosen people from slavery under Pharaoh. . . . —COLLECT AT THE EASTER VIGIL, p. 289

Out of the meaninglessness imposed on them by their servitude in Egypt, the people of Israel fashioned the memories that would empower their deliverance. And then their deliverance itself, the central memory for the Jewish people, that which forever after sang to them of God's regard for them: "Sing to the Lord, for he has triumphed gloriously," they sang, and remembered how they had crossed the Red Sea on dry land. They understood the importance of their song of memory when they were led away from their homes into exile. How can we sing the Lord's song in a foreign land? they asked each other. How can we keep our memories alive, even though we are surrounded by a culture which is not our own? They made sure they remembered.

The prophets among them kept the memory of who they were alive. They lived among the Babylonians. Learned to speak Babylonian. Became useful and valuable members of Babylonian society, some of them, even became rich and powerful in that society. But they always remembered that they came from somewhere else. Their traditions mattered. Their stories mattered. Their language mattered. And they taught it to their children. And when it was time to go home—years and years later—they still knew who they were.

May 2

. . . forasmuch as without thee we are not able to please thee . . .
—COLLECT FOR PROPER 19, p. 182

God doesn't give us ministries we cannot perform. God calls us to ministry and gives us the gifts we need to do what needs doing. We are sometimes amazed at what we are able to do in the service of the God who empowers us with the Holy Spirit.

I have noticed, though, that people can talk themselves out of their ministries. They can focus on their inadequacies and be overwhelmed by despair at what they see. And so they never make a start.

I'm very aware of my inadequacies. I could run up quite a list of them if I wanted to do that. But I don't. I focus on God's sufficiency for my needs and the needs of those I am called to serve. God didn't put me where I am so that I could wallow in my own shortcomings and do nothing. I was put here so that I might glorify God in my words and deeds. That's why we're all here, and we will have the gifts we need, to do what God wills for us.

I derive a great deal of peace from thinking these thoughts. If I thought that the world depended on me and people like me for its salvation, I'd be a nervous wreck, for I know that I possess neither the wisdom nor the strength on my own to save the world. We have another savior, who has chosen to use us in the great and graceful plan of the world's transformation.

May 3

Thou shalt not make to thyself any graven image. . . . —THE FIRST COMMANDMENT, p. 318

Idolatry in the dying twentieth century is not a matter of golden calves or statues of the Roman emperor. It is different now—more subtle and more difficult to name for what it is.

The first and most obvious to me is our idolatry of money. We view the right of an individual to make money as the most important right he has. Other rights are fine as long as they don't impede that most sacred one. The right of a worker to a job is all very well, but not if it interferes with the more basic right of a corporation to post a profit. Safety on the job is important, but not if it drives prices up. The rights of a spouse and children are important, but they shouldn't get in the way of a go-getter's sixteen-hour workday and six-day workweek. Public services are all very well, but not if we have to pay for them with higher taxes. The environment is important, but not as important as short-term profit.

And what happens when we idolize the accumulation of money in this way? What happens when profit becomes our god, whether we are talking about the earth or the nation or the corporation or the family? What happens? The same thing that has always happened when human beings have worshiped an idol: we find that the idol cannot save us. We pray to the idol, and it is silent and powerless. Short-term monetary gain is an idol, and an idol cannot save us.

May 4

Sin is the seeking of our own will instead of the will of God. . . .
—THE CATECHISM, p. 848

Why does it happen that a nation of immigrants finds it so easy to turn our backs repeatedly on the newest strangers in our midst with fraudulent assertions about a racial and ethnic purity that does not exist here and never has? The natural bond of relatedness, the natural love of family and locality, all become ugly idols when they are allowed to cross the line between self-affirmation and denigration of the other. Ugly idols, indeed: this century has seen more ethnic bloodshed than did all of the centuries that preceded it, combined. Our methods of killing have become more efficient; we have become able to spread more death across a larger area in less time.

People as smart as we have become should know better than to continue to hate, and yet it goes on. We have witnessed genocide after genocide. We have even watched it on TV. It has destroyed whole countries. It is quite capable of destroying this one. I see a terrifying increase among us of tolerance for bigotry, an alarming willingness to ignore and forgive—or even to applaud—racist and anti-Semitic behavior on the part of political leaders. We cannot let these things pass. For us, the unity of the human family is not merely a political issue; it is a theological one. God has an investment in our oneness, and God will not be denied.

May 5

Look favorably on your whole Church, that wonderful and sacred mystery. . . . —ORDINATION OF A BISHOP, p. 515

The people of the early Church thought the end of the world was near. When they talked about the coming kingdom of God, this was probably something they thought was imminent. Time was short for them. That is why we hear little, if anything, in the words of Jesus that survive about what the Church should be like or who should run it. Jesus did not understand himself to be founding a church. He was proclaiming the kingdom of God.

That was the way they were. We are different people. We don't know when the kingdom is coming. Some people have given up on it altogether. But time is short for us, too, even if we don't base our behavior on the end of the world being near. We, too, are running out of things: air, water, money, opportunities. Running out of time. When is the end of the world? I don't know. But we need to reclaim the consciousness that those people had, the sense of running out of time that they had. Because that is the truth: we are, each of us, running out of time. Today will never come your way or my way again. When it is over, it will be gone forever.

So we must live it mindfully. Wring it of every drop of sweetness and meaning we can. Find in it every gift it contains—even if it turns out to be a day on which something bad happens.

May 6

I ask your prayers for all who seek God, or a deeper knowledge of him. —PRAYERS OF THE PEOPLE, p. 386

How do we begin to believe? Each of us has a story of how it was for us, and each story is different, but in all of our stories there is the sense of a personal call to follow Jesus. In all of our stories, there is the birth of a sense that our lives have a spiritual meaning. For many, many people, this sense is powerful and unique, an explosion of grace into a life that seemed aimless and random. For many, many others, it was a more gradual dawning. But for all believers, the beginning of the conscious journey was the sense that our lives mattered to God. The sense of being held dear.

And then the journey progresses. Another person finds us, or we find another person—interesting, the way we find each other, isn't it?—and we begin to be instructed in the faith. We begin to live in community. We come to know that we cannot do this alone, that the spiritual life is not a life that can be lived in isolation. In spiritual relating of any kind, the joy of the community is our own joy, whether the community is a community of two married people or a congregation of hundreds. Unease within the community uneases us. Joy within it makes us happy. Deeper and deeper into our hearts goes the penetrating love of God, and wider and wider spread the wings of our own ability to love. Our capacity for joy in one another grows. Our capacity to feel one another's pain grows, too. One does not come without the other.

May 7

We praise you for your saints. . . . —PRAYERS OF THE PEOPLE, p. 387

There have been people whose love spread its wings so wide that they could give their lives for someone else. We are amazed. And yet that is the journey we, too, are on. A journey into God's love. Always deeper and always wider.

What will this love produce in us? We lift our hands and make the sign of a cross upon our bodies: our foreheads, our breasts, one shoulder and then the other. The paradox of the deep and wide love of the cross is imprinted on our bodies thousands and thousands of times. I must have made that sign on my body a million times by now.

Our heroism may be of a very quiet sort. There is a heroism to the unsung performance of thankless boring tasks, too. A heroism appropriate to wading through the mud. Most of us know something about this: the daughter whose elderly mother's care falls entirely on her exhausted shoulders; the man who slogs through months of unemployment, looking for work so he can feed his family; the disabled adolescent who tries and fails and tries again and never gives up; the woman who works at a job she hates just because her family needs to eat. Martyrs? Not exactly—not technically, anyway. But good and faithful servants of a God whose primary self-revelation is not in self-seeking, but in self-giving.

May 8

. . . that they may be faithful ministers of your Word and Sacraments. —*PRAYERS OF THE PEOPLE,* p. 387

Leaders in the Bible are ambiguous people. I think of Moses' reluctance to lead, of his people's reluctance to leave the relative comfort of captivity for the uncertainty of the desert wandering that lay ahead. I think of the beginning of kingship in ancient Israel, of the many failings of the kings of Israel, of the biblical writers' attempts to understand what went wrong in this or that reign to produce war, or famine, or suffering among the people, of how often the tale of leadership corrupted is told in Scripture. I think of every prophet's protest of the call to prophesy: I'm too young, I'm a man of unclean lips, my people are unclean, too. Let God call us to lead, and right away we can think of a set of pretty compelling reasons why God should get someone else. I think of the deep shame of Paul when he was called by the one whom he had persecuted, of the feet of clay Peter frequently displayed as his call to lead was being developed.

Every occasion in which power is assumed carries with it the seeds of the undoing of power. Our will is so good. We want to do so much. And yet we know what can happen: power tends to corrupt, the saying goes, and absolute power tends to corrupt absolutely. That's for sure. No human being has absolute power, and we cannot behave as if we did without disastrous results.

May 9

Almighty Father, who didst inspire Simon Peter, first among the apostles, to confess Jesus as Messiah and Son of the Living God . . . —COLLECT FOR THE CONFESSION OF ST. PETER, p. 187

Poor Peter never quite got it right. He is often presented by the gospel writer as a good-natured, bumbling Everyman, expressing a limited human approach to Jesus so that we may see Jesus patiently correcting it. Peter says the things you or I might say, and Jesus challenges him to go beyond his parochialism to grasp the enormity of what is happening in his world. Peter's life will never be the same.

We now know what Peter was to become. While we see him fumbling along behind Jesus in those early years, we also know that his ministry, and that of his friends, began the community of faith in which, two thousand years later, we still live. Peter did not always get it right—at least not at the beginning—but the spirit of Christ was in him, and he persevered. I doubt if any of the things that Peter got from Jesus were clear in his mind at first. I don't imagine his own martyrdom was part of his game plan. But when the time came, our tradition records, Peter was ready. His focus on himself, so much a part of the early years, yielded to something more, a power beyond him. And the Church was built upon this rock.

May 10

Father, we now celebrate this memorial. . . . —HOLY
EUCHARIST, p. 374

Our ancient concepts continue to inform us. We are a people
that looks back to the tradition for help as we move forward.
We know that the whole of human history is in God's hands,
that the thread of the divine providence runs through all the
situations in which human beings find themselves, that ancient
wisdom and warnings are not out of date, even if the issues of
our day little resemble those of ancient times. We know that
God will guide us if we are willing to accept guidance, to
teach us if we are willing to learn, and that it is through the
events of human history that we are so guided and instructed.
We face the new century as people of prayer and faith, asking
God for the wisdom to discern truly and the courage to act on
what we, by the grace of God, have discerned.

Into the future we will go, ready or not. We will witness
great change, and we will be agents of great change. New
idols will appear, and new versions of old ones. They will
beckon to us; many will yield to their worship. But let us be
faithful to the God from whom all good gifts proceed, never
worshiping the gift instead of the giver, always remembering
that all things come from God and from nowhere else. We
and the whole creation belong to God, as we always have. Let
us be good and intelligent stewards of all we have been given,
and entrust the future, as we entrust the present, to God.

May 11

. . . for prisoners and captives, and for all who remember and care for them . . . —PRAYERS OF THE PEOPLE, p. 384

We all know that there is a powerful movement in this country against the convicted perpetrators of crime, a vehement desire to punish. I live in New York, a state that has reinstated the death penalty. I was sickened by the ease with which capital punishment, against which the former governor had stood firm for years, was swept into law. I was even more sickened by how many, many people rejoiced in this development, proposing toasts to the electric chair in bars, crowing about it on the radio as if it were a great victory.

We have a message to deliver to our culture: The ability to separate the humanity of a person from the things that person may have done is a rare but essential kind of wisdom, for the responsibility for rendering judgment on guilt or innocence is not ours. We can understand and empathize with the frustration and fear that have given rise to the new vindictiveness, I believe, without becoming part of it ourselves. Our job is the nurture of spiritual growth and freedom in the children of God, even when personal autonomy is appropriately curtailed.

Our advocacy of the imprisoned is not a spineless desire that they be allowed to walk away from the responsibility all God's children have for their actions. We do not believe that people should somehow be allowed to *get away* with terrible crimes; we only insist that even those who committed such crimes remain children of God.

May 12

Grant us grace fearlessly to contend against evil....
—COLLECT FOR SOCIAL JUSTICE, p. 209

The call to holiness is very often coupled with a demand that we avoid political issues. What's wrong with the Church, the argument goes, is that it has become the trendy captive of a purely secular agenda. Many, many people write me to tell me that they want this to stop. Stop talking about issues, they say, and start talking about Jesus.

Now, the condemnation of Jesus and his crucifixion could have been avoided if he had chosen to do that. He didn't have to go into Jerusalem at all, did he? My reading of the passion narratives is that it was his choice to do so.

But that is not what he did. He waded into the fray, a man armed only with holiness. And the outcome did not look to his followers of the time to have been a good thing. The disciples did not think things were really coming together as a result of the crucifixion. They thought things were coming apart.

We do need to recapture our holiness. We do need to commit our lives to prayer, to demand of ourselves personal purity of heart and of action. But we do not need to set a great gulf between ourselves and the world. The world is not served by our becoming a small group of very holy people. Or even a large one. The world is served by our mission into it. God loves the world. Its issues are not a matter of indifference.

May 13

. . . and courage to die . . . —COLLECT FOR THE FEAST OF A *MARTYR,* p. 195

My wife is passionate about a great many things, but Patti prays and works for the healing of the brokenness of the land where Jesus lived harder than she prays for anything else. She travels there as often as she can. She's gone there on crutches. She visits the injured in hospitals, the families whose children are in prison. She talks with those who negotiate for peace.

It's dangerous to go there. Terrorism in Israel is a fact of daily life. In the twisted logic that gives rise to the terrible crimes we hear about on the news, Patti would be an attractive target. A large part of me hates it when she's there; I'm afraid something will happen to her, and that's not a crazy fantasy. I want her to be home where she's safe.

But I know that her destiny, like my destiny and like yours, is not always about being safe. I know that Jesus once turned to someone who was worried about his safety and called him Satan. So if I honor God in her, I must accept the risks that go with her life. I hate the thought of one day living without Patti, or of her one day living without me. But that day will come. A day will come when the love of God is the only love I have left—and perhaps I will realize that it has really *always* been the only love I had. All our loves are pieces of that love. So nothing is lost.

May 14

Let the whole earth also worship you. . . . —EVENING PRAYER,
p. 124

We are rooted in the past, but the past is not where we live. We are about to cross the great millennial divide and it is the future we think of, more and more, as the year 2000 approaches. We are almost in the twenty-first century of our faith, a faith very different from what it was in the first century. The faith that was a tiny, persecuted minority at the beginning of the first millennium is part of the woodwork at the beginning of the third. What does it mean for those of us for whom A.D. 2000 is not just a number, but a marking of sacred time passing?

Most of us would not describe our society as a Christian one. Oh, plenty of politeness attaches itself to our holidays and customs. Banks are closed on Good Friday; everybody wishes everybody else a Merry Christmas; bakeries sell hot cross buns throughout Lent; politicians make sure they are photographed in the company of famous preachers and, occasionally, even in church. But nothing gets in the way. Nothing that would inconvenience us in our pursuit of things that often have very little to do with the household of God and, often, are significantly at odds with its values.

But we are in God's care, whether we are faithful or faithless. It is the Year of Our Lord all over the world, every year.

May 15

Will you persevere in resisting evil? . . . —*THE BAPTISMAL COVENANT,* p. 304

All of us have been shocked by occasions when a prominent religious figure has been revealed in some act of sinfulness or cruelty. For instance, I am thinking of recent cases in which clergy have been charged with the sexual exploitation of those under their care; it is painful to everyone to see these horrors splashed across the front page, to think that the world grows a bit more cynical about the Church every time it happens. As one charged with giving comfort and fairness to the victim and to the accused, I don't think there will ever come a time when dealing with this painful issue will be easy for me. Or for any of us.

It is obvious for visible figures of authority, but it is true for all of us: religious people represent God to the world. When the world sees us, it forms conclusions about our God from our behavior. In a very real sense, the person of faith is not a "private citizen," free to pursue his own interests without representing anything but himself. By our baptisms, we have become "public people," permanent members of a community that will be judged by what we do. Our actions work to dispose others to receive the gift into their conscious lives, to understand God's love for them. Or they work against it. But they are never neutral. We no longer live for ourselves alone, but for God in one another.

May 16

*For the good earth which God has given us . . . —PRAYERS OF
THE PEOPLE,* p. 384

Now, in the springtime, as the leaves burst from the trees and
flowers carpet the ground, when the sun finally shines and the
wind has a new softness, we hear new birds singing in the
morning, birds who have come back again from their winter's
stay somewhere else. Along the walks of nursing home gardens, young people walk slowly arm in arm with the very old,
out walking in yet another of the many springs they have
experienced; the old ones, who have lost some strength, some
ability, have not yet lost life, and they, too, feel it in their
veins, feel the warm kiss of yet another gracious sun on their
faces. Kids beg their parents to come outside and throw them
baseballs. Teenagers start up lawnmowers and walk along
behind them, complaining bitterly all the while but breathing
deeply to get the wonderful smell of fresh-cut grass. This is
the time when we remember how much we love our world. It
is almost too beautiful to bear.

May 17

God our Father, you see your children growing up in an unsteady and confusing world. . . . —PRAYER FOR YOUNG PERSONS, p. 829

I need to work on a graduation address tonight when I get home. I do one or two each year, usually, and I love giving them, looking out at the young faces, the proud parents.

I want the world to be the way it's *supposed to be* for them. They are being prepared for life in institutions that value honest, respectful debate among caring, intelligent people about things that matter, and I want very much for them to enter a world in which everybody is like that. But I know that we are not living in such a world. We are swimming in a much more difficult and dangerous stream, and sometimes those who seek the good find that we have to swim against the current.

But students are not being trained to seek after an easy lie. They are being trained to handle difficult truths. My prayer for them is this: That they will not be discouraged at the truths they hear. That they will find the strength to confront evil squarely, and name it for what it is. That they will be brave, as human beings in every generation are called upon to be brave, each era in its own way. And that they will never forget that all of us are in the service of One who experienced the full extent of human cruelty and still found a way to love the world.

May 18

Lord, who may dwell in your tabernacle? —PSALM 15:1, p. 599

We live in a country, founded upon the principles of freedom and equality for all, in which the great divide between black and white, starkly revealed in recent headlines, imposes terrible limitations to that equality. We can no longer ignore the fact that there are two Americas, two American realities: one for white people and another for people of color. We must assert the wrongness of this unflinchingly, not retreat from it when people are angry with us for bringing it up. Joining with the rest of the religious community, we must stand for reconciliation. That Jesus Christ is enlisted by some claiming to speak for the Christian faith as a cheerleader for the current division in society is a scandal to the cross upon which he died for all, and we must say so. If we do not speak this prophetic word to our beloved country, we abandon it.

The protection of the weak has ever been the priority of the God we serve. It was to the weak and the poor that the Son of God showed himself first. Let us take comfort from the limitless love of God for the human race, a love in which there are no outcasts. Let us drink deeply at the well of that love. Let us love and care for one another. Let us do these things so that we will have the strength to bring healing to a bleeding world, for this cannot be done from a position of weakness.

May 19

. . . may its fruit flourish like Lebanon. . . . —PSALM 72:16, p. 686

By now, people's gardens are mostly in. Into the wet, dark earth went the little seeds. A profound gesture of hope, the planting of seeds: a vote of confidence in the orderly and predictable power of life. Put those little brown specks in the ground and add water, and you'll get plants.

Of course, they don't all make it. When they're a couple of inches high, you have to thin them—pull about half of them up by their tiny roots and discard them, so that the ones remaining have a better shot at the nutrients in the soil. The birds, who were watching you as you planted the seeds to see where you put them, did some of that thinning for you. Maybe a rabbit did some, too; in fact, maybe you got a little more help from the rabbit than you really needed. The impulse toward life is strong, but a lot can happen along the way. Growth into fruit-bearing maturity is not a sure bet.

God as a farmer: not an image we think of right away. We're used to God as a mighty ruler. God as a father. God as a judge. Those are images we've seen and heard a lot. But God as a gardener, investing love and labor in us, God placing us here in the garden, with everything we need in order to grow, sowing us into the earth, from which we spring into our season of life under the sun—to think of God as a farmer offers us an aspect of the divine character we usually miss. It gives us a glimpse of God as one who hopes for us.

May 20

But we turned against you, and betrayed your trust, and we turned against one another. . . . —EUCHARISTIC PRAYER, p. 370

Ever since that moment almost twenty-five years ago, when I first saw a beautiful picture of the earth as seen from the moon, our lovely, lovely world, hanging like a jewel in the blackness of space, I have known that we are very close together, all we who ride through the immensity of the universe on this small planet. Neighbors. What is out there is so much bigger than all of us; we are dwarfed by the vast stretch of everything that is. We huddle together for warmth, whether we know it or not, under the same blanket. We need the earth, need the air and clouds in which we have been so tenderly and protectively wrapped.

All of us, our differences so minute in the face of infinity that they mean almost nothing at all: to think that we spend even a minute in anger at a fellow citizen of this small, beautiful world is a terrible waste. We cannot afford to be without compassion. We cannot hold one another at arm's length, turn our backs on one another, pretend not to be related. There isn't time. And there isn't room.

May 21

And grant that every one of us may enjoy a fair portion. . . .
—COLLECT FOR THE OPPRESSED, p. 826

People sometimes criticize the environmental movement for being antihuman, for caring more about owls, say, than about other human beings. They also sometimes criticize it for being racist and classist, seeing environmentalists as people of the elite, who have gotten their overlarge share of prosperity and now wish to deny it to third-world people, to farmers, to workers, all so that they can wear expensive hiking gear on exquisite picnics in an unspoiled wilderness created just for them. We need to face the complexity of this clash squarely and honestly, and assert in a believable way what we know to be the truth: that the love of the earth and the love of other human beings are not two different loves at all. They are the same. That issues of peace and justice are not fully considered if the claims of the environment are not among them, and that the poor and the oppressed lose much more in the spoiling of air and ground and water than the middle class ever does. That the injustices done in the history of Anglo and Native American life together, for instance, are not undone by making the Native American the tame icon of an environmental movement that is essentially Euro-American, as if by doing that one were absolved of the responsibility of actually listening to what Native Americans have to say. We need to assert environmental claims as the issues of justice and righteousness for everyone that we all know they really are.

May 22

Through the ages, Almighty God has moved his people to build houses of prayer and praise. . . . —*THE DEDICATION AND CONSECRATION OF A CHURCH,* p. 567

It isn't hard to experience the presence of God in an old church; everything we see and we hear is intended to make the reality of God mightily present to us. Every stained-glass window shows us God at work in human life—in the life of Christ, the sacraments of the Church, the lives of the saints, the lives of the nameless faithful. The sound of the mighty organ fills the space in which we sit—we are surrounded by it. We are also surrounded by history: the history of faith and the history of the human family. And it all works; we are filled with awe.

Every grand old church, though, sits on a site that was once just another spot in the wilderness. Urban historians say that the designation of sacred space was the first thing the people of antiquity did when they founded a city. We also know it was one of the first things our colonial ancestors did.

Would that have been *our* first thought? To build a church out in the wilderness, when so many other things were needed to make life sustainable? Perhaps not—ours is a different age. It would be hard for us to think about building a church before we'd even put up a McDonald's.

But even we don't live by bread alone. Everyone needs a spiritual home.

May 23

Grant, O Lord, that the course of this world may be peaceably governed by your providence. . . . —COLLECT FOR PROPER 3, p. 229

The Bible is the story of a people struggling to become righteous, and of God's active role in their struggle. It knows about oppression, about freedom for the slave and the captive. It speaks powerfully of the love of God for the poor and the obligation of God's people to stand with them. The Bible knows the heart of the tyrant and the terror of war. It knows what despair is and holds out the vision of hope in its midst.

This treasure of knowledge is in our custody, and we hold it for the benefit of all people, not only for those who believe as we believe. When people of faith speak to our culture, we do not speak as political leaders. We speak as the custodians of a moral witness, a spiritual tradition of prophecy older than our nation by many centuries. Our power is not diminished by our separateness from the official structures of secular power; the disestablishment of religion actually frees us, allowing us the critical detachment necessary for true prophecy. We are more able to comment on a system we do not control.

In the Bible, it is usually not the royal prophets, those who work for the king, who speak the truth. It is the ones from outside. In modern American culture, we are outside. Perhaps our temporal power has decreased. But our moral power is greater.

May 24

Grant that by your inspiration we may think those things that are right. . . . —COLLECT FOR PROPER 5, p. 229

The Information Revolution, it is called: so much information, so readily available to us. It has made most of us many times more productive, and it has made some of us very, very rich. But has it made us better? Has the information revolution that has changed human life so profoundly made us more humane, brought us closer?

"What hath God wrought?" Samuel Morse telegraphed his colleague in the first-ever transmission of human language through the airwaves, certain that this epoch-making new tool was the work of the divine creator through human hands, certain that the speedy sharing of words and thoughts would lead with certainty to an increase in human felicity. Has it? Do we now recognize the truth better because we can see it on TV?

I don't think we do. We can make a lie look so good these days that nobody would take it for anything but the truth. We can make war look so surgical, so clean, that we forget it's all about killing. We can make unemployment look like prosperity. We can buy and sell across thousands of miles in seconds, and we can do it in our sleep. Even so, the gap between rich and poor widens, faster and faster, yawns like an open grave into which the hope for justice in the human family tumbles in a discouraged heap. Things are different, and yet the old familiar enemies remain: hunger, plague, war. Not better. Just faster.

May 25

*O Almighty God, whose blessed Son our Savior Jesus Christ
ascended far above all heavens that he might fill all things . . .*
—COLLECT FOR ASCENSION DAY, p. 174

The Feast of the Ascension acknowledges, at once, the presence and the absence of God. "While he was blessing them, he left them," it says, "and was taken up into heaven." And we stand on the ground, left behind, not at all certain how to discern his presence and his will *here*.

And this is remarkable: With all of our sophistication, we do not go about that discernment in a way that is different from the way it was done three hundred years ago or two thousand years ago. The watchfulness of the spirit for the things of God has not changed. The longing of St. Paul to align his unruly will with the will of God; the longing of St. Augustine for union with God; the unwavering trust of Dame Julian of Norwich in a God who abides in all things and will bless them all; the majesty of Thomas Cranmer's adoration of the great God in heaven and his confidence in the quiet voice of God within; the anguished struggle of Dietrich Bonhoeffer to discern God's will for him in the face of great evil: the walk of the spirit with God in these great souls is easily recognized from age to age as something like our own walk with God. Wherever we are, whenever we inhabit the earth for our brief span of life, our project is the same: to discern God's will for us and live it fully before the time comes for us to die.

May 26

So guide us in the work we do, that we may do it not for self alone, but for the common good. . . . —COLLECT FOR LABOR DAY, p. 210

Early last summer, when my back went out just as Patti was recovering from surgery, we actually had to have a nurse's aide come in for over a week to take care of us. Our house was like a MASH unit there for a little while.

Ironically, one of the things that Patti was working on while we were both confined to our recliner chairs was a talk she was supposed to give to a group of clergy spouses on the topic of wellness. She told me that she should probably call them up and explain that she was hardly the person who should be talking about wellness! But I told her that we don't learn how to take care of ourselves from people who've never had problems, but from people who have. "Just tell them what you've learned from what you've been through," I told her.

So that's what she did. "Of all the things I have learned from this stupid knee," she wrote, "the most important one is this: There are times when I can't be the one who holds everything together for everyone else, when someone has to take care of me. There are times when my desire to handle my own affairs and my duty to handle things for others is simply overruled. This is so hard to accept. I think I would have preferred to learn about it in another way!"

In an easier way. But there are things in life we just can't learn the easy way.

May 27

. . . to suffer gladly for the sake of the same our Lord Jesus Christ . . . —COLLECT OF A MARTYR, p. 195

This century has seen more religious persecution than all the early centuries, so famous for their holy martyrs, combined. It doesn't happen here in America, of course. Nobody is padlocking the doors of American churches to prevent the faithful from gathering. Nobody is putting American priests and bishops and laypeople in jail for witnessing to Christ. Our lives are not in danger because we are Christians. In Rwanda, Liberia, Burma—in many places it's a very different story.

But it is our business, even if it is far away. Our souls will grow soft if we do not engage in the struggle of our brothers and sisters for whom these things are daily realities. If we abandon one another, each to our own local sorrows and challenges, we lose the gift of paradox which is God's primary way of interacting with the human. We cannot know the risen Christ if we shrink from the crucified Christ. We who work in countries where our faith is not officially challenged are especially in danger, for the paradox is often not very available to us. If we allow ourselves to remain in the sunny, complacent meadows of the worldly security our enlightened national governments protect, security will turn to apathy very soon. And nothing saps our spiritual strength more efficiently than apathy.

May 28

Be near me in my time of weakness and pain. . . . —PRAYERS
FOR USE BY A SICK PERSON IN PAIN, p. 461

Christ came as a baby. But he also comes as a former inmate, longing for a job and a home and a family. He comes as a divorced man or woman, a brokenhearted child, an old man in a nursing home. God chose our brokenness in which to appear because it is in our brokenness that we need God. Weak and broken, but trying to live.

What do we see when we behold the weak? All they hold in their hands is their own longing. They are at the bottom of the chain of power, as the world knows power. But what I feel in their presence is awe. And I see that the world's understanding of power is upside down. Power is not the naked ability to coerce. It is the God-given ability to live. It comes from our loving God. In power that works through our weakness, God is with us.

It seems that most people back then did not see the power in the baby Jesus. Or in Jesus when he grew up. Most people saw only the weakness. Most people thought they knew what power was.

But for those of us in whom the spirit of Christ lives, teaching us daily, the categories of power and weakness are forever changed. Seeing the victory of Christ through the embrace of the cross, our own weakness is transformed. Weak, we are strong in Christ. Dying, we live. We live, yet it is not we who live. Christ lives in us.

May 29

. . . seeking the knowledge of such things as may make you a stronger and more able minister of Christ? —ORDINATION OF *A PRIEST,* p. 532

One of my sons is also a priest. It was interesting when he was in seminary. I noticed that a lot of the things he learned were the same things I learned way back then. But I saw a lot that was new to me. New slants on things I've taken for granted. New ways of looking at old truths.

When I went off to seminary some people in my town were concerned I might be educated out of my faith. School would make me question things I had no business questioning. Faith was best if it was untainted by critical scholarship; I might lose my relationship with God if I questioned too far. Some quoted St. Paul: "God chose what is foolish in the world, that the wisdom of the wise might be confounded." But this passage is not an endorsement of ignorance. Quite the contrary. God chooses the foolish, not so they will remain foolish, but so they may acquire wisdom. God intends our search for the truth to be conducted in partnership with the Holy Spirit, who is sometimes called "wisdom" in Scripture. I cannot imagine a question which would frighten the Holy Spirit away from us. God is just not that small.

May 30

Cleanse the thoughts of our hearts by the inspiration of your Holy Spirit. . . . —COLLECT FOR PURITY, p. 355

Purity, to many people, means keeping away from things. People are pure if they have refrained from uncleanness, especially sexual uncleanness, and once it is lost, purity cannot be regained. Impurity is like a stain that won't come out of a T-shirt in the wash.

I think of purity, however, in more positive terms: single, unmixed, focussed. Rather than being a word for unspottedness and avoidance, I think of purity as the singleminded longing of the whole person for the goodness of God. Now, you certainly will see evidence in a person's behavior of that other definition of purity if he or she has this kind of thirst. The manic pursuit of selfish pleasures will not be a part of the person's world, for the focus will not be on the self at all.

But the sign of a person's purity will not be primarily in the things *avoided* during the course of life. It will be in the transformation of the heart into a disciple's heart. This is good news. Purity of heart—the desire to see God—is available to the most fallen sinner among us, as well as to the one who has never fallen at all—if there is such a one.

May 31

Holy and gracious Father . . . —*HOLY EUCHARIST,* p. 362

We, like the ancient Israelites, often seek to understand God by using parenthood as a model. We see the wrath of God as tempered always with mercy and love, never out of control. Life is set up so that we can learn what we need to know from its occasional tap, and if we so learn we can avoid some of the painful experiences ignorance and stubbornness will earn us. Life administers such taps and the painful results of ignoring them. The process of growing up teaches hard lessons. Our children have to learn them, and it can be a hard thing for a parent to watch them suffer the consequences of their actions. How we wish we could spare them this! Why can't they listen to our advice? Well, sometimes they do, but often they do not. They must find things out for themselves.

The difficult things in life are not the result of God's wrath; they are usually the result of human error, or of unhappy chance. There is not one of those difficult things, however, that does not have within it the potential to teach us a lesson we need to learn. In those lessons lies the mercy of which the prophet speaks. I have learned many important things from experiences I would not care to repeat. The same is probably true for most people.

June 1

Plant in every heart, we pray, the love of him who is the Savior of the world. . . . —COLLECT FOR THE FEAST OF THE HOLY NAME, p. 213

I remember, in the years that I served on the island of Okinawa, a community of lepers who lived together there. They were separated by their disease from the rest of the people. Separated from their own families, sometimes. I remember their appearance, as their leprosy progressed: their missing ears and noses, their faces eaten away, terrifying signs to newcomers of what they could expect as the years unfolded.

This colony was a place from which anybody would expect hope to have fled long ago. And yet, exactly the opposite was true. They were joyful people. Generous and joyful, looking out for one another in emergencies, seeing to the children. I used to love visiting them when I was their bishop.

I remember that one man insisted on giving me twenty dollars to take my mother out to lunch once when I was going to visit her in the States. Twenty dollars was a lot of money in that time and place. I kept protesting about the gift, that it was too generous for me to accept. I can still see his ruined face, with its big smile, as he told me how lucky I was to be seeing my mother. No wife, no children—but he nurtured as well as any father I ever knew. He still nurtures me. He confirms in me the central tenet of my faith: hope in every situation. God in unexpected places, grace and power from unexpected people. Joy conquering despair.

June 2

. . . for the help and comfort given one another in prosperity and adversity . . . —CELEBRATION AND BLESSING OF A MARRIAGE, p. 423

On the radio today, I heard an interview with the elderly widow of a famous ball player. She talked of his career and what baseball was like in the old days. She and the interviewer reminisced pleasantly—until the subject of her husband's forced retirement came up. Then she spoke with indignation and real anger about the unfairness of it. "Oh, I was angry. I still am. I am this morning when I talk about it. To see a proud man so humiliated . . . ," she said. It was clear that the incident was very fresh in her memory.

Once my son Peter was at a Church convention. Stopping at one organization's table to look at their pamphlets, he saw a flyer very critical of me. "I guess I kind of let them have it," he said to me a little sheepishly on the phone later. "I asked them how they would feel if they saw something like that about their father." I didn't say much. I wished my visible position didn't invite such things, but of course it does. If our positions had been reversed, I would have been furious.

People can say what they like about me, but I won't stand for attacks on the ones I love. I think most people who love are that way: the pain of our dear ones is our pain, and we will fight to protect them from it if we can. More, perhaps, than we would fight to protect ourselves.

June 3

You only are immortal, the creator and maker of mankind; and we are mortal, formed of the earth, and to earth shall we return. —BURIAL OF THE DEAD, p. 499

At one time Manhattan was an island covered with trees. The people who lived here were hunters and farmers, and the rhythm of the land and the seasons was the rhythm of their lives. Now, as I hear the subway rumble under my feet, and the faint honking of automobile horns far below, I have another rhythm for my own life. Tense. Too busy. Too loud. The city that we have built has become the island of Manhattan, and the rhythm of the land is almost silent.

It is hard to believe that someday none of this will be here. No Empire State Building. No Statue of Liberty.

It makes me a little sad to think of this. I don't know why it should, though—did I really think the Empire State Building was eternal? Of course not. But the passing of solid things like buildings reminds me of my own greater fragility. Someday I won't be here, either, and of the two of us—me and the Empire State Building—I'll probably go first. God alone endures, and my enduring is in God alone. Do I know what form my life will take when I am with God eternally? I haven't a clue. But I have the promise of the God who rules history and all that is created. All in me that is conformed to God will endure. All that is not will pass away.

June 4

Look with favor upon the world you have made. . . .
—*CELEBRATION AND BLESSING OF A MARRIAGE,* p. 429

We read in Genesis that God saw the world that he had made and that he thought it was very good. Some aspects of that creation make some of us nervous, though. More than any other single facet of the religious worldview, the Church's ambivalence about the goodness of human sexuality has made it seem an inevitable and eternal enemy to many people. The negative face of this ambiguity is so thoroughly documented in American culture that successful Broadway musicals have been created to lampoon it. Many times the Church has been enthusiastically portrayed as burdening the faithful with inappropriate sexual guilt.

Most observant religious people imbibed a distrust of human sexuality in their religious education as children. But when they have found themselves in a position in which their actual experience of a person came into conflict with their training, many have chosen to learn from their experience. Mothers, fathers, brothers and sisters, nuns, priests, caregivers: many people in the forefront of religious AIDS advocacy and service were once unable to make common cause with the AIDS community because of what they once were taught about sex and sin. They changed their minds because of what they saw and experienced.

June 5

Bring them to the fullness of your peace and glory. —HOLY
BAPTISM, p. 306

The soul speaks quietly. Her voice can easily be drowned out
by all the other noise of our days. Let her speak. For just as
you hear with your ears and see with your eyes, so you pray
with your soul.

Those of us who have time to think about it at all want to
pray in a way that nourishes us. But we race guiltily through
familiar prayers and hope that this will suffice, promising ourselves that we'll come back to them and do it right when we
have more time. Many times, we never do.

It's not that God doesn't hear us when we are praying in a
way that does not touch our own hearts, only that we long to
pray in a way that does. We want to be nourished in our
souls. So we enter our dry, rushed little prayers. And make
ourselves some promises:

*I will give myself some quiet time in the morning or evening.
No radio. No TV.*

*I will read something nourishing each day. Maybe only a page,
but something.*

*I will reflect, each night before I sleep, upon the blessings I have
had during the day. I will also reflect on those actions of mine that
were less than they should have been.*

This simple discipline works. It brings back the warmth in
prayer. And God intends prayer for our joy, to bring us closer
to him.

June 6

Fill them with your holy and life-giving Spirit. —PRAYER AT
HOLY BAPTISM, p. 305

If you're like me, here is what often happens: I'm in a place
where I'm actually free to listen to my soul, and my mind will
begin to jump ahead, to grab at a dozen things to worry
about—to plan a meeting, to remember something I forgot at
the office. Trivial things, often. I can respond in either of two
ways: I can become angry at myself for allowing these distrac-
tions to enter into my thoughts, or I can make prayers out of
them. Are we going to get through our meeting agenda? My
soul can answer, in her quiet way: How blessed you are to
have dedicated people with whom to work. How blessed you
are to have lived your life in the Church and been nourished
there. What a miracle each one of those dear people you have
known in your ministry has been—how blessed you are to
have been guided through your ministry by wise mentors and
good friends.

So worrying about an upcoming meeting becomes a
prayer. So can washing a car. So can doing a very disagreeable
sales report. How blessed you are to have work. How blessed
you are to have the strength to complete something you do
not enjoy. Your soul takes your worldly concerns and speaks
them in the language of the spirit: everything comes from
God, and everything returns to God. Look at this, she says to
you wonderingly about some perfectly ordinary thing, can't
you see God plainly in it?

June 7

Mercifully grant that we may walk in the way of his suffering, and also share in his resurrection. —COLLECT FOR PALM SUNDAY, p. 219

Another way to quicken our spiritual lives, although this one takes some doing in a society as competitive as ours: We can allow our souls to speak of our defeats as well as our victories. Victories are easy; you feel wonderful, everyone congratulates you. Thank God! you say, and you really mean it. Defeat is different; we are ashamed of failure, alone in our defeat. No one else speaks of it to us; they don't want to make us feel worse. But it is in defeat that God longs to come close to us. We need feel no shame in allowing our souls to cry out in pain. God knows what has happened.

In the honesty of our pain, whatever it is, the soul's way of speaking to God is what gets us through. Our spirits grow through what we endure, if we will allow our souls to speak of them to the God who loves us. Look at yourself—at your own life. Isn't it true that you have grown from having suffered the sorrows you've suffered? Perhaps—no, I think probably—even more than from your joys. We don't know why we suffer, always, but we can always know that spiritual growth comes out of such times. We may rather have learned what we know in another, less painful way, but we cannot deny having learned it. And we have learned it in our souls.

June 8

We thank you, almighty God, for the gift of water.
—*THANKSGIVING OVER THE WATER AT HOLY BAPTISM,* p. 306

The Bible never lets us forget that our faith arose among the people of the desert, where water was scarce, and people were extremely careful with the water they had.

People who write about the spiritual life sometimes speak of "dry" periods. Dry periods come to every person who takes seriously the call to a life of prayer. They have come to me, and they will surely come to you, now and then, if they haven't already. You set aside your prayer time in the right way, you say the right things, you *want* to pray and be filled with the Spirit of God as you have so many times before—and nothing happens! These times can be brief or long.

Teresa of Ávila had a theory about what she called "sterile prayer." She thought it must be *most* pleasing to God because to persevere in it showed such devotion! She knew how easy it was to pray when feelings of closeness to God flowed abundantly. But in sterile prayer, she felt no reward at all. She prayed out of a desire for God with no glimpse or touch of God to sustain her.

When I have a dry period I think of Teresa. Sterile prayer is always rewarded, she said, with the return of the fullness that gives such joy. Life! Streams of water in the desert.

June 9

Therefore, Father, through Jesus Christ your Son, give your Holy Spirit. . . . —ORDINATION OF A PRIEST, p. 533

Episcopalians assign a place of great importance to the Holy Spirit in our ecclesiastical life, for we have a specific set of beliefs about the way in which the power of the Holy Spirit has been shared and multiplied throughout the ages in the Church. It is probably because we believe so much in the reality of the Holy Spirit that we have argued so much over who may and who may not be a priest or a deacon or a bishop. We think the laying on of hands in ordination is *real*. We think the ordained ministry is more than just a job. The mitres our bishops wear—those pointed hats—are intended to symbolize flames of fire, the sign of the Spirit's presence in the Church.

But the Holy Spirit is not on sabbatical in between Episcopal visitations and ordinations. We also believe that the Spirit permeates the life of each of the faithful, yearning to be made explicit in everything we do, however simple and ordinary. You were led by the Spirit to pick up this book, and the Spirit will take my frail words and speak to you through them in a way that is unique to you. Sweeping through the whole of creation and giving it life, the Holy Spirit comes to rest upon you *this moment*. You are being filled with the Spirit's power *right now*.

June 10

Give them wisdom and devotion in the ordering of their common life. . . . —*CELEBRATION AND BLESSING OF A MARRIAGE,* p. 429

This is the month when a lot of people get married. I've had three weddings in a row on more than one lovely June Saturday. I never perform one, of course, without thinking of our own wedding.

I have loved Patti for more than forty years. She is part of my body and my soul by now. When she dies, a part of me will die, too. And if I go first, the same goes for her. But, though we are so joined, we are also not the same person. I can see her as she cannot see herself. And she can see me. And we each are occasionally called to confront, to call each other to account for his or her own good, for the health of our bodies and our souls. Our marriage vows do not allow us to continue along a path of illness: through overwork, overeating, over-anything. It is my job, and it is her job, to keep us along a path of nourishment and health. It is our job to make a home together, a home from which we both go forth into the world refreshed. A haven that strengthens us. A place of quiet and of truth. We promised before God that we would do that for each other, a promise no more and no less binding than the promises I made in ordination. Both are made in church. Both are made to God. And both are made by fallible human beings who cannot possibly keep these vows without constantly seeking after the grace of God.

June 11

. . . who forever sing this hymn to proclaim the glory of your Name. —HOLY EUCHARIST, p. 367

One of the things I love most about church is the music. To lift our voices together and praise God in song is probably the most thrilling thing we do together in liturgy. Even people who don't sing very well can join in congregational singing, and the music of the assembly of the faithful carries them along.

Every Sunday afternoon I have a hymn running through my mind. Something from the morning's worship just stays with me, and I sing it all day. Sometimes out loud. I can't get it out of my mind, and I really wouldn't want to. The song in my mind keeps me centered in the Eucharist I shared with my brothers and sisters earlier in the day. The words and music meander through my consciousness, and in my mind's eye I see again the wine and the bread, the faces of the people who were there, the different parts of the service. Then I think about the words themselves, words I may have known since I was a child, and I hear them in my mind as if they were new. Almost without noticing it, I have started to *pray* the hymn. The one who sings, prays twice, St. Augustine is said to have remarked, and it's blessedly true.

June 12

. . . our Lord Jesus Christ took bread; and when he had given thanks to you, he broke it. . . . —HOLY EUCHARIST, p. 362

Isn't it remarkable that so many people who knew Jesus so well during his earthly ministry seem to have had a hard time recognizing him when he appeared after the resurrection? Mary Magdalene thought he was a gardener. Thomas thought he was a ghost or a mirage, I guess, until he saw the wounds on his hands and feet and side. Luke tells us that two of the disciples walked along the road with Jesus for what sounds like several miles, talking about Scripture just like they used to do in the old days, talking, in fact, specifically about prophecies of the promised deliverer of Israel, all without a clue as to who he was. It is not until they sat down to their evening meal and Jesus broke the bread that they realized who he was.

Jesus was not known by sight. He was not known by Scripture. Jesus was known in the sacrament of his continuing presence in the Church, that liturgical act which, even in Luke's time, only a few dozen years after the events of that first Holy Week and Easter, was performed by the faithful using the very words we use today: "He took bread, and blessed and broke it, and gave it to them. . . ."

June 13

... the Church is the family of God, the body of Christ, and the temple of the Holy Spirit. —ORDINATION OF A PRIEST, p. 531

The author of the Gospel of Luke believed that the Spirit was present in the Church. He believed that the Spirit was present in the Church in exactly the same way that it was present in the earthly ministry of Jesus. This is good news for us. Luke wrote his gospel toward the end of the first century. Most of the people who had been alive during the earthly ministry of Jesus, who had known him then, were dead now. Luke himself was not one of them; he was younger. He had been converted to Christ by the Christian community, and he knew what he knew from his experience of the community. Fascinated by the stories of Jesus' life and death, his resurrection and the events which followed it, the courage of the first preachers of the Good News, he knew that the Spirit was alive in the Church. He wrote the stories of Jesus' life, so that future generations would also know, so that we would not think we were at a disadvantage in our faith because we did not walk with Jesus. Luke hadn't walked with him either, but he had experienced his continuing risen life in the Church. And he wanted us to experience it, too.

We wish we'd lived when Jesus lived. Seen him. Talked with him. But he is here among us. That part of him recognized by those who knew him once is also recognized by us today.

June 14

O God, the strength of all those who put their trust in thee.
—COLLECT FOR THE SIXTH SUNDAY AFTER THE EPIPHANY,
p. 164

It's impossible to be completely good. We can try and try, but there is always more we could do. We are finite. We always fall short of God's perfection. If we did not, we would not need Christ. We need to remember our falling short. Our awareness of that in ourselves is what keeps us calling upon the Lord to help us. We cannot do this by ourselves.

People are sometimes afraid to say this, as if the certainty of our falling short were permission not to try. But I don't think there is danger of our sinking into despairing paralysis. Our temptation is not to do too little. It is to try to do too much. I think our problem is that we feel as if the whole ride were up to us, as if there weren't other people on board who know how to drive the bus. As if we had no help from a loving God. And when we can't do it on our own, then we feel terrible about ourselves.

The healing of all human sorrows will wait for the coming of Christ, and we cannot assume that we will heal them all. We can accept the impossibility of our task and our inability to perform it, asking for the grace to do what we can and the patience to wait on Christ for the rest. This will not make us lazy or selfish. It is only an honest admission of the way things are.

June 15

All baptized people are called to make Christ known as Savior and Lord. . . . —ORDINATION OF A PRIEST, p. 531

When I was in seminary forty years ago, I was taught that a good priest was to be all things to all people, supplying the deficits of their lives as Jesus would. A wise counselor and brilliant administrator. Devoted pastor to the old and lively friend of the young. Spending long hours in hospital rooms and nursing homes, yet somehow always around the office for an unplanned chat with people who drop by. Handy with tools. Spending every available hour at the church but also present and attentive to my family as well. I longed to be faithful—no, I didn't—I longed to be perfect! I longed to image Christ to my people and to serve Christ in my people.

But I didn't know then, as I know now, how important it was to let other people be Christ to me. Or how effective people would be in being Christ to one another. That is what the Church is: it is the body of Christ. All of us have the ministry of this body, all of the ministers, lay and ordained. This is a ministry we share. From where I sit, that is very good news.

June 16

. . . therefore let us keep the feast. . . . —THE BREAKING OF THE BREAD, p. 337

What is heaven like? One thing keeps coming up in Christian tradition: that life in heaven is like a banquet, a celebratory meal to which all the beloved of God are invited.

I do remember foretastes of the heavenly banquet from my boyhood; times when all of us were together, and my mother made something wonderful, and we all ate and then just sort of stayed at the table, talking and enjoying each other. At those times, my heart was so full of love for my family that I almost told them so, which probably would have embarrassed them to death.

Later on, my own large family at the dinner table was another such hint of heaven. It could be loud when all the children were around the table, and there was a period back then when it seemed as if somebody knocked over a glass of milk just about every night. But the feeling of safety, the joy of watching our children eat—I was acutely conscious of the palpable presence of love in the room.

I wonder if heaven is not just like that, only more so: the acute consciousness of great love. My flashes of heaven-consciousness only lasted a moment or two—until somebody knocked over the milk and I was on my feet, headed for the kitchen to get the dishrag. The eternal consciousness of the heavenly banquet never ends.

June 17

For my yoke is easy, and my burden is light. —COMPLINE, p. 131

Sometimes what we need is a good dose of reality. I, for one, don't want to lose my sanity—or even one precious day's portion of my serenity—trying to excel in everything people expect of me and everything I expect of myself. I don't want that for any of us. My forty years in this ministry have taught me that we need to do three things, and I think they are probably pretty much the same for all of us: First, we need to choose between what must be excellent and what need not be. Second, we need to reach out for the help and support we and our families need. And third, we need to assert and protect the boundaries of our lives, those places in our families and in our marriages that are not public property. Only God can really be everywhere for everyone, equally intimate with everyone. We are not God, and so we must have private places for our intimate lives. If we don't, those lives will suffer.

June 18

That it may please thee to inspire us, in our several callings, to do the work which thou givest us to do with singleness of heart as thy servants, and for the common good. . . . —LITANY, p. 151

Remember the Israeli doctor who went berserk and sprayed a mosque with machine gun fire, killing dozens of people before he was killed himself? I was struck by the cruel irony of it: one sworn to do no harm became a killer. I wonder if the doctor whose calling went so terribly astray might have been saved—along with the dozens of people he killed and maimed—if he had found the blessing of supportive and honest friends who could have helped him see the truth, rather than the ideological fanatics with whom he surrounded himself, people who located all evil in their common enemy. How things might have been different if he had been able to accept his own imperfections and limits, if he had somehow gained a sense of himself as an individual, apart from his group and its expectations of him. I wish that had been so. I wish a heart that passionate and devoted could have spent itself into old age, serving God in peace, with the education and skill that were God's gracious gifts to him, instead of leaving the world prematurely, in a murderous blaze of hatred and death.

I wish that all of us had the support we need, the blunt honesty of a caring friend when we need it, the private space for the family and marital and personal intimacies we need. I pray for this, for you and for me. And I work for it, in my life, and I hope you do, too.

June 19

O God, your unfailing providence sustains the world we live in and the life we live. —COMPLINE, p. 134

Trust in God is not always easy for modern people to have. Many things in life worry us, and we have a hard time turning them over to God. Besides, we're Americans: we're supposed to be strong and self-reliant, the captains of our own fate. Our society is not strong on developing trust; we are much better at maintaining a healthy cynicism about other people and their motives. But then we remember that our society, that world of power and wealth and competition, is not the only America there is.

The society that arose first in our country allowed itself trust in God and his creation and lived in this trust for centuries undisturbed. This society that has suppressed it has lately begun to ask itself some hard questions, begun to wonder if something important was not allowed almost to disappear. In our heritage, one which understood the spirit of God apart from the revelation in Jesus Christ, we find many of the things Jesus Christ revealed: the primacy of love over self; the simplicity of the relationship between the human being and nature; the interconnectedness between people which transcends selfish concerns. All Americans need these values. And now we realize that many of them were here when the Europeans first arrived, thinking themselves to be converting people from heathenism, unaware that conversion is a two-way street.

June 20

. . . you have promised through your well-beloved Son that when two or three are gathered together in his Name you will be in the midst of them. —EVENING PRAYER, p. 126

The essentially solitary way of contemplation is habit-forming: make it part of your life and you will not want to live without it anytime soon. But it would be a mistake to think that it exhausts the possibilities of living the spiritual life. The aspect of spiritual life involving you in community is equally necessary; it feeds that part of you that needs other people.

From its earliest expression, the Judeo-Christian understanding of God's action in human life has been a corporate one. Famous individuals arose in the history of Israel, but God chose the people as a whole and raised up famous figures for the sake of the whole of Israel. The Christian understanding of Jesus as Messiah would be meaningless if there were no people of whom he was to *be* the Messiah; his life is not lived for himself, but for us, and it is poured out in death for us as well. It is not too much to say that there is no such thing as a Christian alone, and the same is true of a Jew. Neither my worth nor my happiness rests entirely with me; they can be complete only in the company and service of others. We may encourage, support, annoy, or bore one another, but we cannot be *without* one another. Our souls are in danger if we try. While it is true that the cultivation of one's spiritual life begins with the self, it cannot stay there.

June 21

O Lord our God, accept the fervent prayers of your people. . . .
—*COLLECT AT THE PRAYERS OF THE PEOPLE,* p. 395

What do I pray for? Prayer isn't just about "Let me get better" or "Let me get the job." To allow my spiritual life to be circumscribed by the test of physical well-being or personal material prosperity would be to deprive myself of something I need: a context for my life that is larger than I am. To enter through prayer into the world's suffering, to take its joys and sorrows as my own—for indeed, they *are* my own—is to become more and more who I am designed to be.

Perhaps you remember what it was like to be in love for the first time; how immediately you felt the joys and sorrows of your beloved, how much his happiness mattered to you. It is that heightened relatedness—minus the butterflies in the stomach we remember so well from first being in love—that characterizes the spiritual life as it is lived in relationship.

In the life of prayer, this sense of interrelatedness is expressed in what has traditionally been called "intercession." "I'll pray for you," one person says to another as they part. I will join myself to you when I sit in the presence of God. I will intend your good in the stillness of my soul. I will long for your joy as I long for my own.

June 22

. . . where we may be still and know that thou art God.
—*PRAYER FOR QUIET CONFIDENCE,* p. 832

I walk along the city street in a clerical collar. "Pray for me, Father," a homeless man says as I pass him, and I stop to talk with him for a moment. "What is your name?" I ask him, and he tells me it is Calloway. He has inferred the availability of my prayer from my style of dress; he has done so without knowing anything of what is in my heart. He has the right to do so, I think to myself as I walk on and ponder this exchange; people shouldn't wear funny clothes if they don't want other people forming judgments about them on the basis of their attire. To him, the black shirt and white collar advertise my willingness to be in relation with him and with God. I ask God to make me worthy of that assumption, immediately remembering three or four recent occasions upon which I have been quite unworthy of it. I always fall short of the self-giving love that called me into being as I move through my world, and I always will. My love for others, however absorbing it may be, will always fall short of God's love for them. My prayer for them, though, imperfect and halting as it is, connects me with them spiritually.

June 23

Almighty God, who hast promised to hear the petitions of those who ask in thy Son's Name . . . —FOR THE ANSWERING OF PRAYER, p. 834

Some researcher somewhere has determined that people who pray, or who have people praying for them, have such-and-such-a-percent better chance of recovery from gallstones than people who don't. Good. I often pray that sick people will get well.

But I also pray for many people who don't get better. If my prayers do not turn these things into the releases and healings for which I long, does that mean they've failed? Does it mean I didn't pray right? Didn't pray hard enough? Only if the narrow test of immediate historical change is the only test of prayer's efficacy. If the only useful prayer is a prayer that works right here and right now, in just the way I want it to work, we're in trouble. Prayer is not a way to get around human sorrow, a special incantation that produces a desired result God would otherwise withhold from us. It is a thread of holy energy that binds us together. It enables the communion of my soul with the souls of others, whether I know them or not. "I could feel myself lifted by all the prayers," someone will often tell me after a serious illness. Get enough of these holy threads wrapped around a person, and she *will* feel them, quite apart from the issue of whether or not she gets what she wants.

June 24

In peace, we pray to you, Lord God. —*PRAYERS OF THE PEOPLE,* p. 392

Some people keep a list of people for whom they're praying in their pockets. I know some people who keep such a list on their computers. I know of an on-line group that shares prayer requests with one another; they log on and see who's on the list and what concern has prompted the request. Most churches have a prayer list in the bulletin they hand you when you go there on Sunday morning, and most of them will put the name of the person you'd like remembered on the list if you ask them to. A list of names and sorrows: Mary who has cancer, David who suffers from a mental disorder, Peter in prison.

What is happening to all these people on all these lists? What are we doing when we pray for someone?

We are lifting them to the God who loves them. We are active when we pray for someone, and that is why, in many churches these days, the ordinary posture for intercessory prayer is standing: it is the posture of readiness for action, the posture from which a person walks forth into the world. In prayer, we walk forth, joined with those we love and worry about and also with those we've never met, commending them and their need to that infinite love and healing that holds us all in its embrace.

June 25

. . . make no peace with oppression. . . . —COLLECT FOR SOCIAL
JUSTICE, p. 209

A while back, I traveled to Mexico to participate in the celebrating of that Church's transition into independence. For
years, the Anglicans in Mexico had lived under the jurisdiction
of the Church in the United States; now they were at last
claiming their own autonomy. It was a joyous celebration. It
has been centuries since the prosperity of the Mexican people
matched the great natural wealth of this rich land. Mexico is
large. The land is rich. The people have lived here amid that
richness and seen it siphoned off to the benefit of others. That
is now changing.

It will fall to the Church to be the strong, clear voice of
Christ. The Church always occupies an uncomfortable seat at
the world's table: if we find ourselves sitting there too com-
fortably, it is certain that we have overlooked something.
There have been many times in human history when the
Church has walked easily hand in glove with the rich and
powerful, when it knew all the time that Jesus chose to walk
hand in bare hand with the poor. We know better than to
regard prosperity as a God, worthy of any ethical sacrifice that
might be asked of us. Economic prosperity is not God. Only
God is God.

June 26

Almighty God, who hast so linked our lives one with another that all we do affects, for good or ill, all other lives . . .
—COLLECT FOR LABOR DAY, p. 210

I listen to a news report: a young woman with two children is telling the reporter about having to give up her schooling as a practical nurse because Workfare demands that she clean the sidewalks in the park when she's supposed to be in class. She is in despair; she has been a straight-A student and looked to becoming a nurse as her way out of welfare altogether. Then a politician comes on; he is crowing about yet another victory over the shiftless poor. His audience cheers.

How can it be that so many Americans heartily approve of the plan to keep the children of the poor in poverty, as if the deadly combination of youth, anger, and ignorance were no threat to the common good? For let us make no mistake: a person who knows that his society has no stake in him will feel no stake in his society. If we break the cycle of obligation that binds us together in society, it will be broken on both sides. The one to whom nothing is owed, owes nothing.

Although the world feels free to ignore the poor, we can never feel that freedom. All of our actions, including our political actions, are informed by our faith in the God who chose poverty and obscurity as the means by which to enter the world as a human being.

June 27

If the Lord had not been on our side, when enemies rose up against us . . . —PSALM 124, p. 781

I was not in the war myself—I was not old enough. I was very absorbed in it, though, as all of us were in those days. I listened to the radio every evening, listened to those foreign names—names like Anzio and Bastogne. I remember saving pieces of tin foil—it wasn't made of aluminum then—and turning in big balls of it to be recycled into something the army could use. I remember my dad saving motor oil to be reused. We saved everything, I think. I remember not being able to get new shoes for two years in a row, because the leather was needed for combat boots, and I remember worrying about what would happen if my feet grew out of my shoes and there were no new ones to be found. I never said anything to anybody, though; I didn't want to give aid and comfort to the enemy by seeming to begrudge our soldiers the boots they needed to win the war.

I remember—and it is painful for me to remember this now, but it was true—how easy it was to hate the Germans. I remember nobody called the Japanese anything but Japs. I didn't know, then, that we ourselves had rounded up Japanese Americans and forced them to live in camps; if I had, I might have had an easier time believing the news about the death camps in Europe. I like to remember the feeling of common cause we all had—it is rare today. But it is important also to remember that even a just war is really not glorious.

June 28

When observed, the ceremony of the washing of feet appropriately follows the Gospel and homily. —RUBRIC FOR MAUNDY THURSDAY, p. 274

For me, the most powerful teachings of Jesus were his actions of inclusion: eating with the tax collector, talking with the prostitute—the representatives of those who had been outcast by a rigid, righteous, and pious society. He opened his arms to the incurable, the sinful, the powerless. Jesus' words inspire and his actions embolden me to do the same.

The account of Jesus washing the feet of his disciples is a dramatic illustration of this style of leadership. After dining with his followers, Jesus takes a towel and bowl of water and washes their feet. This is the action of a slave. The deeper I find myself in prayer and reflection on this act, which summarizes all his life, the stronger the servant role emerges. It is not only in what Jesus did that I find guidance and nourishment, it is in what he became. He became a servant. He became powerless. Jesus became an outcast.

In the person of Jesus, Christians have claimed a special revelation of God. And Jesus allowed himself to become an outcast. Chose the simple and the sinful as his friends. We are so anxious about our prestige and position. We've got a ways to go before we become like him.

June 29

I am in an unusual walk of life—most people who are not clergy, or close to clergy in some way, don't realize that it is as hard for us to connect with Jesus as it is for them. That, in some ways, it can be even harder: if we are not careful, we can get so busy about the Lord's work that we have little time or energy for the Lord himself. We can spend ourselves facilitating other people's religious experiences, and unless we take explicit care of our own souls, everyone gets fed but us.

I realized early in my forty-something years of ministry that my walk with Christ was mine. That I wasn't going to be able just to "do church" and pretend that this public ministry was all that was needed for a spiritual life. I love the public parts of my work. But if there is no private part, I am not complete.

I realized that I am called to this life in order that I may find God in it. So wherever I have gone, I listen for the presence of God. I watch for the signs—not just the obvious signs, the ones you find in churches, but the unexpected signs of God's presence. And, in forty years, there has never been a time when I did not find them. Of course, there wouldn't be, would there? God is not in the business of hiding from us. If we are willing to see Christ in unexpected places, we will never miss him.

June 30

Lead us, who know you now by faith, to your presence. . . .
—COLLECT FOR THE EPIPHANY, p. 214

I found Christ recently in a very unexpected place. The person who brought me face-to-face with Jesus turned out not to be a Christian at all. She was a Buddhist. She was Daw Aung San Suu Kyi, the spiritual leader of the democracy movement in Burma. She was held under house arrest for six years, kept from her husband and children, by the military junta that rules the country with an iron hand, all because she would not abandon the cause of democracy.

But she holds no grudge against the men who imprisoned her. "They did me no harm," she says, and she means it. It is clear that she simply does not worry about her house or herself. She does not allow fear to hold her back from her calling, even fear of death. "Everyone must die," she says, very calmly, with good humor. After all, she is a Buddhist. "We do not believe in permanence of any kind," she says.

As I listened to her, a person whose life has been in danger more than once for her beliefs, I thought of Jesus, on his way to Jerusalem, knowing what lay before him. Now here was this tiny, courageous Buddhist woman, sitting in the semi-darkness of her bare living room and talking softly about freedom, her country, her own death. I had the sense of being with Jesus. He is truly Lord of all. There is nowhere on earth where we cannot find him.

July 1

. . . to have and to hold from this day forward, for better for worse . . . —CELEBRATION AND BLESSING OF A MARRIAGE, p. 427

We had a letter from a dear friend—just a little note, really, to say how nice it had been to be together at a conference the week before. Patti and I have known her and her husband for years and don't see nearly enough of them. She wrote, "Learning to talk about our differences sure takes a lot of determination. . . . Unless we want to get divorced, which we don't, we might as well learn to talk civilly to one another."

Marriage joins people who may be very different. Never again can plans be made or dreams dreamed as if the union did not exist. When you are married, you cannot one day just decide not to be.

I was touched by the pain and the courage that I read—between the lines, mostly—in my friend's letter. She didn't say she was in pain, not in so many words. She is not given to complaining. I responded at a very deep level to her fierce protectiveness of her marriage, to her willingness to endure pain for its sake. That is not the floppy love of sugar-sweet greeting cards. That is love that will not let go. And it is that tough, wiry love that is asked of us, for it was that kind of love that brought us all here. Love that did not shrink from the cross. No easy thing. But this vowed relationship that unites two human beings, with all of its difficulties, is also a primary way in which we learn what joy is.

July 2

O God, the life of all who live . . . —A COLLECT FOR
PROTECTION AT EVENING PRAYER, p. 124

To love God with all our hearts, to hold our neighbor's good
with the same urgency with which we hold our own, to give
place in love to the brother or sister with whom we vehe-
mently disagree when every competitive fiber of our being
aches for the thrill of victory: no easy thing. To yield up our
power, the world's shiniest treasure, becoming a servant
instead of a master, a partner instead of a boss: most unnatural behavior, according to the canons which govern the world.
No wonder we fail at it so often. We are often tested for the
depth of our desire to live together in this way. We all know
that it will not be easy; nothing of any real importance ever is.
But I can imagine no more potent comfort than the presence
of the God who has shown us this difficult love. I wouldn't
trade it for anything.

July 3

. . . restore me to the blessed company of your faithful people. . . .
—*RECONCILIATION OF A PENITENT*, p. 450

I never forget that Christ died for the one with whom I disagree as well as for me, and that in Christ the pain of disagreement will be comforted if I am open to it. This can be so hard! But God calls us to show the world what love is by loving our enemies.

How on earth do you do that? How do you love someone who has hurt you and is likely to hurt you again, someone the mention of whose very name makes you angry? Perhaps it will help to note that we don't have to like a person to show him the love of Christ; it is a decision, not a feeling. In fact, the very dislike you are feeling can form the basis of your prayer for the one with whom you find yourself at odds; this situation of enmity is hurtful to you and can be offered to a loving God in prayer.

It may be that you and that person will never be on intimate terms. You may rub each other the wrong way for the rest of your lives. Not everybody is everybody else's best friend. But praying for an enemy drains the venom out of your heart, and nobody needs a heart full of venom. The love God plants in your heart may indeed be love from a considerable distance, but there is no heart in which God cannot plant love if we are willing.

July 4

For seasonable weather . . . let us pray to the Lord. —PRAYERS
OF THE PEOPLE, p. 384

It's been awfully hot today, but I see that tremendous dark
clouds are forming: we're going to have a cloudburst any
minute now. Three different people have come back into the
office from lunch and remarked upon it. The weather reminds
us of who we are. We are not the ones who run the world.
Forces far beyond our small strength determine a great deal of
what happens to the human race. No wonder people in
ancient times worshiped the forces of nature. They're a lot
bigger than we are.

We don't worship trees and storms. I think, moreover,
that most of us have moved beyond the childish analysis that
attributes natural disasters to God's agency as the direct and
immediate punishment for human sin. God doesn't send us
tragedy to teach us a lesson.

But that does not mean there are not lessons to be learned
from the things that happen in history. We often have very
little say over what will happen, but we have sole power over
what we will do with it. God will move with great power in
our lives if we allow God to do so, but nobody has to allow
God's power. It has always been quite possible to live one's
life with absolutely no reference to God's presence in it, and it
still is. Nobody's going to force us to be Christians. The ball is
entirely in our court.

July 5

O God, you have made of one blood all the peoples of the earth. . . . —COLLECT FOR THE MISSION OF THE CHURCH, p. 257

While I was bishop of Okinawa, it became clear that the Church would need to stand on its own as an independent part of the Church in that area, rather than as a part of the Church in faraway America. A delegation of leaders from Japan then visited us with a proposal: the Okinawan Church could become a part of the Church in Japan, with the proviso that I would remain as the bishop, rather than an Okinawan being elected. "No way," I said. This was not to be a colonial church, whose own leadership does not lead it, or a church that embodied the second-class citizenship of the Okinawan people in the eyes of the Japanese. The time when the Church baptized cultural and ethnic prejudices was coming painfully to an end back here at home—this was the mid-1960s—and I wasn't about to be part of perpetuating that approach in the Church overseas.

Needless to say, this was disconcerting to some. But the church on Okinawa *did* become independent of America, and an Okinawan *did* become its bishop. The larger culture of the Japanese Church *did* allow itself to be enriched by the smaller one of its island neighbor. From a cloud of sinful realities—the fracturing of a society by war, the painful reality of ethnic and cultural prejudice—God brought forth something better. The forces of domination and prejudice did not get the last word.

July 6

For the kingdom, the power, and the glory are yours . . . —THE
LORD'S PRAYER, p. 364

Jesus ran away from an admiring crowd once, we are told,
because "he perceived they were about to take him by force
and make him a king." He rejected that kind of power all his
life. "My kingdom is not of this world," he said to a man who
knew a lot about how worldly power worked, and Pontius
Pilate didn't understand what on earth he was talking about.
Power that ennobles the people of God, power that dedicates
itself to their empowerment, power that is not all about its
own conservation—an earthly king doesn't understand that
power. The metaphor of kingship, once so useful in the human
groping for words to describe the power of God, suffers now
from our consciousness of the centuries of oppression kings
have wrought on their subjects. And the modern, eviscerated
king, that quaint and slightly embarrassing polite figure of
contemporary constitutional monarchies, is a poor communi-
cator of the awesomeness after which we seek when we try to
speak of God.

We struggle to understand power—the power of God and
our own power—as the human definition of power changes
and develops through the ages. It is not what it was. History
only moves forward, and while we are in the body, we move
forward with it.

July 7

Almighty God, whose will it is to be glorified in your saints . . .
—COLLECT FOR THE FEAST OF A MISSIONARY, p. 248

I've been looking back over my life recently at the different eras of my forty-plus years as a priest. Has being the Presiding Bishop been the hardest thing I've ever done? I think of the missionary work that was my early ministry, the rickety church buildings and the window fans that didn't work and all the resources we didn't have—that was hard. But I remember how the people filled those rickety churches with flowers every week, how soft and dark and lovely the nights on Okinawa were, how it was to raise children who knew for a fact that the world was splendidly full of diverse people because they'd experienced that diversity firsthand—what a gift it was to do that work! It was hard, but good.

And that's how I'd have to sum up this work, too. Hard, but good. The buck usually stops on my desk, and that means that not everybody is thrilled with me all the time. But to travel around this Church of ours and see how ordinary people love their churches, how good they are, how hard they work—it is a great joy. And to experience firsthand the courage of our brothers and sisters overseas—living their lives in Christ under the thumb of religious persecution, some of them in danger of their lives—it has been awesome to know them. I wouldn't have traded it for anything.

July 8

But I have squandered the inheritance of your saints, and have wandered far in a land that is waste. —RECONCILIATION OF A PENITENT, p. 450

The ancient Israelites believed that God was revealed to them in the law. When they talked about the righteous reign of God, it was primarily in ethical and legal terms. But the prophets constantly pushed them—and us—to go further than the letter of the law, beyond the dryness of legalistic self-definition to the living reality of God's presence in human life. Not just What must I do in order to avoid punishment? but What can I do in order to be truly righteous? To seek God's presence in our lives in a personal way—not to just follow God's operating instructions for the world and the society, but to believe in God among us.

Some people have given up on that idea altogether. But I have not given up. God is with us, and we must make ourselves ready to inhabit a world that more resembles the God who made it, a world whose heart is not of stone, but a world with a living heart.

We must prepare ourselves for that world, that household of God, that new, living heart. For we cannot continue to live with hearts of stone. A child hopes to escape punishment, but an adult walks into the world full of hope and trust in the God who challenges her to be righteous and will show her how. One is passive, the other active. One is timid, the other is brave.

July 9

Almighty Father, whose blessed Son before his passion prayed for his disciples that they might be one, as you and he are one . . .
—COLLECT FOR THE UNITY OF THE CHURCH, p. 255

Is unity really important? Is it worth the trouble and pain spent in trying to maintain it? What if we just said, to those who disagree with us, "Well, all right then, the heck with you, I'm leaving!!" Why do we spend so much energy and time and—yes—money, trying to find a way to stay together? The Lutherans and the Anglicans have been separate for nearly five hundred years; why try to find a way to worship again in institutional unity now?

Because the Body of Christ is a living body, not a statue. We are flesh, not stone. Each united with him, we cannot *not* be united one with another. It would be like brothers and sisters in the same family who do not speak. You may know a family in which this situation prevails, and if you do, you observe that their silence doesn't affect just them; the whole family is injured by it. Connected in Christ, we do not choose whether or not to be related; we just are. And if we are not relating to each other, we cannot accurately say that we are relating to Christ. We waste precious time grooming our differences instead of nurturing the love of the sisters and brothers to which God calls us. We puzzle outsiders and obscure the liberating message of Jesus Christ that we are called to proclaim.

. . . to preach peace to those who are far off and to those who are near . . . —MORNING PRAYER, p. 100

I remember once, when I was a boy, a traveling revival came to town. They set up a big old tent. I'll never forget the heat: the ladies fanning themselves with fans from the funeral parlor with Bible scenes printed on them, the men in their shirt-sleeves, sweating. I can see the preacher now, and I can hear him, holding his Bible up in the air and shouting, and then dropping suddenly almost to a whisper, his face gleaming in the heat, his voice full of emotion, like he was ready to burst out crying right there.

I was an Episcopalian, and I had already listened to a lot of sermons in my short lifetime, and we sure never had any like that in my church. When he called for people to come up front and be saved, I found my feet walking me right on up. The next morning, I woke up in my room and looked around. I thought of the night before, of the heavy hands of the preacher on my head. And then I thought of the rector of my parish church, a man who was like a second father to me, and I pulled the covers back up over my face. Why on earth had I gone up there?

The next day I got a letter from the rector. He told me how proud he was of me. I was safe calling upon the name of God, no matter where I did that. Nothing had been lost. I had not ceased to be myself. God is large enough to be met in some pretty out-of-the-way places.

July 11

Help us to heal those who are broken in body or spirit. . . .
—*PRAYER FOR THE POOR AND NEGLECTED,* p. 826

Several times, I have participated in the reading of names at a memorial service involving the AIDS quilt, the gigantic communal needlework project that arose out of the sorrow of the AIDS epidemic. The epidemic grinds on and on. The quilt gets bigger and bigger. The flower of a generation has been deprived of the God-given right to live and love and work and grow old. The number of the bereaved increases; there are more orphans, more mourning parents and partners. Every stitch of that quilt speaks of heartbreak.

But every stitch also speaks of sweetness. This ongoing tragedy has brought about the largest sustained expression of compassion the world has ever seen. People are often moved to acts of kindness by tragedy, but it is usually the case that the action is taken over a relatively brief period of time. The response to AIDS has been sustained. Many people here today have, in some way, made their response to this epidemic a permanent part of their lives. They are in it for the duration.

As beautiful and stirring a memorial as those bright acres of memory are, the quilt is not a more beautiful memorial to the martyrs of AIDS than these consecrated lives of service. Sometimes sorrow makes a person shrink into bitter isolation. But their sorrow has not made them shrink. It has made them grow in compassion to a needy world.

July 12

Almighty God, the giver of all good gifts . . . —COLLECT FOR
THE MINISTRY, p. 205

Everything is a gift from God. The people we love, the skills we have, our possessions, our physical health—we hold no entitlement to any of these. I visit a hospital in the Holy Land and talk briefly with a young man who has lost a leg in a bombing, a mother who waits to hear if her son will live or die after surgery. In other countries the same: young people, whose strong young bodies are ripped by bullets or explosives or the anonymous withering of extreme poverty. I think of my own children, of their healthy bodies, of how good Patti and I always felt after a medical checkup, or even just after watching them eat a good meal; it is a wonderful thing to be able to protect and nourish our children. It is the most important thing in a parent's life. And it is a gift of God.

And not everyone has it. Every baby who comes into the world comes in the image of God. Every child merits love and nurture. I am struck, when I visit a difficult place, by the great gulf between my many advantages and the great want of others, separated from me by only accident of birth.

For this reason, we end every blessing at every meal with the words "and keep us ever mindful of the needs of others." We are the hands and feet of Christ, the primary mechanism by which the hungry will be satisfied. We are not here simply to enjoy our own gifts. We are here for one another.

July 13

. . . that their home may be a haven of blessing and peace . . .
—*CELEBRATION AND BLESSING OF A MARRIAGE,* p. 431

Sometimes I travel to countries where much of the landscape is desert. Even traveling by car through the desert, I am parched, longing for water. A little green is a welcome sight.

I think of the oasis, sometimes, as a model for what a home should be like: a haven of blessing and peace. But you do not stay at the oasis in the desert; you rest and drink, and then you go your way again—back out into the difficult and dangerous desert. As precious a thing as it is to be safe at last, the purpose of the oasis is not itself; the purpose of the oasis is the journey. The oasis is part of the desert.

The beauty and lushness of the oasis is intimately related to the great thirst of the traveler. The world is thirsty. The world longs for God, mostly without even knowing it. We see how that longing plays itself out in our culture, how we try to slake our thirst with the salt water of compulsive consumerism, compulsive use of alcohol or food or sexuality or any number of other pleasurable things. We long for truth and love, all of us, and our advertisers promise us falsely that we can buy it at the store. Each purchase creates a new need for some future purchase. Each compulsive act increases our addictive longing for more and more and more. We can never be satisfied in our search for love until we know that what we long for is God.

July 14

The Lord will guide our feet. . . . —BURIAL OF THE DEAD,
p. 483

I was lucky enough to see part of the Olympics when they were in Atlanta. I marveled at the spectacle, the physical strength and grace, the speed. The perfection of the young bodies. And at the discipline: what you see in athletic competition is the fruit of a willingness to enter into pain and struggle in the pursuit of excellence. Athletes are powerfully self-motivated people. They're willing to sacrifice whatever it takes to know the joy of being the best they can be. The drive to be simply the best comes from within them.

Life is something like that. You don't have to be an Olympic athlete; nobody's going to make you. You can be a couch potato. And you don't have to involve yourself in the sorrows of the world; nobody is going to make you. You don't have to give a dime or a thought to anyone but yourself. But our greatest good lies in our willingness to enter into the struggle for the good. It is there that we experience ourselves as most truly human, most fully alive. We are most joyful and most nourished when we nourish others who are in need, most connected to life when we do not shrink from death, most aware of blessings when we bless others, strongest when we allow ourselves to see and respond to the weakness of others. Most connected to God, the source of our strength, when we allow ourselves to be connected with our brothers and sisters in the world.

July 15

O Lamb of God, that takest away the sins of the world, grant us thy peace. —AGNUS DEI, p. 337

Some say war is the inevitable product of a competitiveness with which we are born. Others point to studies of cultures who are not competitive to say war is not natural. Yet we continue to wage war.

Why is it that we never talk of waging peace? Why is it that we think that peace is merely the passive absence of armed hostilities? Why cannot peace be something we actively pursue, something for which we campaign, something for which we plan and strategize? Why is it that we do not study ways of making peace, and why do we not have a technology of peace to match the technology of war upon which we spend such vast fortunes?

If war is something we have to learn, then perhaps we can learn peace, too. The pursuit of peace is not something we can afford to leave to the experts. Every Christian is commissioned in baptism to be a peacemaker.

There are powerful signs among us that people of all nations are beginning to see peace and justice as issues in which they have a right and a duty to take vigorous initiative. Perhaps we can come to our senses and realize that we are profoundly weary of warfare and coercion as a way of solving disputes. Let us watch carefully and pray faithfully, that in all these initiatives the power of love overrules the power of anything else.

July 16

Those whom God has joined together let no one put asunder.
—*CELEBRATION AND BLESSING OF A MARRIAGE,* p. 428

There is hardly anyone among us who has not been touched by divorce and its pain, whether in our own families or in those of our friends. For a variety of reasons, divorce is a significant factor in our life together. Nobody would argue that this is a good thing—just ask those who have been through it. But it can provide us with an opportunity to show the compassion and empathy by which we want to be known as the people of God.

Those of us who are happily married know we are greatly blessed. Let us not say to those who are not that they are damned. There was a time when my Church withheld the sacrament of Holy Communion from those who had divorced and remarried, in a hard-hearted refusal to offer healing to some who needed it most. Blessedly, that time is past. We believe that healing can happen, and we believe that the Church—and all of us in it—is empowered and called to show forth this transforming grace among all men and women. We can condemn if we wish. But the way of compassion is a more familiar path for us, and it is the one upon which we are more likely to meet Christ.

July 17

. . . give your angels charge over those who sleep. —COMPLINE, p. 134

Dreams are filled with messages. They are like the best prayers: honest. Sometimes they are signals to us that we are troubled by something to which we would never admit in the daytime. Sometimes they are expressions of anger or sorrow or fear of which we are consciously unaware, and sometimes becoming aware of those feelings can liberate us from them. Sometimes dreams are wishes, and sometimes dreams give us the solutions to problems over which we have puzzled to no avail when we were awake.

The ancients believed that God spoke to people in dreams. Long before Freud and Jung, they sensed the importance of what dreams have to tell us. It seems to me the most natural thing in the world that God should speak to us in our dreams. God speaks to us in everything, why *not* in dreams as well? It is a good thought to have as we fall asleep each night. Even in our sleep, God is close to us, speaking to us in ways we cannot hear when we are awake.

July 18

Create in me a clean heart, O God, and renew a right spirit within me. —PSALM 51:11, p. 657

I remember listening to the Nuremburg trials. Listening to the Nazis' laconic descriptions of their work, I had a terrible feeling that was new to me: it seemed that the human race had somehow changed character during the war, had actually changed what a human being is, as if a leopard had changed his spots. Where had our goodness gone? I had no place in my experience to fit people who could put living babies in flaming ovens in the morning and listen to a symphony in the afternoon. I felt as if I had been a fool, believing that the world in which I lived was a good place. I felt as if my town, where everybody knew me and everybody spoke kindly to everybody else, was like a stage set for a play; that probably the people who incinerated those babies were pleasant people, too, cheerful with their neighbors, loving to their children as my folks were loving with me. I just couldn't make sense of the human darkness I was hearing about on the news. Fifty years later, I still can't.

There is evil in the world. There is just no way to make this terrible chapter in human history make sense.

Where is the hope in such a thing? Only in the resolve of those who remain to guard humanity against such a thing again. Only in our capacity to become more loving because we have seen such cruelty. To let God work in us against evil, to be part of life and not of death.

. . . a broken and contrite heart, O God, you will not despise.
—*PSALM 51:18,* p. 657

Preparing for a sermon I have to preach next week, I reread the parable of the prodigal son this morning.

I think of the way the family was before and the way it is afterward, at the beginning of the story and at the end. I think of the superficiality of what we are told about the family; it is mostly in terms of their roles and expectations. The two sons stand to inherit. The father is a man with money. Not much in the way of personality.

It is not until the prodigal confronts himself in the wreckage of his life that any of the people in the story become real. Then the narrative in the story gives way to interior dialogue. At first we just watch the prodigal do things, go from one thing to another, journey, carouse. It is not until he crashes and burns that we begin to hear him talk within his own soul, begin to argue with himself, begin to despair, decide to reach out for love and forgiveness. From the darkness of despair he grows and deepens. He would never have done so from sunshine.

Everyone else grows, too. The elder son learns something about the limits of ordinary righteousness, and the father learns what it is to find hope when all hope was gone. Everyone learns, through pain, what joy is. What more do we need to know?

July 20

Make him/her a bishop in your Church.... —*ORDINATION OF A BISHOP, p. 521*

It is my privilege to participate often in the consecration of a new bishop. It is an awesome occasion—someone new takes his or her place in a line of succession that stretches back to the earliest days of Christian history. I feel the presence of all those colleagues, the living and the long-dead. I know, though, that while the feeling of being joined to those bishops who lived so long ago is very real to me, I probably would be just about unrecognizable to them. Who we are and what we do today would shock them. The hardware would fascinate them first: our magical lights that go on all at once when we flick a switch, the huge sound of the organ that seems to come from everywhere, the heat that comes magically out of our walls without a flame in sight, the magical devices that amplify our voices. These things would shock them first. Then they would have to absorb the sight of women in the role of priests and bishops. We would talk, brother and sister bishops visiting across the centuries, and I would try to explain America to them—concepts like the separation of church and state, or denominationalism, or religious and cultural pluralism—and they would shake their heads. We would talk numbers, and they would be amazed. We would compare a typical day in my life and one in theirs, and the differences would amaze both of us. We are joined, but we are not very much alike.

July 21

I give you this ring as a symbol of my vow, and with all that I am, and all that I have, I honor you, in the Name of the Father, and of the Son, and of the Holy Spirit. . . .
—CELEBRATION AND BLESSING OF A MARRIAGE, p. 427

When I first went to Hawaii Patti and I went to Marriage Encounter. They have a custom called "ten and ten": you take a subject, write for ten minutes on it, and then share what you've written with your spouse and talk about it. It's an exercise to help you stay in communication. This was years ago that we first began doing this, but even now—often—I'll go into the bathroom in the morning to shave and there will be a ten and ten waiting for me on the mirror. Maybe it will be a real moment of critique—or it might just be a letter of deep support and love. Sometimes I know it's coming. Sometimes it's a surprise. But each morning, I move slowly into the bathroom to see if there's anything on the mirror!

It's so easy to get out of touch. It's always amazed me how little physical proximity has to do with that; people can sleep side by side for decades and really not talk. And other people can be separated by a continent, confined to letters and the infrequent phone call, and communicate exquisitely. Near or far, it all comes to the same thing: being close doesn't just happen to a couple. It's a choice.

July 22

As he grows in age, may he grow in grace. . . .
—*THANKSGIVING FOR THE BIRTH OR ADOPTION OF A CHILD,*
p. 445

My eldest son was angry at me for accepting my election as Presiding Bishop of the Episcopal Church. It would break up our family geographically, he said, and expose me to all manner of slings and arrows of public criticism. And he meant it, too; when our plane landed back home after my election, there were two hundred cheering people at the airport to meet us, and Mark wasn't one of them!

I like it that he is willing to be that angry about something I might do, even though I didn't take his advice that time. I like it that he feels free to tell me the truth as he sees it. I even like it that he is honest about the ways in which my professional path has had a cost for the family.

Most of all, though, I like it that it's a two-way street. Once he and his brother were at our cabin and decided to take his kids out on the lake. They stayed too long, and the weather got bad. I was beside myself with worry, and I lit into him when they finally got home. "Don't you ever take my grandchildren out in conditions like that again," I said. And, of all things, he actually told me I was right.

Love is like that—not always sweet and affirming. Sometimes, if it's really love, it's pretty confrontational.

July 23

We give you thanks for the blessing you have bestowed upon this family in giving them a child. —THANKSGIVING FOR THE BIRTH OR ADOPTION OF A CHILD, p. 443

Before our daughter was born, Patti and I were beginning to think we'd have nothing but boys—and then along came this beautiful baby girl, looking just like her mother. I was ecstatic.

I assumed there would be a difference. Vague, stereotypical thoughts about gentleness and fragility and domesticity came and went; the women with whom I'd been surrounded all my life were certainly not frail, so I don't know why I would have thought this one would be. And she wasn't, either; her brothers' nickname for her was "Doberman pinscher." The same combination of fierceness and grace that I love in her mother, I love in her.

Why is it that so much of the religious imagination has opposed this combination—as if good people were never angry people, as if righteousness and passivity always went hand in hand? Why do we gravitate toward the gentle Jesus, when the early Church left us so many stories of the angry young man: Jesus in the temple overturning the furniture, Jesus lashing out at one of his best friends and calling him "Satan," Jesus calling his enemies names like "vipers."

We are afraid of anger. But righteous anger, sanctified and submitted to the judgment of Christ, is never ultimately hurtful. It is ultimately healing. If we offer our anger to the service of God, God will take what is righteous and use it to our good.

July 24

Sanctify, O Lord, those whom you have called to the study and practice of the arts of healing. . . . —PRAYER FOR DOCTORS AND NURSES, p. 460

I always *thought* my son Philip would become a doctor—he must have broken every bone in his body when he was a kid. He practically had his own room in the ER, we were over there so much.

It was awesome to watch him during those long years of preparation to become a physician. I thought I knew what perseverance was, but he enlarged the concept for me considerably. I was no stranger to long hours, either, but to become accustomed to people's lives resting in one's hands for twenty-four hours at a time requires a certain kind of strength and staying power.

We don't have it at first. We grow it. We grow it the way an athlete develops a muscle: in accordance with the demand placed on it. The very fact of being pushed beyond the limits of one's capability is what makes the growth; like a muscle, we expand and strengthen to accomplish what is required of us. "Gosh, I could never do that," someone says about a herculean task. You could if you had to, is the answer, and it's the gospel truth.

July 25

. . . grant that we may so use our leisure to rebuild our bodies and renew our minds. . . . —PRAYER FOR THE GOOD USE OF LEISURE, p. 825

We were surprised when we found out our fifth child was coming. I remember, in fact, that Patti was more than surprised; livid would be a better word to describe her feelings at that time. Four kids and forty thousand dirty diapers had seemed like enough to her.

God is good, though. Our experience of an unexpected dividend was like that of most families who get one: a wholly gracious thing, another chance at a job we'd come to realize we were pretty good at. There is a bittersweet quality to watching your children get older; you want their independence and growth, of course, but every milestone marks a place in a journey that leads inexorably away from you. And now there would be another chance, a chance to slow that journey toward the end of life down a little.

He did slow down the journey, most graciously so. It seemed that every moment with him was dessert, an unearned bonus. We were better able to savor it because it was such a bonus, and because we knew that this time really *would* be the last time. The life we have lived together has had the quality of play, the kind of play that explores a person's potential and offers growth in unexpected directions.

And his profession, now that he's all grown up? He's still facilitating play in everyone he meets: he's a tennis pro.

July 26

Send us, we entreat thee, in this time of need, such moderate rain and showers, that we may receive the fruits of the earth. . . . —PRAYER FOR RAIN, p. 828

Car tires hiss along the wet street outside the door; it is raining in New York City. It has been debilitatingly hot for more than a week; we are hopeful that the rain will break things up a little.

The sound of the rain in the city is so different from the sound of rain in the country. There, it begins with the plop of fat water drops on broad leaves, each one a discrete sound until the moment when there are too many of them for me to hear each one, and the rain becomes an undifferentiated fall. Inside, upstairs, I awaken to the sound of rain on the roof and feel an ancient, safe feeling. Patti is still asleep; I creep out of bed so as not to awaken her and go around the house, checking the windows.

In the city, rain makes life harder. In the country, it seems to make things easier, less urgent. So many urban intensities are absent there. The spirit relaxes and stretches out. It is good.

I want to carry my country self back into the city when I go. I want the rain to bring peace and safety, not annoyance. I know that whether or not this will happen does not depend on the rain; it falls alike on the country and on the city. Everything that happens in my life is received by me, and I am the one who will characterize it, for good or ill. In large measure, my inner peace—or lack of it—is a decision I make.

July 27

Give them an inquiring and discerning heart. . . . —*HOLY BAPTISM*, p. 308

We have a fancy phone system in the office. My staff tries to protect me from it, but every now and then I come up against it. I also don't yet know what a RAM is if it's not a male sheep. I am in awe of my grandchildren, who seem to have been born knowing how to do all manner of electronic things; their grandfather lags sadly behind. I understand from Patti that I'm going to learn how to do all these things when I retire, that I'm going to E-mail my grandchildren. Just thinking about it makes me tired.

It's remarkable to me that very young children seem so able to manage this technology that is so mysterious to me. But then I remember their parents, years ago when we lived overseas. Patti and I worked so hard to learn the languages of the places in which we lived. I really struggled. And then the children would wander off to play next door for a few hours and come back fluent. They seemed to pick it up without any effort at all.

They are programmed to learn. They absorb knowledge like little sponges. When Jesus said the kingdom of heaven must be approached like a little child, surely this quality that they possess—this eminently teachable, open-minded readiness to receive—is one of the things he meant.

July 28

We thank you for giving him to us . . . to know and to love as a companion on our earthly pilgrimage. —COLLECT AT THE BURIAL OF AN ADULT, p. 493

The kitchen was always a wonderful place in our house when I was a boy. I remember the way the wonderful smells of dinner would begin to permeate the downstairs of our house while my mother cooked. My brother and I would talk to her while we set the table, getting hungrier and hungrier, until at last it was time to sit down.

It's funny: any kitchen I'm in makes me think of our family in those days. Even our sleek modern kitchen reminds me of them, although it is nothing like the kitchen in our old house. I walk into our kitchen while dinner is cooking and I miss my brother.

Ordinarily, my family would eat dinner in the kitchen. We saved the dining room for Sundays and special days. After dinner, my brother and I would do our homework on the kitchen table; it would be dark by then, and the light of the lamp was a warm yellow. We must have passed hundreds of evenings that way.

I never thought, in those days, that one day we would be separated by death. That those evenings and our lives together in that house would take their places in my past. Of course I didn't; kids don't think of those things.

July 29

. . . make us mindful of the needs of others. . . . —GRACE AT
MEALS, p. 835

The traditional obligation of the religious community is to care for the weak and the oppressed. How will we be judged? Jesus says it will be on whether or not we bestirred ourselves on behalf of those less fortunate—nothing more. The old saying, often attributed to the Good Book—"The Lord helps those who help themselves"—is, in fact, nowhere to be found in holy writ. The overwhelming message in Scripture is not that at all; it is, rather, that God helps those who need help.

In the pages of the Christian and Hebrew Scriptures, as well as in the Koran, the duty of the believer is to come to the aid of the poor, the hungry, the sick, the widow, the orphan. We are to be merciful because God is merciful. It is true that the theme of divine judgment is also a strong element in the major religious traditions of the western world. But we sometimes ascribe to God a distaste for this or that lifestyle or practice—a distaste that we actually invented ourselves. The people who wrote the Bible sometimes did this, too. But there is much less warrant in Scripture for punitive behavior toward people or groups who differ in some way from the majority than there is for a consistent posture of compassion based on the simple fact of the other's need.

July 30

The earth is the Lord's and all that is in it. —PSALM 24, p. 613

If everything goes according to plan, I am on vacation at this time of year. We have a cabin in the woods to which we flee to recharge our batteries. I relax immediately and completely the moment we turn into the drive.

One of my favorite things to do there is to have morning devotions outside—early in the morning, when the birds are celebrating the new day and the air is cool and the grass is still a little wet with dew. The early sun filters down through the leaves and dapples the ground like stained glass.

It is a cathedral. The hand of God is so visible in the woods, and I am so powerfully reconnected as part of the earth God has made. I begin the old prayers, prayers I've said all my life, prayers that have bracketed every day at its beginning and again at its end, and they take on an eternal quality. Everything around me is a combination of new and old: ancient trees, new grass, old prayers, young birds. Old earth and young me, grandfather that I am: old earth, earth that was here long before I came and will be here long after I am gone. The oldest among us is here for such a short time.

July 31

Make their life together a sign of Christ's love to this sinful and broken world. . . . —CELEBRATION AND BLESSING OF A MARRIAGE, p. 429

Marriage is work. Patti has pointed this out to me from time to time, especially early in our ministry, when it was easy for me to think that my important ministry was the only work for which I was responsible. She refused to allow us to slip into the work pattern that was common in those days: the husband devotes himself solely to his career and the wife solely to the home, and once in a while their paths cross. We had to pay attention to us, not just Ed and not just Patti, but us. I don't know how she became so wise so early, wise enough to see that our marriage itself was a living thing that needed nurture.

But it isn't just marriage that needs nurture. Every kind of human community needs it. Sometimes you'll hear a person who's frustrated in a romantic relationship joke about entering religious life. "I'm gonna become a nun and forget about all this," and everybody laughs. But talk to a sister or brother and they'll tell you: it's no easier to live in a community of twenty than it is in a community of two. In some ways it's harder.

Two or twenty or two hundred: there's no such thing as a free lunch in human fellowship. To have a friend, at whatever level of intimacy that friendship works out in your life, you must also be one.

August 1

Into your hands, O God, we place your child. . . .
—*THANKSGIVING FOR THE BIRTH OR ADOPTION OF A CHILD,*
p. 444

It has always been true that kids having sex too young are playing with fire. Pregnancy has always been a central fear, of course, but the rape of self-worth involved in too early an entry into intimacy is every bit as profound. Girls in one way, boys in another: girls coming to see their sexuality as a coin that could buy them what passed for love and power, boys coming to see women as instrumental to their pleasure. And both using the powerful feelings unleashed in them to separate themselves from their parents: *This is what true love is. No one has ever felt as deeply as I feel at this moment. And if you don't get it, Mom and Dad, you just don't know what love is.*

Young men and women have always faced these hazards. They have always made mistakes—whoppers, some of them—and they have learned, painfully, from them. Sexuality has always been laced with danger. "Safe sex" is a contradiction in terms; sex is anything but safe. That's why every human society has hedged it around with rules—not always the same rules, but all cultures have recognized its power.

But you didn't used to die from it. Parents of adolescents now live in fear: what if she experiments with sex and gets AIDS? They sit their teenagers down for a talk; the kids roll their eyes and look bored. The parents learn a lot about prayer, very quickly. *The Lord bless you and keep you. . . .*

August 2

The vines in the window boxes spill luxuriantly over the edges; the flowers crowd together. By eight in the morning it is already in the seventies—another hot one, like yesterday and the day before. A double line of children, each holding the hand of a partner and a rolled-up beach towel, watchful counselors fore and aft, makes its way down into the subway: a trip to Coney Island for the day. Already groups of men have assembled in the park around the chessboards.

The city is less hectic on August mornings than it is at other times of the year. Those who can get away have done so, and the streets are left to those who can't.

In the evening, people are outside walking, sitting on the stoop if they have one—a lightheartedness lives on the street. Children stay up late and it doesn't matter—no school. It will all begin again soon enough: new Broadway shows, new lunch boxes and school uniforms, new semesters, new energy at work after the late summer slowdown.

In so many of the places I visit, most people never have a vacation. They are too poor even to imagine such a thing. They may never venture beyond the confines of their own neighborhoods throughout their entire lives. They have only this kind of break: the walk at the end of the day, the chess game in the early morning, the idle talk on the stoop at night. Whatever respite is theirs, they savor it. Even God needed a little Sabbath.

August 3

Watch over the child, O Lord, as his days increase....
—PRAYER FOR A BIRTHDAY, p. 830

Our tradition has always known that it is in the poor and those in need that Christ can be found. The message of longing and hope is easily heard by those who know they are in need.

But there are many who have stifled their longing, who have papered over their need of redemption with the urgent drive to consume more and more, as if happiness were to be found in possessions. We worry about this in our children, we who are fortunate enough to be able to give them the material things they enjoy. We are caught between our desire to give them these things and our desire that they grow to be people who know about the life of the Spirit, people who long for the gifts no amount of money can buy. We don't just want them to be successful or financially secure, although we do want those things for them. We want them to be good men and women, joyful men and women, generous and loving men and women in whom Christ is clearly visible and alive. And sometimes we wonder if, in this world with its addiction to material things, we can raise such men and women.

If we are such people, we can raise such people. Of course they will be enticed by the bloated consumerism of the world, but the apple never falls too far from the tree. If our values are in order, theirs will be too, sooner or later.

August 4

Heavenly Father, in you we live and move and have our being.... —A COLLECT FOR GUIDANCE AT MORNING PRAYER, p. 100

By now, my grandchildren are beginning to be bored with summer. Their parents are beginning to feel the heat, too; they're running out of creative things to suggest to their lively offspring. We offer sympathy; we remember just what it was like to need a little space by the time the end of the summer rolled around.

The people of the Old Testament did not believe in an afterlife. The immortality of the soul was an idea whose time had not yet come. But they did have one thing that represented immortality to them: they would live on in the lives of their children, and their children's children, and their children's children's children.

I understand how our forebears found it possible to locate the ultimate meaning of their lives in their children, for I know the love that parenthood has brought to my life. Oh yes, at this time of year, they can drive a person nuts. Parents pray for school to begin. But the thought of not having them makes our blood run cold.

Still, as precious as they are, my children cannot be my god or my heaven. This mortal life is one piece of a much larger puzzle. It contains us, and them, and all who have ever been or ever will be.

August 5

Give us grace seriously to lay to heart the great dangers we are in by our unhappy divisions. . . . —PRAYER FOR THE UNITY OF THE CHURCH, p. 818

With five children, there was no shortage of arguments to settle at our house. Some of the things they chose to fight about were small things that made not much sense: who was going to sit in which seat in the car, for instance, or who would have which color paint first for a rainy-day art session. Later on the stakes were higher; they argued passionately with us about ethical problems, staking out positions that I sometimes thought were chosen mostly because they were different from ours, positing insoluble moral dilemmas and demanding solutions to them. The arguments grew more complex as the children grew older.

The ones about the paint or the car seat were easy. Adult battles are harder. I used to wish that the situations my children encountered were not so ambiguous, since they themselves were so pure in heart. I wished that there were fewer shades of gray in human moral choice, so that their battles would be easier. I wished for them what I do not and never have had for myself: clear and easy choices. But life is not like that. Anglicans understand moral choice to be a struggle—rarely a clear-cut confrontation between obvious good and obvious evil. A much muddier enterprise. A struggle with another person, sometimes, but always a struggle with the self.

August 6

If thou bring thy gift to the altar, and there rememberest that thy brother hath aught against thee, leave there thy gift before the altar, and go thy way; first, be reconciled to thy brother, and then come and offer thy gift. —OFFERTORY SENTENCE AT THE HOLY EUCHARIST, p. 343

We feel uncomfortable when we are at odds with someone to whom we once were close. I have known people who went for decades not speaking to someone to whom they once confided everything. Even if they still believe themselves to have been in the right in whatever dispute separated them, this estrangement cannot be but painful. It is not God's will that we should live in enmity.

When we see a command like the one above—drop everything and go to your estranged neighbor for reconciliation before you come to worship—we come into contact with a dimension of human enmity beyond the individual pain it causes those directly involved: it is also an offense against God to live in enmity with one another. The God whose image we all carry is distanced when I distance my neighbor from myself. God continues to love me and long for my return, but I keep both God and neighbor at arm's length.

"But the whole thing was not my fault," the estranged one cries, full of righteous indignation. "Why should I have to be the one to make the first move?" Perhaps it was not. But in the end, it will matter less who started a quarrel than who has the courage and love to finish it.

August 7

Bless them in their work and in their companionship. . . .
—CELEBRATION AND BLESSING OF A MARRIAGE, p. 430

I have always felt that I was part of a ministerial team. Patti and I had the privilege of working in a number of out-of-the-way places that helped us define who we really were, and what our ministries might really be, by giving us the remarkable experience of evaluating them in the setting of cultures very different from the one that nurtured us. I don't think there was a single assumption about life and relationship that went unchallenged in those years of living and ministering in other countries. I wouldn't have traded it for anything. I cannot imagine us apart from the experiences of those years, and I cannot imagine us in those years without each other.

Yet, in those same years, and in all the busy years since, it has always been important for each of us to nurture a sense of ourselves and our ministries as individuals. I am a part of a team, and I love being part of that team, but that is not all I am. God does not only speak to us, to Patti and me, but God speaks to *me*. I have a destiny that is for me alone. In prayer—even though Patti and I have morning devotions together every day—I sit in God's presence in a way unique to me, and I puzzle over God's word in my own way. God has a ministry for me because I am me. We serve best, and most joyfully, as the complete and whole women and men God calls us to be.

August 8

Lord, in your mercy, hear our prayer. —*PRAYERS OF THE PEOPLE,* p. 389

Prayer frustrates some thoughtful people. What's the point, they say. Is God someone who wants to withhold good things from us until we mutter the right incantation? Does God send bad things to us if we're bad and good things to us if we're good, rewarding us and punishing us as we might our own children?

I don't think God punishes us in such a way. Often, we do a pretty good job of that ourselves; many of the things that happen to us happen as the perfectly predictable result of an action of ours. Other things do not; there are many tragic things that just happen to people because they are at the wrong place at the wrong time.

So then what *does* happen when we present the desires of our hearts to God in prayer, if it's not a magic incantation guaranteed to get us what we want? In my own life, praying about a problem or a desire has served to open my heart to God's love for me in a given situation, regardless of what does or does not happen subsequent to my prayer. Maybe my prayer did not always change the situation. But it always changed me.

August 9

Make you perfect in every good work to do his will. . . .
—*BURIAL OF THE DEAD*, p. 487

You often hear someone say that if something is worth doing, it's worth doing well. Well, maybe so—but it's also true that not everything needs to be done perfectly. Modern life is a busy proposition. Some things must be done in a hurry, and some of them will just have to settle for *good enough*.

This is more spiritually important than it may seem. The world is full of people who are afraid to begin any task because they fear they will do a less-than-perfect job. Not only must they live in constant fear of their own mistakes, but they must also deal with their growing sense that they actually have not accomplished anything because of this fear.

Was everything I tried to do a howling success? Certainly not—and because my life has been a public one, I have never lacked for people who were all too willing to let me know just where and how I have fallen short!

But my shortcomings don't make me want to stop trying. I *expect* to be imperfect; only God is perfect. And I expect God to work in me to heal my imperfections, one by one. I will probably run out of life before God runs out of things to fix, so the bulk of them will have to wait until later! It is hard to imagine myself perfect, completed in the presence of God's eternal love. I'm so used to my frailties, and God is so good at helping me to manage in spite of them.

August 10

Do not forget the trust committed to you as a priest of the Church of God. —ORDINATION OF A PRIEST, p. 534

In airports, in taxicabs—very frequently a stranger will see that I am a clergyman and strike up a deep conversation about difficulties he or she is having with faith. I can tell that they assume that I have my faith all figured out. They see my white hair, and they think that I long ago laid to rest any difficulties I was having in putting God first in my life. That, of course, is far from true; for me and for every other faithful Christian I know, the life of faith is a daily challenge. The things that happen in this old world puzzle and sadden me. I do not understand God's plan much more often than I understand it.

To me, faith is not very dependent on understanding. It is, rather, a decision about where I will put my life's energy. I choose to live with reference to God, and that choice orders other choices in my life. So the question of faith is not so much What do you think? as it is Whom will you follow? Not so much a matter of the intellect as a matter of the heart and will.

August 11

O God, who on this day taught the hearts of your faithful people . . . —COLLECT FOR THE DAY OF PENTECOST, p. 227

My kids used to have a firm belief that it was bad luck to step on a crack in the sidewalk. I know people with advanced degrees who consult their horoscopes in the newspaper every day, and I know some awfully bright people who knock on wood if they find themselves talking about something bad that might happen in the future.

I know that our faith seems like that to some outsiders—a superstition: You're afraid of death and chance like everybody else, and so you've bought into a lot of ancient mumbo-jumbo about resurrection so you'll feel better. Many thoughtful modern people think that religion is what you do if you're too dumb or too timid to face life honestly—that it is a way of avoiding unpleasant truths. And it's certainly the case that legend and superstition are woven into our faith tradition.

But the religious project itself is not superstition. Superstition is all about magic: controlling events in this world by drawing on the power of another. Faith is not about controlling anything. It is based on the undeniable fact that human existence is brief and fragile, and on the careful hope in a larger reality. These days, it has little interest in just what kind of gold bricks pave the streets of heaven or in surefire methods for averting life's tragedies. People of faith know they're going to experience the same sorrows as everybody else. We just affirm that we never face them alone.

August 12

. . . who on the first day of the week overcame death and the grave. . . . —PREFACE OF THE LORD'S DAY, p. 377

The people who wrote the Scriptures believed that God was revealed in human history and in the natural world. So do I. Their writings are full of vivid descriptions of moments when the laws of nature were suspended by God for some reason directly related to human destiny. A bush in the desert burns continuously and is not consumed. The sea parts so that the Israelites can walk across it on dry land. Five thousand are fed from five loaves and two fish. A virgin conceives a child.

Regardless of one's attitude toward the literalness with which they should be taken, all of these miracles and the many others we find in the Bible prepare us for the one great event to which the whole thing points: the defeat of death. That ancient enemy of ours, visible in the distance from the moment we draw our first breath until the moment when he snatches our last, determines everything that is human; almost everything we do, we do to escape him. The human experience is colored by fear.

It is in this that Jesus destroys death: Henceforth, we see it as a moment in a life that continues beyond it, not as the end of life itself. There is a life that contains the life we are living. So we need not hoard the crumbs of this life, clutching it fearfully to ourselves because we are afraid of losing it. We can spend it freely and lovingly; there is always more.

August 13

Come to me, all who labor and are heavy-laden, and I will give you rest. —COMPLINE, p. 131

I arose early this morning to catch a train, so I could be in Washington, D.C., in time for a full day's worth of meetings and appointments. The train is crowded and quiet; it is still dark in the towns we hurtle past, stopping to pick up knot after knot of quiet commuters on our way down the east coast.

I have some papers to go through, and I get them all arranged on my lap. I find my pen and the little book I use to write notes to myself. The engine throbs throughout the train, though, providing a kind of gentle rocking motion, and the heat is working well, so it's pleasantly warm. When I wake up, papers still neatly on my lap, pen and notebook at the ready, we're almost in Baltimore.

Oh, well. I must have needed the extra shut-eye, or I wouldn't have been so easily ambushed by it. I remember being able to study all night, if I had to, when I was young. It didn't seem at all important to husband my strength in those days— all of us just knew the energy would be there to meet the demand. Middle age is different: the body begins making some demand of its own, and you have no choice but to listen.

I call Patti from Washington to let her know I got there in one piece. "I went back to bed after you left," she said, "and I really just got up." I tell her I sort of did the same thing.

August 14

Will you do your best to pattern your life . . . in accordance with the teachings of Christ? . . . —ORDINATION OF A PRIEST, p. 532

Near our office building, there is a man who always stands on the street corner. He is always dressed in a clerical collar. He holds out a paper cup, and people put coins into it. He thanks them and blesses them with a priestly dignity. But he is not a priest; he is a beggar.

What gave rise to his choice of costume? Perhaps the confused hope that people will think he really *does* represent a church and be more generous. I think it unlikely that they will; he is so shabby, and looks so unwell. I think it is something else: The clothing of the religious functionary seems to him to betoken a closer walk with God than he would otherwise have, a more direct connection to the power he needs, a straight shot at overcoming the deficits that have placed him so far behind in the race. I will wear the clothing of someone who is strong and close to God, he reasons, and I, too, will be strong and holy.

But the Italians, living as they have for centuries with the enormous wealth and power of the Vatican right under their noses, have a saying: The habit doesn't make the monk. Our clothing or our offices or our possessions don't make us strong or good. Possessions and earthly powers come and go, and they have little to do with who we really are while they are ours.

August 15

Restore to them the assurance of your unfailing mercy.
—*PRAYER FOR THE VICTIMS OF ADDICTION*, p. 831

People with some expertise in the world of therapy have often told me that I must be angry about my early life with my dad. I've listened to them, and I've examined myself many times. There is absolutely no doubt that my father's enslavement to alcohol affected everyone in my family very powerfully. I must say, though, that anger is not what I feel toward him. Somehow, I never have. Denial? That's not the case either. I'm very aware of the potent effect that early experience had on me. I know my scars. I well remember them all, and I burn with longing for the healing of others' pain.

I have an idea about this: maybe powerful things are what happens when anger is sanctified. Maybe sanctified anger acts mightily to heal the world. That painful memory. That remembered sorrow. Maybe sanctified anger is anger so transformed that it doesn't feel like anger any more, but like the potent healing touch of an infinitely compassionate God.

Maybe that's where my anger went. And maybe all anger has the potential to bear good fruit in that way.

August 16

Give to us, your servants, that peace which the world cannot give. . . . —COLLECT FOR PEACE AT EVENING PRAYER, p. 123

We didn't spank our children when they did something wrong. We used the time-out approach instead, in which the child spends some time in a private place thinking his own thoughts before being allowed to rejoin the group. Since there were five of them and they all had lively imaginations, somebody somewhere would usually be needing time-out a fair amount of the time. I'd go into a room and often there in the corner would be an angry little back facing the room, its owner facing the wall, enduring the passing minutes as best he or she could.

After a spell—ten minutes, maybe even less—enough emotion had subsided that we could really have a conversation about whatever it was that had happened. There would have been no way to do that right off the bat—either for us or for the young offender. Children can make you angry; they are not the only ones who find it hard to control their behavior at those times. The time-out was every bit as much for us as it was for them.

Do we seem like that to God? Rambunctious and unable, at times, to control our emotions sufficiently to behave as we really want to? Forever testing the limits? I think we must. It is oddly comforting to think of myself in that child's role, and of God waiting patiently for me to calm down so we can talk.

August 17

Almighty God, give us grace to cast away the works of darkness. . . . —COLLECT FOR THE FIRST SUNDAY OF ADVENT, p. 211

When we are passionate in our beliefs, how can we be sure that what we think is faith is not really fanaticism? How will we protect our hearts from being co-opted and deceived in the service of evil when we think we are doing good? The chief priest who condemned Jesus thought he was doing a good thing. The man who shot Prime Minister Rabin thought he was doing a good thing. Hitler and his cohorts thought they were doing a good thing. Look what evil the pursuit of good can bring about! How can we arm ourselves against such a delusion creeping into our own hearts?

I believe we must return to the sacred texts of our faith with our eyes wide-open. We must discern within them the great themes of redemption and love that breathe through them, and resist the use of pieces of them to baptize violence. No godly program involves killing people. One that claims to do this is simply not godly, and it doesn't matter whose program it is. Death is our ancient enemy—it can never become our friend and ally in righteousness. That is a lie. And we are not supposed to be in the business of lies. We are supposed to live in the truth.

August 18

Sunday at eleven o'clock is the most segregated hour in the American week. The history of every religious denomination in our country is shot through with the scars of racism—fresh scars and older ones. Racial bigotry frequently cloaks itself in religious language. We all recoil from this in its extremes, like the Ku Klux Klan or the Aryan Nation, but we must acknowledge the link between even the politest prejudice and violence. It is a short step from holding a group in contempt to considering the members of that group less than human. If it is true that the longest journey begins with a single step, it is true for ill as well as for good, and small hatreds are the first steps toward great ones.

The custodians of a society's religious and moral traditions are precisely the ones who constitute the greatest danger: we are the ones people look to for moral guidance. If we begin to lead those who seek God down a path leading to hatred, or stand quietly by while others lead them there, they may well follow. And the judgment against us in heaven will be more severe. Our God of love can only be served with love. God's glory can only be protected and honored with love. If we, of all people, succumb to the virus of bigotry and hate that afflicts so much of the world, our state is a grievous one indeed.

August 19

Sanctify us also. . . . —*THE HOLY EUCHARIST,* p. 363

So many people look at the headlines of the day, so full of human sorrow and injustice, and despair of faith. Or at their lives, also full of sorrow. And there is abundant reason for sorrow—evil is real, and it is widespread. But we can choose whether we will be part of the evil or part of the redemption. Ultimately, God's purpose for the world will prevail, but we will decide what our position toward it will be. The world offers us this choice every day: the choice between love and hate, between bigotry and inclusion, between war and peace. I could not choose whether or not my father would remain in the grip of his addiction, but I could choose how *I* would behave and how I would use that sorrow in my life. We cannot manage other people's actions, but we can always choose how we will act. Will we be the chief priest in the world? Or will we be Jesus? The choice is ours to make, today and every day. Part of the problem or part of the answer? Defined by despair or by hope? We can choose.

August 20

O God, in the course of this busy life, give us times of refreshment and peace. . . . —PRAYER FOR THE GOOD USE OF LEISURE, p. 825

I spoke at a friend's retirement celebration recently. It was a loving occasion; people from all of the churches he's served over a long career came, and his whole family was there. There was a video presentation of pictures, and people laughed at the 1950's haircuts, the youthful face of the guest of honor in the old snapshots.

He spoke briefly, too, thanking everyone there for being part of his life. Now he intends to turn himself to those pleasures he has often had to forego, and he says he is so eager for those moments he can taste them. He talked about fishing with his grandchildren and going for long walks with his wife. He talked about his gratitude to God for preserving their lives to this point.

We all felt that odd mixture of joy and sorrow you always feel on those occasions: What a treasure life is, and how short the years seem when they are over! Back then, I thought I had all the time in the world. My career seemed endless and boundless. And now? Forty years feels like a month or two.

If I could do it again? Most of the things I've done I'd do again, with one thing more: I would be keenly aware of the precious gift each minute was, how irrevocable its passing. Once it's gone, it's gone, and it happens fast.

August 21

*. . . a perpetual memory of that his precious death and
sacrifice . . .* —*HOLY EUCHARIST,* p. 334

When I read about this or that group denying that the Holocaust happened, I always wonder what, exactly, motivates the denial. Is it simply an inability to believe that human beings could be so cruel, that incredulity I remember so well from the days immediately after the war? Or is it, as I fear, the first small step toward the chance to be that cruel again? These hideous stories have become too much a part of modern experience for us to deny them. After all, we have seen what occurs when we do deny them: they happen again. I have heard that Adolf Hitler, talking to his staff about the feasibility of the Final Solution, convinced them with this irrefutable argument: "After all, who today remembers the Armenians?" He had a point.

We remember our moral triumphs very well—we are somewhat less photographic in our recollection of our moral compromises. But we need to remember—it is our only protection against ourselves, all that stands between us and evil. Human beings are capable of great good and great cruelty; we must never allow ourselves to think ourselves immune.

August 22

Thou shalt not take the Name of the Lord thy God in vain.
—THE SECOND COMMANDMENT, p. 318

When I was a boy, I had a rudimentary grasp of what blaspheming involved. I had heard some blaspheming, here and there, on the lips of adults I knew in town; you could usually hear some when a hammer hit a thumb instead of a nail head, or when an outfielder missed an easy one, or when a car engine overheated.

That was before I knew that blasphemy meant much, much more than just a list of words. To live blasphemously is to live as if God were dead. In speech, to be sure, but more than just words: it is blasphemous to walk in the world as if there were no God, no judge of our hearts.

It is safe to say, I think, that by that definition our culture is a blasphemous one. Much of what happens among us happens as if there were no God: business deals are consummated, treaties signed and broken, cheap and sometimes deadly intimacies exchanged, children raised from birth to adulthood without any reference to God at all besides the explosive ones I remember hearing when I was little.

To live as if God were dead. That can be forgiven. It can be fixed. People don't have to live their lives that way. The aimlessness of a godless life can be infused with meaning by the creator of all that is. There is no one standing outside the house of God who cannot be invited in.

August 23

We are truly sorry.... —CONFESSION, p. 331

Repentance is an active thing, a turning from sin toward righteousness. God's forgiveness is active, too; it is not a flabby sort of oh-never-mind-that's-okay attitude toward sin. God's forgiveness is piercing, demanding honesty. Sins forgiven are not sins that didn't happen. Who we are and who we have been is never rubbed out; it is transformed. All the sorrow of our estrangement becomes the glory of our new life. It has happened in my life, and I know it has happened in yours. I have learned much, much more through repentance and forgiveness than I have ever learned from my own righteousness. We can still see the scars of our old lives, and they remind us all the more of the great gift that has been given us.

I think of the scars on us: each scar is a remembered pain. Some of these injuries are still quite fresh; others happened long ago, and the Spirit has had years in which to heal them. But they are who we are; our history is a permanent part of us. Our history has happened, and is happening as we stand here today. We cannot help being part of it. And it doesn't move backward. It moves forward. Is there a chapter in it that the Spirit cannot heal and use to build the body? No—there is no injury God cannot heal, no anger the Spirit cannot bend to the will of our loving God.

August 24

. . . be present with those who take counsel . . . for the renewal and mission of your Church. —PRAYER FOR A CHURCH CONVENTION OR MEETING, p. 818

General Convention happens every three years, bringing together delegates from every diocese and all our bishops. I always need to give a number of addresses, and my office helps me prepare by sending out a request for information, so that the group I am addressing can let me know what concerns ought to guide me as I write my speech.

At one convention, I was to address a women's society of the Episcopal church. They sent back the information with a request: "Tell us how we can pray for you."

I looked at the form for a long time before I began to write. I don't know when was the last time anybody asked me that. As a matter of fact, I'm not at all sure anybody ever has.

I asked them to pray for the peace of the world. I asked them to pray for the Church we all love. And I asked them to pray for me. To pray for Patti and our life together. I asked them to pray that I might continue to experience God's call to me with joy. That I would never allow the anger of others to overwhelm me, and that I would always lift up my own anger to God so that it never got in the way of my wisdom. That I might grow in wisdom and stature all the days of my life. And I asked them to pray these things for themselves, so that at the last we all might hear the greeting we long to hear: Well done, good and faithful servant.

August 25

. . . may the Holy Spirit, who has begun a good work in you . . .
—*ORDER FOR REAFFIRMATION OF BAPTISMAL VOWS,* p. 419

Sometimes a child who finished the previous year in utter defeat returns to school a new person: four or five inches taller, ready to concentrate in a way he was not able to before. Teachers count on it: kids grow up a lot during the summer.

Maybe adults do, too. Most of us don't get the entire summer in which to grow up: we get two weeks, perhaps, or maybe just one week. But work often slows a bit during these months. The daylight lasts longer; we stroll the streets and sit on the porch, feeling a little more leisurely than we feel in the winter. A little more breathing room, a little more time to stretch.

My mother used to tell me you could hear the corn growing out in the fields during the night at this time of year, that it made a rustling sound as the stalks stretched taller and taller. Imagine: you could hear corn grow. Nourishment and sun aren't everything: corn also needs the quiet dark to grow in.

I sit in a chair in the yard and think about the past year and the year ahead. I think about what didn't go well and what I might do to make it better. I think about things in myself I might usefully change. The days are still hot, but the nights are starting to be a little cooler. It is late summer: growing time.

August 26

Eternal Father, who didst give to thine incarnate Son the holy name of Jesus . . . —COLLECT FOR THE FEAST OF THE HOLY NAME, p. 162

I'm the only person I know to have been named after a hardware store. Flato's Hardware, largest hardware store in the south. Owned by Edwin Flato—my dad was working at Flato's at the time of my birth. My mother wouldn't let Dad name me Flato. Thank God. So I was Edwin, until I changed my name.

I changed my name to Edmond because it was my father's name and I wanted to be named after him instead of after a hardware store. Not much of a change, from "Edwin" to "Edmond," I guess, but it mattered enough to me to go down to the courthouse and see to it.

I changed my name to my father's name because I loved him. He's been gone for thirty years, and I still love him. The communion of the saints is like that: the love we bear one another never ends. It's one of the reasons I believe in a world beyond the realities of this world.

August 27

. . . you have blessed us with the joy and care of children. . . .
—*PRAYER FOR THE CARE OF CHILDREN*, p. 829

The divine work of bringing good from sorrow and pain often proceeds painfully. I was blessed with the chance to be part of a people's journey toward independence while I was on Okinawa. This was thirty or more years ago, but the process continues there, as the Okinawan people take steps to assert their autonomy further. Slow steps, and painful sometimes: you remember, I think, the shameful events of last year on Okinawa, when the realities of oppression were terribly embodied in the assault and rape of a young girl by three American servicemen. I cannot adequately describe how horrible a thing this would be for the Okinawans, who value family above almost everything else, and who view children as sacred. Yet, from this horror, new energy for self-determination arises there.

Nobody would say this terrible crime was a good thing. The fruit of racism and colonialism is anything but good. But God is good. This outrage is part of a more and more unacceptable political reality, and the pain of it will galvanize the people to quicken their steps toward autonomy. God brings good from evil. We can count on it.

August 28

. . . work through our struggle and confusion. . . . —*PRAYER FOR THE HUMAN FAMILY,* p. 815

Recently I was thinking about St. Augustine. Today is his feast day. During his time as bishop of Hippo, the Roman Empire fell. People the Romans called "barbarians" entered the Eternal City itself and laid waste to it. The structure that had for centuries provided the framework by which the Western world had defined virtually every area of life was gone. To what might we compare it? To our world if the United States should suddenly disappear.

We live in a world like the world Augustine lived in—not in its particulars, but in its disturbing unfamiliarity. Our foundations have been shaken, as theirs had, and we feel the tremors of change beneath our feet. And what does the Church say to a world that has lost its mooring?

We say what Augustine said: "Here we have no abiding city. . . ." Until the end of our time on earth, we will be plagued with uncertainty. It is the way of life. Whenever we think it is not, whenever we think that everything is very, very clear and certain, that life is clear and unambiguous, that choices are simple, it is only because we have overlooked something important. Let us not deceive ourselves about the security the city of this world offers. It offers none. Hold it lightly while we still have it, because one day it will all be gone. People, possessions, money, power, life itself—not ours to keep.

August 29

In the modern age, we are always looking for the lie. Always sceptical, always wondering what's the catch. Ever vigilant for the hypocritical, ever suspicious of the easy platitude. But God provides no easy bromide for human doubt and fear. God is not so simple that he is defeated by the worst humankind can offer. That is why the events of Holy Week are so powerful; they happen every day, all around the world. Human suffering is real, not some divine drama enacted out as an allegory. So real that the Son of God himself did not escape. And now we stand at the empty tomb and look inside and do not understand, for there is another reality, one about which we know next to nothing: the reality of God, the larger reality that contains ours and is not contained by it. That knows our sorrows and is not defeated by them. That is revealed to us, not deduced by us. We don't figure it out. It comes to us as a gift from the God who has walked with us all these years and walks with us still. We do not understand.

August 30

Give us calm strength and patient wisdom as we bring them up. . . . —PRAYER FOR THE CARE OF CHILDREN, p. 829

To be the one who models love for another human being is one of life's greatest privileges and joys. It is certainly life's greatest challenge! When a young adult is somewhere in the twenties, and one finally gets a sense of having done about all there is to do in the launching process, there's a feeling of something like shock. *You mean he's on his own?* It is an odd joy: just a hint of bittersweetness.

We develop such intimacy with our children, love them with a love we didn't know we had in us until we had them— and then they leave home. Our purpose in parenting is to teach them to live and to love, and we have only half succeeded if they cannot leave us.

The challenging yet nurturing love of God for each of us is just this mixture of moving out and staying close that we model in the goals of our human mothering and fathering, with the important difference: it has no bittersweetness. We lose our children somewhat if we have parented well, and they lose us, somewhat, in their new adulthood. But we do not lose God. Challenge and nurture cause no tug-of-war in God's heart, utterly good and utterly creative heart that it is.

August 31

Restore our fortunes, O Lord. . . . —*PSALM 126:5, p. 782*

The Color Purple is the story of an African American woman's life and the way she overcame the many trials she faced. The film is one you just want to stand up and applaud at certain points. I remember one exquisite scene in particular. When she was very young, the heroine had given birth to two children who were taken from her. She knew that they had gone to a good home, and she buried the pain of losing them deep within her. Not long afterward, she was separated from her younger sister. Loneliness mixed with a persistent hope for the return of her lost family.

At the end of the film, her family is restored to her. Handsome young adults now, the children walk across a field of flowers to their mother, joined in that joyful walk by her sister. The sun shines on the golden flowers and the green grass, and the African robes of the children and the sister flutter gorgeously in the breeze. I could watch that beautiful scene a hundred times without ever tiring of it.

The joy of this reunion is the same joy looked for by the people of Israel. They sustained themselves with the anticipated hope of it. We rejoice in sure and certain hope of it.

September 1

Applause is appropriate. — RUBRIC ON THE CELEBRATION OF
A NEW MINISTRY, p. 563

It is the joy of life in Christ that calls people into it. What else but joy would make people get up and follow? I know that many people feel uncomfortable with the idea of themselves as evangelists. But let us not sell ourselves short. Our own lives can call others into relationship with God just by showing forth the happiness that is to be found in the community of God's people.

Joys and sorrows come to all people, the churched and the unchurched. We know that our faith does not cushion us from unpleasant realities. A talisman against evil is not what we proclaim. But we *do have* an ongoing reality beyond that which circumscribes our physical lives. We *do* think that there is more to life than meets the eye, and we *do* feel supported by a loving God who cares and acts for the world. In short, we are people who know that we are not alone, and that we never will be, no matter what.

And we are people who think it important to band together to celebrate what we know. When we are deliberate about doing this, we have a wonderful time. And we go forth into the world to share this wonder in our words and deeds, so that our joy may be complete.

September 2

Surely, it is God who saves me; I will trust in him and not be afraid. —CANTICLE 9, p. 86

Jesus means "Yahweh Saves." This was the name he was given before he was born, at the moment when the angel announced his miraculous coming to his mother. A sign of the meaning of the birth, the name of Jesus summed up the history of the Jewish people.

The oldest book in the Hebrew Scriptures is not Genesis, even though we may read it first. The oldest account by the Hebrew people of God's action in their lives is the story of the deliverance from Egypt in the book of Exodus. It is, above all, the story of God's acting to save the people of Israel. They did not drown in the Red Sea; the people of Israel crossed safely to the other side on dry land and lived. This experience of deliverance was so profound that the Israelites never forgot it. It came to define them as a people forever: the chosen people of God, those whom Yahwah saves.

Jesus. Yahweh saves. It is a statement of belief, a creed. It is also a prayer. You are the God who saves your people, the Holy Name of Jesus cries. Move with might among us and save us now. And God hears the prayer, again, and God does move mightily in Israel, more mightily than anyone could have predicted.

September 3

All that we are and all that we have is yours.
—*CONSECRATION OF A CHURCH,* p. 568

Dear Mr. Browning. Dear Minister. Dear Rector. Dear Father. I smile as I read all these greetings in the letters that come to me everyday. Some of them haven't been true for years; it takes a while, I guess, for the mailing-list people to catch up.

The emotion of a worship service, the deep peace of private prayer, the excitement of a good Bible study: these are the highs of religious life. The business letters and schedules, the budgets and planning meetings: those are the rest of the story. However we may feel about them, they are inevitable. Corporate life requires corporate work, and not all of that work is exciting.

I began my life as a priest many years ago. I was so excited about the things I would be doing! I wanted to be a faithful pastor, a good preacher, a good teacher of the young, and a compassionate visitor of the sick and the old. I wanted to combine a strong private prayer life with a prophetic life of public worship and witness. When I pictured myself as a priest, I don't think I ever pictured myself filling out an annual report or negotiating the price of a new oil burner.

The early church was full of the Holy Spirit. So is our church today. So are you. So am I. But they had their business to administer, and so do we. We will not be able to do the wonderful things of which we dream without a good, strong structure in which to do them.

September 4

Christ is risen from the dead, trampling down death by death, and giving life to those in the tomb. —BURIAL OF THE DEAD, p. 500

The earliest Christians only had what we now call the Old Testament as their holy book; the New Testament hadn't yet been assembled and written down. They all knew those Scriptures well, since they were still very close to their Jewish origins. Some of them hit upon the image of Jesus as the new Adam, through whom redemption would come. Sin and death entered the world through Adam; through Christ we would at last be free of them.

Of course, death is our enemy. Modern Americans know that very well, and do everything in our power to whisk it out of sight every time it comes too close. "I called the hospital in the middle of the night," my friend told me when her father died, "to see how he was doing, and the nurse told me he had 'expired,' as if he were a library card." We're afraid to say the word even.

About sin we are not so sure. We're not always even sure of what it is. But the ancients linked sin and death, not because disease or accident comes as punishment for human wrongdoing, but because sin robs the living of the sweetness of life. It gets in between us and God and blocks our view. And so, though we live and breathe, we are denied the fullness of joy we could and should have before we leave the earth.

September 5

The Minister of the Congregation is directed to instruct the people, from time to time, about the duty of Christian parents to make prudent provision for the well-being of their families. . . .
—RUBRIC ON THANKSGIVING FOR A CHILD, p. 445

It was quite an undertaking getting all five kids ready to go back to school. Buying shoes and dozens of socks for feet that had grown a whole size or even more during the course of the summer, buying pencils and rulers and composition books.

We were certainly not poor, but neither were we rolling in money in those early years of our ministry. The necessary expenses of September put a real dent in our budget every fall. I remember now how sweet our children were about that: considerate of our feelings beyond what you'd expect of young people. They really didn't complain about not having the latest style of everything. Sometimes there were things they wanted we couldn't get them right away, or even at all, and I remember how gracefully they accepted that. They knew we were a large family living on a clergyman's salary. And they knew that we would have given them the whole world if we could have.

We always hated it when we had to say no. We knew we were richly blessed in not having to deny them things they really needed, for we'd served in countries where many parents had to endure that sorrow. But giving them things that delighted them delighted us, far beyond the pleasure any self-indulgence might have brought us. It does to this day.

September 6

. . . multiply the harvests of the world; let thy Spirit go forth, that it may renew the face of the earth. . . . —PRAYER FOR THE HARVEST OF LANDS AND WATERS, p. 828

I guess a person has to have been brought up in a farming community to understand immediately how urgent a thing harvesttime is. The harvest, of course, is the moment to which the whole agricultural enterprise leads; the months of hoeing, sowing, watering, thinning, staking, pruning, all culminate in the moment of ripeness when it is time to gather the fruit.

The urgency is not just because there's a tremendous amount of fruit to gather. The real urgency comes from the fact that this tremendous volume of work needs to be done in a very short time. If you wait, the fruit will rot on the vine. If you don't get the harvest in now, you won't get it in at all.

In farming communities, everybody understands this. Students are routinely excused from school to help bring in the harvest. People often band together and use each other's machinery and animals and families. Nobody does anything else until the harvest is safe and dry in the barn.

Jesus could assume that his hearers knew what the pressure of a plentiful harvest was. So he talks about the kingdom of God in these urgent tones. This is not something we can mull over as we mosey on down the road. There are opportunities to be a part of God's work that only come our way once. We can't afford to let them pass.

September 7

Look with mercy, O God our Father, on all whose increasing years bring them weakness, distress, or isolation. —PRAYER FOR THE AGED, p. 830

When my back went out a year or two ago, decades of things I had taken for granted were suddenly impossible. I was utterly dependent on the people around me. The sickbed was not a mystery to me, since I had done a lot of hospital calling in my years in the ministry, but it was a different animal to be the one *in* it.

To experience radical weakness changes a person. In a funny way, that painful coming to the end of my own rope occasioned not the terrible anguish I might have expected, but something else: a kind of a gentle settling down. It turns out that I was never in charge, all along, that all my energy and my capability came from God and always had. And that, if God couldn't supply my needs one way, they would be supplied in another way. God certainly has a lot of different ways of doing things! More than I have.

I don't know what the end of your rope looks like, whether it's physical or emotional or spiritual or a little bit of all three, like mine. But I know we each have one, and I know that God is waiting there, as God has walked with you throughout your journey. When I come to the end of the next one, I hope I'm able to see God there more clearly and more quickly because of what I've learned this time.

September 8

May the Lord who has given you the will to do these things give you the grace and power to perform them. —ORDINATION OF A PRIEST, p. 532

As clergy we need to remind ourselves that power does not come from within us, but settles upon us as a gift in trust to us from God. Any Christian who has power has it only for the sake of the brothers and sisters, not as a possession in his own right. Just as the power of a parent is focussed on helping a child grow to independence, so that he can leave home and live on his own, so the leadership of a Christian is always focussed on the empowerment of others, never on itself and its own conservation. It is not rule. It is service.

There is tremendous personal freedom in this recognition. I need only be faithful and focussed on the love of the Body of Christ committed to my charge, and God will provide the power needed to serve it well. When we lay aside our self-interest for the empowerment of the other, whether it be in the work of the Church or the privacy of the family, we are free to receive blessings we would never know if we had to claw and grasp after them. For love cannot be commanded. It can only be freely given.

September 9

Bless this child and preserve his life. . . . —PRAYER FOR A CHILD NOT YET BAPTIZED, p. 444

It seems like only yesterday that our kids were babies. I will never forget my shock at how small they were—it didn't seem possible that a person could be that little and still be all right! I was nervous about holding them at first. I was afraid I would do something wrong and the baby would break! People had to talk me through it until I got the hang of it. It wasn't until I had to baptize a very, very premature baby in the hospital that I realized that our kids were actually big. That little tiny human being, lying in a carefully watched incubator, had arms smaller than my finger; his whole body would easily fit into a man's hand. I was awestruck by his tiny perfection. Such fragility. So tiny. But fighting to live. Everything in him working away at the new business of being alive.

To see a little baby is to see what the shepherds saw, what the three kings saw, what Mary and Joseph saw. Just a little human being: weak, fragile. Never again could people dismiss the weak and the fragile as unimportant. God's own self chose this form in which to come among us: a decisive choice of the weak as the vessels of God's love for the whole of creation. God chose weakness.

September 10

Strengthen your servant, O God, to do what he has to do and bear what he has to bear. . . . —PRAYER BEFORE AN OPERATION, p. 459

We have been busy, back in New York, with the coordination of relief efforts for our churches in the Virgin Islands. The roof was ripped right off the cathedral in St. Thomas and then sucked back into its nave in a million pieces. Hardly a structure is intact. People's homes. Schools. The tourism industry, economic lifeblood of the islands, will take years to recover. This is a tremendous loss.

In many places throughout the Caribbean, the Hurricane Prayer is a regular part of the liturgy. It asks God's protection in that dangerous season. They know that God is with them. From this they summon the courage to rebuild. They've done it before. They will do it again.

In large ways and in small ways, that is how faith carries us. That knowledge that our lives are contained by God no matter what happens to us. That willingness to see God's hand at work. That eagerness to be connected with God and with one another. You can live your life in that faith or outside of it. You will face the joys and sorrows of life whether you believe or not. When the hurricane comes, both the people of faith and the people who have no faith have to dig themselves out of the mud. Faith is not a way out of facing the hurricane. Faith is how you will face it: alone, or with your brothers and sisters in Christ.

September 11

Thomas Gray lived in the eighteenth century. He was well-born and well-off, an educated man, a history professor at Cambridge. He visited a country churchyard once; the elegy he wrote about it at the end of a summer day stands as one of the best known and best loved poems in the English language.

The shadows of early evening had begun to fall; the simple stones marking the graves of the poor leant against one another, poorly supported by the settling ground. Gray was struck to the bottom of his soul by the anonymity of the poor in death. In his extensive travels, he had seen magnificent monuments to statesmen, poets, and artists; kings and queens; popes and princes. Here, though, in the fading light of a country evening, each rough stone testified silently to a life equal in value to that memorialized by the most opulent of marble tombs. What was the difference, Gray asked himself, between these unknown dead and the long-remembered great figures of history? Only opportunity. What gifts never had the chance to grow and flower before their possessors were gently laid to rest here beneath the tall trees?

> Perhaps in this neglected spot is laid
> Some heart once pregnant with celestial fire, . . .
> Full many a flower is born to blush unseen,
> And waste its sweetness on the desert air.

September 12

You called on me in trouble, and I saved you. . . . –
p. 704

I have served in this conspicuous office in our Church during one of the most tumultuous eras in our history. It has often been difficult, for the issues facing the Church are the same ones facing the society, and they generate high emotion. "How do you want to be remembered?" Sometimes people ask me that, and I know that they are thinking of this or that wrenching controversy, this or that betrayal of trust somewhere in the Church.

But I know that one of the things that happens when trust has been betrayed too often is a hardening of the spirit. We become suspicious and fearful when we have survived betrayal. We want to protect ourselves. In our nation, in the Church, or in any human society, we are apt to turn upon the weak, the poor, the stranger, when we ourselves feel insecure.

I would like to be remembered as one who resisted that fearfulness. I want to be one who continued to trust in God even when human beings let me down, and I want to be one who can encourage that trust in those committed to my charge. I know that I cannot always control the behavior of others, but I want to be remembered as one who was willing to go beyond disappointment and fear to embrace the hope Jesus endlessly offers us. I do not want us to circle the wagons in a spasm of self-protective fear. I want us to open our hearts as faithful people.

Strengthen, O Lord, your servant with your Holy Spirit. . . .
—*THE ORDER FOR CONFIRMATION,* p. 309

If we look at the role of the servant in Jesus' day, we see that the central reality of the servant's life was the setting aside of his autonomy. In most cases, this loss of personal autonomy was not a voluntary thing; a person was born into it. But however the servant became a servant, his first duty and his first thought was not to himself, but to his master. His well-being was not something that existed apart from the well-being of the master. This was a very different thing from the rugged individualism we experience as normal in our culture. Here, a song entitled "I Gotta Be Me" is sung in cocktail lounges across the country, summing up a basic cultural attitude. Here, cowboys ride off into the sunset alone at the end of movies. We admire self-determination.

But there are relationships among us in which we yield that ruggedness. Marriage is one: I cannot be happy if Patti is unhappy. I am not all right if she is not all right.

Parenthood is another: we perform all kinds of tasks for our children we would not perform for other people. We give them baths, wash their clothes, feed them—the sorts of things a servant would do for a master. But we do not do them out of a spirit of servitude. We do them out of love. Love makes us servants of those we love. And almost everybody experiences this kind of living as a great joy. Almost everybody wants to have somebody for whom the barrier of self-interest falls away.

September 14

In the midst of life we are in death. . . . —*THE COMMITTAL AT THE BURIAL OF THE DEAD,* p. 484

We begin at the empty tomb. It is silent in that rocky place as we approach it. Not a soul around. We look inside. When our eyes have become used to the darkness, we see that there is nobody in the tomb.

If the hallmark of modernity is the loss of meaning, as many have said, then this silent, ambiguous scene at the empty tomb is a very modern moment. It is surreal; a dead body was laid there and now is gone. Nobody is on hand to explain it all to us. This is something the world has not seen before.

Those people have been dead for almost two thousand years. They were not modern. They didn't worry about whether or not the world had meaning. Nobody thought the human race was just here by accident, adrift in a meaningless universe without moral significance beyond what human beings fashioned for themselves. And yet, as different as we are from those first believers so long ago, they did not behave so differently from the way we might have behaved had we been there instead. What did they do? Proclaim the resurrection from the housetops? Not at first. They kept it pretty quiet, for all kinds of reasons, paramount among which must have been that they just didn't understand what was going on.

September 15

Grant us, O Lord, to trust in you with all our hearts.
—COLLECT FOR THE PROPER 18, p. 233

I am listening, as I write this, to the Gershwin opera *Porgy and Bess*. Porgy, the indomitable man who loves Bess with a strength that cancels out for them the fact that he is unable to walk, has lost her to the evil Sportin' Life, who has enticed her away to the big city. Porgy forgives her; she belongs with him, and he knows that if he can find her, she will come back. He sets out for the city in his mule cart, singing "Oh Lawd, I'm On My Way." That song is my favorite part of the whole opera: it's full of hope, courage, trust in the power of love, and trust in the self. Good will triumph over evil. Sure there's trouble, and sure it's dangerous, the song says, but I'm on my way! In spite of the betrayal and sorrow that Porgy has known, this is one of the most joyful songs that musical theater has ever produced.

Porgy and Bess is not a religious work. But it is certainly a work about faith, and the kind of love and courage Porgy shows in it is the kind of love and courage to which we are called. Does our salvation show in the grim circumstances in which we sometimes find ourselves? Maybe not, but it is close at hand. Nearer to us now than when we first believed. We're on our way!

September 16

He will come again in glory. . . . —THE NICENE CREED, p. 359

The first Christians believed Jesus would return during their lifetimes. That turned out not to be the case, of course. Now it is almost *two thousand years* later. What does the witness of someone who thought the world would end so long ago have to say to us today? It says that we live in expectant, jubilant hope, that life should be lived so that it will have been fully lived when it ends . . . *whenever* that may be. The time to reach out is *now,* the time to forgive is *now*; you may not have another chance. The time to enjoy the sweetness of life is *now,* for none of us is immortal; and all of our sweetnesses will have an end.

Sometimes when I awaken early enough to watch the sun come up over the tall buildings of the city, I stand at the window feeling the beauty of that particular dawn soak right into my soul. I feel as if it were eternal, and I feel as if I were, too. But the dawn fades away as the sun comes up, and, one of these days, so will I. It wasn't eternal after all, and neither am I. But I felt it as if it *were,* and the happiness of that sunrise filled me completely. May we be aware of the beauty of this world and sense the eternal moment when we can, for of such is heaven made and we do not know when the Son of Man is coming.

September 17

Give us grace to heed their warnings. . . . —COLLECT FOR THE
SECOND SUNDAY OF ADVENT, p. 211

Jesus often used images like the suddenness with which a flash
flood can overtake a desert area to talk about the need to be
ready for the coming of the kingdom of God. The desert can
be literally bone dry one minute and dangerously flooded with
water the next, with hardly any warning at all. But the people
were living their lives without any awareness of their actions,
and so when they were swept away they were not ready.

It should not be so with us. As we have been created to
love and savor the world God has given us, so we have also
been created to care for each other, to serve whom we can
while we can. While God's goodness does not depend upon
ours, and God's plan unfolds whether we go along with it or
not, we are intended to mirror the love which created us in
the love we bear one another. If we do not, we will have a
well-earned sense of unfinished business about our lives.

We are free to live as if the kingdom of God were not at
hand. Nobody is going to *make* us anticipate it. But if we live
and die as if we were less than the image of God we are called
to be, something inside us will know this, and that something
will mourn the loss of the wholeness we might have known.

September 18

The peace of the Lord be always with you. —THE PEACE AT
HOLY EUCHARIST, p. 360

"And a little child shall lead them." I have always loved the
image of the wild animals walking tamely behind a little child,
who leads them unmolested and unharmed. Our grandson
Jacob would be delighted to set off at the head of a parade
of lions, leopards, and tigers, for Jacob does not yet know
much about danger. People who love him make sure he is all
right, and it never occurs to him that it could be any other
way. Thank God.

Jacob's trust will be tempered and informed by tough
experiences as he grows. I feel sad when I think about his first
disappointment, his first betrayal, about his having to learn
not to talk to strangers. Thinking about this in relation to
Jacob is somehow even more poignant for me than the same
thought about his dad when he was little, and I am not quite
sure why. Other grandparents have told me the same thing.

I wonder if Isaiah was a grandfather. Why not? We know
he had children. He undoubtedly pictured a world in which it
was safe to be as Jacob is: happy and trusting in the goodness
of life, brave and eager. It was a place in which the hearts of
savage beasts are melted by the simplicity of a little boy until
they follow him around like puppies and kittens. I know why
Jacob tugs at my heart so; I see in his joy a glimpse of what
God intends for us.

September 19

How long will you judge unjustly, and show favor to the wicked? —PSALM 82:2, p. 705

I hear frustration in God's voice. Who of us has not been in an argument with someone we love and felt this way? Some relationships are too precious to us to let them founder without a word of explanation. If we know and love someone and then see behavior which is unworthy of the love we bear that person, we feel entitled to demand an explanation.

We hear the same frustation from Almighty God toward a wayward humanity that we hear in ourselves when a dear one lets us down. It is the frustration of a faithful lover when confronted with the infidelity of the beloved: "How could you do this? Answer me!"

The requirements of our God, as we have seen in the Book of Micah, are really not many. To do justice, to love mercy, to walk humbly. Nothing complex there. It is this simplicity, and the utter generosity of the love of God for us, spontaneously given and unearned, that entitles God to ask this lover's question. God has done well by us and has demanded of us only those things that will truly enrich our lives: not sacrifices, but fidelity to the path that alone leads to true happiness and peace.

September 20

. . . that unity may overcome estrangement . . .
—CELEBRATION AND BLESSING OF A MARRIAGE, p. 429

Everybody who can read a newspaper knows that my church, like every other church, has been wracked recently with terrible scandals involving compulsive behavior on the part of clergy. These cases sometimes end up coming across my desk. I am sure that my intense feeling for the victim in these cases is directly related to my experience confronting addiction in my own father. He was not physically or verbally abusive to us, but our lives were powerfully affected by the fact that so much of his life was beyond his control.

And yet, I also remember the worth that I always saw in him, even though he was not the master of his own actions. I have a photograph of him as a teenager, returning victorious from a football game. Such a broad, sweet smile—it's jarring to me now, seeing that innocence on a face I would later know only as sad.

The one whose life has spun so destructively and profoundly out of control was innocent and confident once, like my dad was. And now he is fallen so far that he hurts the people God has given into his care. I long for the healing of the one who has victimized another with a fervency I probably would not feel if I had not been forced to confront the need for reconciliation every day in my own home. Bitter things for a young person to know, but I am glad I know them.

September 21

We give thanks to you, O Lord our God, for all your servants and witnesses of time past. . . . —THANKSGIVING FOR THE SAINTS AND FAITHFUL DEPARTED, p. 838

True story: when the late John Walker was bishop of Washington, D.C., he was visiting a rural parish in southern Maryland. The church was old, set in the midst of tobacco farming country. A couple of its windows were dedicated to men who had fallen during the Civil War defending the Confederacy. Bishop Walker was the first black bishop of that diocese, and one of only a handful of African American diocesan bishops in our history. After the service was over, the bishop was standing at the church door, shaking people's hands as they left the church. One large, grim-faced white man stopped in front of John and pointedly ignored the bishop's extended hand. "Bishop," he said in a low voice, "Why don't you stay with your own people?"

John looked up into the man's face and broke into a broad smile. "I am with my own people," he said, gesturing around him at all the white men, women, and children waiting in line.

And so he was.

September 22

Preserve those who travel. . . . —*PRAYER FOR TRAVELERS,*
p. 831

On the airplane, I settle into some correspondence. I go through three or four letters, until I am interrupted by a little voice saying, "You sure get a lot of mail." My seatmate looks to be about six. Her mother leans forward and tells her to leave me alone. But something makes me want to put the mail aside for a little while. We talk about her school and her favorite subjects, her two cats and her little sister. She makes me tell her all my grandchildren's names. She wants to go on with a guessing game about what her mother's first name is, but I beg off. So instead we talk about her first trip to Disney World and what she expects to see there. She is astonished to learn that I also have never been there, even though I am very old. I redeem my image by listing for her all the countries I *have* visited.

When the flight is over, her mother apologizes to me for her daughter's interruption of my work. "It'll all still be there tonight," I tell her. It was so natural for her to strike up a conversation. Most of us would have passed the entire trip in silence; maybe an "excuse me" or two, but not much more. I loved the way she assumed my interest in the things that interested her, that open-hearted expectation of common cause. I wish we stayed like that—but then, there is really no reason why we can't, is there?

September 23

Almighty and everlasting God, you made the universe with all its marvelous order. . . . —*PRAYER FOR KNOWLEDGE OF GOD'S CREATION,* p. 827

Just a day or two into fall—the summer lingered for a long time this year, and most of the leaves are still green. But a pale orange-yellow is beginning to show among the green, the first signal of the riotous color to come.

What is the purpose of the autumn leaves? We know why they need to fall: it is so the tree can rest during the winter, and so the soil can be renewed by their decomposing. But why, before they die, do they burst into this glorious song?

It is hard for me to imagine any other reason besides the disposition of God toward the good and the beautiful. Many things need not be lovely, but they are: the Painted Desert, for instance, or a snowflake. Once I saw a school of dolphins leap from the water over and over and over again, graceful arcs of silver gray in perfect formation. There was no need for them to be so beautifully synchronized, but they were.

The psalms are full of the wonder of the natural world. I remember being overcome by it when I was a boy. I would be down by the water at sunset, or staring up at the sky through the branches of a tree, and for a moment I would be acutely aware of just how glorious the world is. And it never gets old; more than six decades' worth of autumns, and I am shocked by the beauty of each one, every time.

September 24

Holy God, heavenly Father, you formed me from the dust in your image and likeness. . . . —*SACRAMENT OF RECONCILIATION,* p. 450

I have a secret ambition for my retirement: I want to become a potter. All my life, I've admired the ability to bring a shape out of inert clay. I've tried my hand at it a few times and, unlike a lot of things, it really *is* as much fun as it looks. When I get a little time to myself, I'm going to get good at it.

One of the great things about it is that if you don't like the way something is turning out, you just take it off the wheel and remake it. You keep the clay wet so that it will remain pliable, and you can work with it and work with it until you get it right.

The prophet Jeremiah compared God to a potter and humankind to the clay. Great image—that is *exactly* the way we are formed by our lives: shaped and remade, shaped and remade by the things that happen to us. And we are like the potter's clay in another way: it is important that we remain pliable. Let the clay dry out and it can't be molded anymore; it will break uselessly. Life can't form us gracefully if we won't allow ourselves to bend. But we will become beautiful and strong if we do.

September 25

Lord Jesus, for our sake you were condemned as a criminal. . . .
—*PRAYER FOR PRISONS AND CORRECTIONAL INSTITUTIONS,*
p. 826

It is a great gift to be able to see Christ in another human being. In some, he is clearly visible. In others, his image is faint; the scars they bear obscure him from our sight. But he is there.

He has said himself, though, that it is in those people that we should look most diligently for his presence. Jesus is Lord of all, not just of the good and the beautiful. The one who allowed himself to be betrayed and abandoned by people who called themselves his friends is not surprised by our sins and unloveliness. He proved stronger than the worst they could do; sin and betrayal are no match for him.

So how do we see Christ in the unlovely? By becoming familiar with him as much as we can in the expected places: in church, in meditation, in talk with other Christians, in prayer. By remaining fervent in intercessory prayer, that prayer that remembers those in any need or trouble and makes common cause with them. You cannot pray for someone and retain a feeling of distance from her for long. When we know Christ's face well, we will recognize him even in places where goodness is conspicuous only by the need of it.

September 26

Grant us, Lord, not to be anxious about earthly things. . . .
—COLLECT FOR PROPER 20, p. 234

This weekend I'm going to lead a Quiet Day for the clergy in a diocese in Florida. That's where a group gets together in a conference center or monastery for a resting and refreshing day apart. A Quiet Day *is* quiet, for sure, but it is busy all the same; usually there are three talks to prepare, plus a sermon. It never fails, just as I'm struggling to get out of the office the day before I have to lead a Quiet Day, something urgent breaks out that prevents me from focussing as much as I want to on the talks I'll have to give. I grab my suitcase and head for the airport.

Often it's tense at the airport, too, with not quite enough time to be what you'd call comfortable in making the flight. And flying itself is tiring. It would be easy to allow these road-blocks and annoyances to dominate the getaway and set the tone for the whole event, so that the hoped-for day of rest and refreshment turned out to be anything but that. But I have noticed something: that never happens. No matter what anxious things have happened on the way to a Quiet Day, once everybody gets there and settles in, God takes over. We are not brought all the way out to a convent in the middle of nowhere so that we will not be rested and refreshed. I am never happier than on one of these days. I leave rested, myself. We are there for the good of our souls. And God sees to it.

September 27

. . . to work together with mutual forbearance and respect.
—*PRAYER IN TIMES OF CONFLICT,* p. 824

In the Bible, people often find themselves gracefully involved with other people with whom they would ordinarily have expected to be at odds. Pharaoh's daughter goes swimming in the Nile and finds a little Hebrew baby whom she raises as her own, even though her own father has ordered all Hebrew baby boys killed. Paul of Tarsus, ardent persecutor of the first Christians, abruptly becomes one—and finds himself preaching the gospel to people he wouldn't have sat at the same table with before his conversion. The lion lies down with the lamb: the Biblical writers regard the healing of ancient enmity as a powerful sign of God at work in the world.

The spirit of God is about whenever people decide to interact as real people, rather than as cartooned members of a group. All manner of possibilities open up for those who approach others that way. For when I reduce others to a set of stereotypical characteristics based on what they are instead of who they are, I reduce myself. Bigotry shrinks the spirit. Love enlarges it.

September 28

Where there is hatred, let us sow love. . . . —A PRAYER
ATTRIBUTED TO ST. FRANCIS, p. 833

So many toys marketed at little boys are based on aggressive-ness and fighting. Toy guns, toy grenades, toy weaponry of all kinds: most parents I know are torn between their desire to give their children the things they want and their desire that their children grow up to be men of peace, not men of war. There is an aggressive and competitive spirit in each of us . . . but people sure manage them differently!

One of the hardest things about being a parent is this bal-ancing of values: the family values of peaceful cooperation and fellowship and the values of the culture into which we send our children every day. It's tough to have to tell your child he can't do what "everybody's" parents allow. Ask around, though, and it usually turns out that "everybody" is a pretty select group of people.

Coming back to the States when our kids were young teenagers after raising them abroad thus far was an eye-opener. My kids felt as if they were from Mars. Many, many things here were new and strange to them, and their peers weren't always kind. "They just don't like us because we're Japanese," I heard one red-haired son console another, and I realized that some serious culture shock was going on. That was an extreme case of what we all experience: every family has the task of translating its values into something the children can carry with them into a hard world.

September 29

Lord of all power and might . . . —COLLECT FOR PROPER 17,
p. 181

There are people for whom everything is a "Yes, but . . ."
They are too aware of the possibility of failure to even make a
start, and so they miss out on the possibility of ever tri-
umphing over the limitations of life.

God knows all about our limitations—but they are our
limitations, not God's. I remember reading a story about
a woman—a small woman, weighing less than a hundred
pounds—who lifted *the front end of a car* under which her husband had been pinned in an automobile accident. For the rest
of their lives, they regarded this as a miracle. I'd have to agree;
whatever the adrenal mechanism of that miracle, it certainly
was one!

But there wouldn't have been a miracle if she had stopped
to reason things out, would it? She would have come to the
inescapable conclusion that a woman her size couldn't lift a
car, and that would have been that.

So what's the message? That it is never necessary to plan
ahead, to weigh the options and the resources and attempt
to do the realistic thing? No—ordinarily, the world runs
according to its rules, and we all know what they are. But
sometimes there is nothing to lose by trying, and everything
to gain. Sometimes a miracle happens, and sometimes you can
be part of it.

September 30 ❊❊❊❊❊❊❊❊❊❊❊❊❊

Guide and sanctify, we pray, those whom you call to follow you under the vows of poverty, chastity, and obedience. . . .
—*PRAYER FOR MONASTIC ORDERS AND VOCATIONS,* p. 819

I am always struck by the sense of peace I find whenever I visit a convent or monastery. It's certainly not easier to live that way than in the way most of us live, although some people imagine that it would be. If you think interpersonal relations in family life are challenging, just try living in community with twenty other people! But a religious house, no matter what's going on there in terms of people's personalities, is first and foremost a house of prayer. Those in it spend hours in prayer. The layers of all those years of prayer do something to the spirit of the building itself.

They are houses where detail matters because every work, no matter how small, is a prayer. Where every task of living is performed mindful of the God from whom all things come. Monastic houses have a tradition of hospitality, born of the awareness of the privileged place the stranger holds in the Judeo-Christian heritage. I share their common meals and their common prayer, and I emerge into the world refreshed.

And prayed for: that is their business. They pray for the world, for you and me. They pray for people who are praying for them and for many more who are not. It has always been a minority lifestyle, that vocation of prayer and common life. But it has also always lived, apart from the world, for the sake of the world.

October 1

. . . that the sense of his weakness may add strength to his faith . . . —PRAYER FOR THE SANCTIFICATION OF ILLNESS,
p. 460

It has helped me immensely in my life to remember that it is only hard to have faith if I think I have to summon it all by myself. You've had this experience many times, I know: something happens, something so unjust, so terrible, that your heart just sinks to the floor and cannot arise. And then somebody says something about there being no God, obviously, because if there were one, such things wouldn't happen. And you look at that event, that terrible thing, and indeed—you don't see a single good thing about it.

At times like that, faith is impossible for us to summon by ourselves. At times like those, whatever faith we find is a gift from God. We don't make it ourselves; God gives it to us. Our pain is such that it paralyzes our hearts and they cannot move. It is not a human creation, the faith that emerges out of such darkness; only God can make it.

It is a gift of God. And it comes to us precisely at the disappointed places: the empty tomb. The deepest of sorrows, the places in which we need it most. We do not know why things happen the way they do, but we know that God can yet bring life out of the darkness and silence of death. When we are in the grip of sorrow, we doubt God's goodness profoundly. But then God moves and the possibility of joy becomes real again.

October 2

In your infinite love you made us for yourself. . . .
—EUCHARISTIC PRAYER, p. 362

We know that the love of God is strange to our culture. This is the land of the prenuptial agreement, the careful negotiating of territory, the angry defense of right and privilege. Well, the love of God was also strange to the culture in which Jesus lived. We know that it took even his closest friends a long time to grasp it—in Scripture, Peter, James, John, Mary Magdalene, were not always able to understand its limitlessness. We see them unable to recognize the risen Christ, so gutted by the agony of their friend's death on the cross that they had no eyes to see his risen glory. We see their doubt and feel a little better, maybe, about our own; it is not our distance in time that makes it hard for us to follow him. It is our humanity that makes it hard for us to glimpse the divine love in a human history so full of pain.

We hear someone say about this or that terrible headline in the newspaper, "How could a loving God let this happen?", forgetting that God's love is signified for us by a cross. Even God, the only one for whom pain is not a necessity, does not escape. In the midst of that which breaks our hearts in two, God abides and comforts. God waits to enter our hearts and transform the ashes of our sorrows into greater love.

October 3

. . . united in one holy bond of truth and peace . . . —PRAYER
FOR THE UNITY OF THE CHURCH, p. 818

When St. Augustine experienced his conversion to Christianity,
it seemed to him to be the answer he had been looking for all
his life. This brilliant scholar and rhetorician experimented with
the most arcane philosophies of his age, applying his intellect
to their study. Nothing satisfied him. In Christianity, a faith
whose simplicity seemed laughable to Augustine's sophisticated pagan friends, he found what he was looking for.

The first thing he did was to form a community. He went
to Ostia, then a bustling seaport and now an arid stretch of
ruined buildings, and he took his mother and his son and
some of his friends. They formed a community structured
around their faith, encouraging one another in their spiritual
journeys, praying and talking together as they imagined the
first Christians had done. He writes about it in his famous
autobiography, *Confessions,* as an idyllic time of fellowship and
personal and spiritual growth. He never forgot his time in
Ostia. He understood what community could do in the life of
the individual believer and leader, because he had experienced
it in his own life. Augustine was brilliant, all right, but his
brilliance was not what brought him peace. It was from his
community that he got his strength and support.

October 4

Lord, make us instruments of your peace. —*A PRAYER ATTRIBUTED TO ST. FRANCIS,* p. 833

Our gentle brother from Assisi is traditionally held to be the author of this famous prayer. One of the many things we know about Francis is that the people who knew him loved him dearly. Their stories of his life, of his simplicity and commitment to poverty and holiness, have a friendly, self-deprecating humor about them often missing from the daunting tales of other great monastic figures written by the respectful subordinates who memorialized them. There was a striking joy present in Francis's austere life, and an equally striking absence of competitiveness. He would have shrugged and laughed at the idea that he might boast of anything.

I think of Francis's simplicity and sweetness. Of his desire to die naked, on the bare ground, as a symbol of his radical powerlessness. I think, then, of some Franciscans of a later age, the ones who accompanied the Spanish conquest of the New World, an enterprise made in equal measure of human greed and religious zeal. Eventually, every renewal comes itself to be in need of renewal. Nothing human is immune from human sin. In all of our striving, we stumble into the ditch of compromise as often as we walk on the road. Left to our own devices, we cannot always be trusted. We have nothing of which to boast. All that is good within us comes from God. The same God has hold of us all, and God does not let go.

October 5

For the beauty and wonder of your creation . . . —A LITANY OF THANKSGIVING, p. 837

Autumn is such a lovely time in so many places; to be outdoors during this time is to have an inescapable sense of the beauty of the earth that God has made.

Now, in the autumn, when nature is perhaps its most beautiful before it seems to die in the winter, when the evenings are cold and the darkness comes early and the wind has a wild edge to it, when we walk along and kick up a flurry of golden leaves as we go, the most jaded among us feels a bittersweet love for the earth as it prepares for its rest. We feel life humming through our veins a little more as we behold earth's last glorious salute of color before it slips away from the trees and flowers for another winter, feel the sense of smell and hearing become a little more acute as we think about the time when they, too, will come to an end. This is the time when we remember how much we love our world, when we see that it is about to go to sleep.

When I was a young man, I remember thinking that I was pretty strong. I wanted to be even stronger, to be able to handle everything. Didn't want to have any weakness or vulnerability. Certainly didn't want anybody else to see any! Now that I am older, I know that I am not really very strong at all. It is God who is strong, not me. One day the world will cease from created existence. It is not eternal. It is created. It had a beginning, and it will have an end.

October 6

Walk in love, as Christ loved us and gave himself for us, an offering and sacrifice to God. —OFFERTORY SENTENCE, p. 343

Have you ever noticed how many of Jesus' teachings are about money? Lots of them. We see people doing all kinds of financial things in his parables: people managing vineyards, people storing up treasure, people investing money wisely and other people investing it foolishly, people buying and people selling. We see them giving money to the temple, and to the poor and suffering. We see people finding buried treasure. We see them borrowing and lending money, and then we see some of them paying it back and others not.

Jesus thinks that the way people are with money tells us a lot about the way God is with us. And it makes sense that this part of human life should be revealing of the love of God—Jesus observes that our hearts are where our treasure is, every time. Money is important to us. Money matters to us. And so we are like money to God. We are treasure. We matter to God.

Much has changed since Jesus told these stories, but we recognize ourselves in them with ease. "Hold on a minute," Jesus says. "Consider the lilies of the field," he says to us. "Don't be afraid to trust in my love for you. You have great worth to me. You are treasure."

October 7

Be always near us when we seek you in this place.
—*CONSECRATION OF A CHURCH,* p. 568

When I visit an old church, I often think about what life was like for the people who first built it. How much hard work it took to build the church. What a different country they lived in from the one in which we live: a country in which uninhabited areas went on for miles and miles, a country in which people lived lives hard, lonely, and short. A country in which families lost children often, to diseases for which there was no remedy. A country in which a man in his fifties was old and so was a woman in her forties. A country in which, at this time of year, everyone who could carry a hayfork was in the fields bringing in the harvest. We drive by the roadside vegetable stands and see the pumpkins, the squashes, the last tomatoes and beans. We buy some of these things and decorate our homes with them, hang ears of corn on our doors, buy a couple of bales of straw and arrange them on our front porches with a pot or two of chrysanthemums. We think they are beautiful. They looked at those things and thanked God they wouldn't starve in the winter to come.

And yet, they found time and energy and wood and trust enough to build God's house. Something in them knew that their trust rightly resided in God. In a time when life was harder and more precarious than our lives are, they found the courage to trust in God.

. . . have mercy on us and forgive us; that we may delight in your will, and walk in your ways. . . . —CONFESSION OF SIN, p. 360

Saul was a persecutor of Christians, responsible for the deaths of many, until one day, on his way to Damascus, he was struck to the ground by a bright light, and heard the Lord talking to him; he then repented of his earlier deeds. He changed so profoundly that he even changed his name: Paul became the most active missionary of the early Church, one of the most famous people of our holy history.

His story is one piece of evidence of something that we don't always like to believe but that is nonetheless true: Nothing you can do will separate you from the love of God. We sometimes resist that truth, either because our guilt about our own lives is so great we can't bear to confess it or because our horror at someone else's misdeeds is so great we can't bear to let him in the door. But it's true, no matter what you have done against the commandments of God, the door through repentance to Christ is always open to you.

God called Paul—and calls us—to repent for the same simple reason we want *our* children to walk a good path through life: It hurts them if they don't. "It hurts you to kick against the goad," the Lord said to Paul as he lay, stunned, on the ground, and it was true. It hurt Paul to be full of hatred. That's no way to live. His conversion set him free from that hurt.

October 9

Almost every public function I attend is a religious one, and begins and ends with a walk, a procession. Usually with beautiful organ music and everyone singing. Usually performed in clothes that were the street dress of an earlier age, now reserved for liturgical functions. Often preceded by candles carried by people in other kinds of special clothes.

In my present calling, I am almost always the last one in line. I like to remember that as we line ourselves up every time, because that position at the end of the line is the position of *least* honor. That is why a bishop walks there—to underscore the Christian understanding of authority as one of many kinds of service. I like to keep reminding myself of that, because with the candles and the special clothes and the singing and the splendor, it would be easy to forget!

It is easy for anyone, I imagine, to begin to feel important if he or she bears great authority. Or, conversely, to begin to feel insignificant if he or she has little or none. The purpose of humility, and its centrality to our faith in a God-man who embodied it as no one has before or since, is to help us to know ourselves as God knows us: just us. Unvarnished. Unadorned. Last in line, but side by side with Christ.

October 10

. . . not as we ask in our ignorance, nor as we deserve in our sinfulness, but as you know and love us . . . —PRAYERS OF THE PEOPLE, p. 394

In a favorite book of mine, *Crime and Punishment,* by Fyodor Dostoyevsky, a brilliant young man commits a terrible murder in order to act out his theory that brilliant people don't have to abide by the same rules as the rest of us. Raskolnikov's subsequent plunge into guilt and near-madness prove him mistaken. He confesses and is sent to a prison camp in Siberia. Justice has been served.

But the author goes further. Sonia, a good and kind girl of great humility who has been forced into prostitution to feed her family and is therefore at the very bottom rung of Russian society, loves Raskolnikov. She goes with him to Siberia and supports him with love and tears and what food she can bring him. She knows the terrible truth about him, and she loves him and forgives him. At the end of the book, we see him coming to understand humility and repentance through Sonia, and we know Raskolnikov has abandoned forever his lonely absorption in his own brilliance.

It would have been just for Raskolnikov to serve his term, alone and unloved, in misery. But love redeemed him. If human love could work kindness even in the face of such guilt, what must be the power of the divine love to work kindness?

October 11

. . . the truth is not in us. —PENITENTIAL ORDER, p. 320

If Jesus were to walk past and say, "Follow me," you probably would. *If* you knew it was Jesus. Most of us would have little trouble obeying God's will if God made it known to us in person. Our love of God, or maybe even just our *fear* of God, would be strong enough to make us do even very difficult things if we knew for sure it was God who was asking. Our problem is that we have to *discern* what God's will is and *then* obey it. And we have to examine the many possibilities God has for speaking to us in the many voices that exhort us to act in our world.

Suppose we choose the wrong one? Suppose we get caught up in an agenda that we truly believe to be the will of God for us and then later find out we made a mistake? Or suppose we never find that out, and we go to our graves mistaken, on the wrong track? We know of many cases in which people did terrible things in God's name—the Inquisition in the seventeenth century, the witch trials at the same time. Might we be caught in something similar, on a smaller scale, and be unaware of it? There are many people speaking today who claim to have God on their sides. We have to choose among them. It's not always easy.

October 12

Open their hearts to your grace and truth. —HOLY BAPTISM, p. 305

People need to develop their powers of discernment, to "work out" spiritually as they might physically in a gym. If I think that I might be acting contrary to the will of God and not even know it, what steps can I take to prevent that?

I can stop filling my prayers with shopping lists ("Let me get the job." "Let that so-and-so get what he deserves.") that arise from my obsession with myself and instead do some listening to God. God has chosen us as people to whom God wishes to communicate. But that's going to be difficult if the level of our spiritual chatter is such that God can't get a word in edgewise. If we are quiet, God will speak to us in prayer.

You don't know what to say to God when you pray? Then say that. Say, "I don't know how to talk to you." And then wait. Mixed in with the jumble of thoughts that crowd your mind will be the calm voice that says, "Don't worry. I heard you. I'll show you how." Read the words of some of the people of prayer who have written for us over the centuries. In their struggles to learn to pray, you will see yourself. Read your Bible and make it a habit like some people do with vitamins or jogging. You will learn to see it fresh each day, and no matter how long you live, you will be surprised by it to the end of your days.

October 13

Give us grace to do your will in all that we undertake. . . .
—PRAYERS OF THE PEOPLE, p. 387

We have just discussed developing ourselves spiritually—through prayer, devotional reading, Scripture reading—so that we will become better discerners of God's will for our actions, so that we will not be unwitting agents of evil when we think we are agents for good. So, then, how will our spiritual conditioning help in keeping us on the side of God in all our actions? We will be explicit preachers of the gospel. The acquaintance we have with God through prayer and Scripture will inform us daily of the love of God, and we will tell people about it. We will exhibit in our demeanor a calm and a serenity that will commend our words to those who hear us. I doubt if the gospel is ever truly preached in a hysterical or agitated manner. The spirit of God is a spirit of order, not of disorder.

And we will be healers. Our activities are not from God if they tear down rather than build up, if they partake of death rather than of life, if they build walls rather than pull them down. Those actions with which we seek to put others outside the sphere of God's love or of our own are not spirit filled.

October 14

. . . the courage to will and to persevere . . . —*HOLY BAPTISM,*
p. 308

In *To Kill a Mockingbird* a small town lawyer took the case of a black man accused of raping a white woman. Believing the man to be innocent, Atticus Finch lost just about every friend he had in that small town in the pursuit of justice.

Sometimes we find ourselves at odds with friends or co-workers because of a moral stand. Perhaps it is nothing more than the decision not to respond to a racist joke at the office, or the decision to call a child to account for insensitivity or cruelty to a classmate who is different from the others. It is not easy to do this. We don't want to be priggish or holier-than-thou. And we truly want people to like us.

But we know that justice is more important than the approval of others. We owe it to ourselves to map out a moral plan for our lives and to pray for the courage to stay on that map.

To Kill a Mockingbird ends with Atticus Finch losing his case, and the young black man wrongly convicted of a terrible crime. Finch walked out of the courtroom defeated. But as he passed his children, seated in the back of the room with the black townspeople, they all rose to their feet—and so do we, mentally, when we read the end of the book—to honor a man who followed justice, whatever the cost.

October 15

. . . *he became incarnate*. . . . —*THE NICENE CREED,* p. 358

The film *The Last Temptation of Christ* portrayed Jesus as imagining living a life like those of other men: getting married, having children, feeling the same desires and joys and fears. Some people were outraged. I think the filmmaker's intent was simple and spiritual: to say that the Incarnation was real. Jesus was *really* divine and *really* human. The way in which that was lived out has always been a mystery. People have often "solved" it by claiming Jesus really didn't feel the things we feel: no doubts, no temptations, no yearning for love and intimacy.

This cannot be. His sacrifice was nothing if his life and its joys were a matter of indifference to him. Part of the glory of the Cross is its sorrow: a young man with everything to live for lays down his life out of a love purer than any the world has known. He gives everything, not just the things he doesn't want. Peter confessed the true identity of Jesus: "You are the Christ." He said this of a comrade, a man he knew well, a man like him in many ways and yet so unlike him—the Son of the living God.

October 16

Seek the Lord while he wills to be found. . . . —*MORNING PRAYER,* p. 86

When Patti and I go to the supermarket, I scan the headlines of those tabloids near the checkout counter. "Lose Twenty Pounds with New Fudge Diet!" "Elvis Talks to Me from Heaven!" "Woman Marries Man from Mars!" We carry our groceries out the door with a smile.

Often the headline is about religion. Sometimes, it concerns a supposedly scientific demonstration of a biblical truth: they've found the core of the apple Eve gave to Adam, or they've figured out Methuselah's real age. There is something touching about this trust in scientific evidence. In our age, an emphasis has been put on empirical reality, things that can be weighed and measured and explained. Some people try to weigh and measure the power of God, desiring to satisfy their scientific way of looking at the world and to believe in God at the same time. God has given us rational minds, and then we use them to see if God is really the truth!

But if we were able to deduce or "prove" God according to scientific methods, God would be diminished and contained by them. God would be finite. This is not the case. Our scientific inquiries, blessed by God, so productive of so many good things, are gifts from God, not ways in which to measure God.

October 17

God looks down from heaven upon us all. . . . —PSALM 53:2,
p. 659

What is it that makes people so intolerant of diversity in matters of faith?

The biggest component may be the lack of a sense of self-worth. When I am truly comfortable with what I am, I will not need to bludgeon you with it. My relating to you will be a conversation rather than a sermon. Sometimes those who need constant reassurance that they are acceptable feel the most need to denounce others. People at peace with themselves are less likely to fall into that.

The Church is a group of people united in gratitude to God for the redemption of the whole creation from the decay of sin and death, not an elaborate set of reasons why I am saved and you are not. We pray for a Christian maturity that will make us *less* focussed on ourselves, not more so.

What will we be asked when we stand before God? *Were you right all the time? Do you qualify for membership?* That is not my image of God's judgment. I think we will be asked if we loved God and tried to show it in the things we did.

October 18

. . . that in tranquility your dominion may increase until the earth is filled with the knowledge of your love . . . —COLLECT *FOR PEACE,* p. 258

I have learned much from living in places where Christianity was a minority religion. I appreciate the gifts of the great non-Christian religions of the world and marvel at the points of contact between them and our faith in Christ. I understand the ways in which God has revealed divine truth in other religions, and recognize elements of our own belief in faiths that arose long ago and far from Palestine.

Yet as Christians we *do* consider our faith claims to be absolute. We believe our God created the universe, and we believe that Jesus was the incarnation of this Creator. We believe that the Spirit of God continues to renew the covenant made in creation. We long for its final perfection when Christ will be all in all. These are claims other religions do not make. Our respect for the faith of others does not detract from our intimate connection with our own principles.

October 19

Give them such fulfillment of their mutual affection that they may reach out in love and concern for others. —CELEBRATION AND BLESSING OF A MARRIAGE, *p. 429*

I have known many Christians who pray every day for the quickening of faith in people they love. Who among us does not want the best for those dear to us? And who among us has not wished for an unbelieving husband or sister or child or friend to sit next to us in church and grab hold of what is so freely offered there? My faith makes me joyful in a deep way, even during hard times. I want those I love to have it too.

Sometimes people want to know what they can do to "get through" to an unchurched loved one. I think the answer lies in being more and more what they are: joyful in the Lord. Our loved ones will see our joy, and they cannot help but want joy themselves. It can be painful for us to see them search for it down dead-end streets, but they may have to. Above all, we witness to them by loving them, and that love makes us influential when we talk about our faith.

Everyone has his or her own journey. God does not want to lose them, and they will not be lost. Our witness, in words and loving deeds, paves the way for God's mighty action.

October 20

The Lord mercifully with his favor look upon you. . . .
—CELEBRATION AND BLESSING OF A MARRIAGE, p. 431

I switched on the television the other night. There was a situation comedy in progress. I was struck by the actors' reliance on sarcasm as a way of being humorous. Almost all of the jokes were sarcastic. There are many types of humor besides sarcasm, but it seems to score the highest on the studio laugh track. I began to think about sarcasm and to ask myself why it is funny. Or whether it is really funny at all.

The word *sarcasm* literally means "to tear the flesh." A sarcastic remark, then, is intended to hurt. It cannot be used in a friendly manner, or it ceases to be itself. It bothered me that this kind of humor was predominant in the show, and I suspect that this show is not unique in that respect. I remember radio comedies at which we roared with laughter years ago. Were they like that? It seems to me now that the feeling was different. More friendly. Merciful. Certainly more innocent in those days. Less negative. Am I right about that, or am I just having a nostalgic day?

"He made my mouth like a sharp sword"—the prophet Isaiah once described his gift of prophecy like that. But not a sword with which to wound people. The sharpness of our wit, the ability to think on our feet—God can use these gifts in us to build others up, to call intelligently for transformation, and—by all means—to make people laugh.

October 21

. . . the firstborn among many brethren . . . —ORDINATION OF *A PRIEST,* p. 533

The older brother figure who must yield to the younger is a familiar theme in Scripture: I think of Jesus' parable of the prodigal son, or of Jacob and Esau. John the Baptist too is such a figure. Unlike the others, though, he makes no protest when his ministry is eclipsed by that of Jesus.

It is good for us to think about this aspect of John's character: his humility, rather than his flamboyance. There is always going to be someone who eclipses *us,* too. There will be someone who is smarter, or stronger, or richer, or more influential. We all have need of John's kind of humility, and it need not cancel out our self-esteem.

"How'm I doin'?" a colorful mayor of New York City used to ask people on the street. I guess we're all asking that question of the world—wanting affirmation and support. Sometimes we get it and sometimes we don't. When it doesn't come from outside, though, we have another source of strength: the loving God from whom all our good works come.

October 22

. . . to equip the saints for the work of ministry . . .
—*ORDINATION OF A PRIEST*, p. 533

I know a young seminary student who did field work in a home for profoundly retarded children. She approached this work with trepidation at first; how would she handle the sad sight of so many terribly handicapped children? One little girl especially tugged at her heart. Unable to see, hear, speak, or walk, she simply lay in her hospital bed, day after day. She had lain there all her life, and there would be no change.

Every visit plunged the student into an angry confrontation with God when she prayed. *You tell me* what purpose this life serves! *You show me* why this child would not be better off dead! One day, wondering what earthly good she was doing, she reached out and touched the little cheek, stroking it with her hand, very gently. And the little girl smiled. From the recesses of her soul, a place without speech, where in a lifetime there had been no light and no other person, the child reached out and acknowledged with joy the gentle touch of a human being. That smile taught the student the most important thing she learned in her seminary career: there is no one whom love cannot touch.

October 23

Give rest, O Christ, to your servant with your saints. . . .
—*BURIAL OF THE DEAD*, p. 499

When the New Testament uses the word *saint*, it is always plural. The saints of the apostolic era defined themselves as members of a community, and they measured their righteousness against the community's standards and in terms of the community's needs. Christian communities in many Asian and African countries represent only tiny fractions of their society. Their churches are peopled with extraordinary Christians who define themselves in terms of their churches, and their churches have a vitality and an urgency that must be like that of those tiny churches so long ago.

Asian and African Christians are also eager to be in community with Western Christians. The worldwide Anglican Communion is not a formality to them. It is a relationship. They feel an urgent need to understand and to be understood within in.

When I was at the Lambeth conference in 1988—where all the Anglican bishops in the world gathered in one place—I had the chance to hear their stories. They came there believing that we would work and talk and pray together about our common life, and they refused to be sidetracked by anything else until we did. I was humbled by the courage and tenacity revealed in those stories. They often pay dearly for their faith. There is a sanctity in our African and Asian brothers and sisters that we might well admire.

October 24

God promised that they would be his people to bring all the nations of the world to him. —THE CATECHISM, p. 847

God says an amazing thing to Israel in a passage from the prophet Isaiah: *It is too light a thing that I should have taken you this far just for yourselves.* Yes, there is more. You are to be a light to the whole world. A shocking thing to say to the chosen people, but it was to come true. Today the people of Israel are scattered throughout the world. Wherever they are, they carry with them the story: the deliverance from Egypt to a small country in the Middle East, the Promised Land which would be their home. They tell it and retell it, singing the old songs and eating the traditional foods. They have told it through the most massive racial persecution the world has ever seen, and those who emerged from it, bruised but alive, tell it still. They know from this story, transposed into many times and places, told in the midst of triumph and told in the wake of tragedy, that Jews everywhere are still a people, still the chosen ones of God, still in the relationship that began so long ago.

Jesus could not avoid thinking of his life in terms of the story. It was a part of him. When people saw him and recognized salvation in him, they called him Messiah, the delivering figure for whom Israel longed. But it was not to be a light thing: not for the people of Israel and certainly not for Jesus of Nazareth.

October 25

The divine Son became human. . . . —THE CATECHISM, p. 850

We have very little to go on when we wonder about Jesus' early life. We see him once at the age of twelve and then not again until his baptism as an adult.

To watch a young adult become aware of his or her powers is a wonderful thing. Gradually they move out of their two decades or so of student status, out of apprenticeship into the driver's seat. The years of preparation begin to pay off, and an adult self-confidence appears on the young face. It is wonderful to see that on the face of a young person whose growth you have watched.

What must it have been, I wonder, for Mary and Joseph to see that on the face of their son? The dawning awareness of his power and his destiny must have been a thunderous dawning for the young Jesus, the son of an ordinary carpenter who was coming to know that he was anything but ordinary. But it must also have been thunderous for his parents, who knew the anxieties that all parents know. We all want our children to live lives that are as free of grief as possible. Mary and Joseph must have watched the spirit quickening in Jesus with mixed emotions; they were human, and they loved him. What was ahead?

October 26

I believe in Jesus Christ, his only Son, our Lord God. . . . —THE APOSTLES' CREED, p. 96

None of us were alive when Jesus walked the earth. If the life of faith were like a court of law, the case for his very existence would be weak: the only surviving *disinterested* testimony to the events was a reference in the writings of an imperial historian named Flavius Josephus—just a brief comment on what a nuisance the first Christians were. All the rest of the testimony about Jesus has come from within the early Christian community—in a court, it would be seen as less than useful, like an alibi provided by a family member. We are biased. We want these events to be true.

But this is not a court of law. And faith is not about that kind of evidence. It is not certified by events in the past, though it is nourished by them. It is certified by events in the present. Although we are the custodians of an ancient and majestic tradition, compiled and preserved by people long dead, each believer can only receive this tradition in light of her own experience. I cannot tell you what to believe.

All I can do is tell you what God has done in my life, and listen to what he has done in yours. That is, after all, exactly what the biblical writers do: they are explaining the action of God in their own times, in their own world, so that we will be encouraged to look for it in ours. It will not be the same— they are two different worlds. But their search informs our search.

October 27

O God, who by the leading of a star didst manifest thy only-begotten Son . . . —COLLECT FOR THE FEAST OF THE EPIPHANY, p. 162

The composer Gian Carlo Menotti remembers lying in bed when he was a boy, listening for the three kings to come, bringing gifts. He would grow up to write the beloved opera *Amahl and the Night Visitors.*

Amahl and his mother live in poverty. They have sold everything they had, and now they are about at the end. All they have is Amahl's flute and his crutch—Amahl is lame. One night, they are surprised at their front door by four unusual visitors: the three kings and their page. Offering what meager hospitality they have, Amahl and his mother welcome the visitors. Later, when everyone is sleeping, the mother finds herself tempted beyond her strength by the gold the kings are carrying to the Christ child. She takes some and is apprehended by the page. To her surprise, King Melchior in an aria says she may keep the gold; the child they seek needs no gold.

Deeply moved, the mother gives it back, wishing she could send a gift of her own to this child. Then Amahl has an idea: he will send his crutch. "Who knows?" he says, "He may need one!" And then . . . but I won't tell the rest.

Everyone loves this story, but the aria of Melchior is my favorite: *"On love alone, He will build his kingdom . . . and the keys to His city belong to the poor,"* he sings. It is full of hope for the humble, sung by a king on behalf of the poor of the earth.

October 28

You are the light of the world. —AN ORDER OF WORSHIP FOR
THE EVENING, p. 109

We are the heirs of many centuries of being chosen, of being
saints, of being careful to nurture our faith in its uniqueness.

But in our joy at having been chosen by God we must not
close our doors to people who are not like us. I have traveled
hundreds of thousands of miles, all over the Church in this
country and throughout the world. What I have seen firsthand
is this: the Church is tremendously diverse. We are not in a
position to decide whether or not we wish to be inclusive: we
are inclusive, blessedly so! Our church is one in which people
who disagree passionately—about things that matter greatly—can share the Body and Blood of the Christ who died *for
all* and made no exceptions.

If ever we could not share in this way, it would be a terrible loss. The Body of Christ is not wounded by people being
different from one another. It is wounded—and wounded
most grievously—by people refusing to be in community with
one another.

I have occasion—fairly often—to plead for this idea. I
cannot think of anything that lies so close to my heart. In
church life, in personal life, in any kind of life in Christ, there
can be no outcasts.

October 29

Almighty God, you have surrounded us with a great cloud of witnesses. . . . —COLLECT OF A SAINT, p. 250

The mythology of the ancient world contains many stories of the births of the gods. But those events were outside of history. Those who told the story of Jesus' birth were the heirs of the concrete historians of the Old Testament, for whom things that happened in the sky were not of much interest. They cared about things that happened on the earth. Their New Testament legatees inherited a responsibility to explain history in historical terms that made the action of God in the world clear to their readers.

Joseph and Mary and Jesus were real people. When much of the New Testament was written, there were people alive who had known them. The story of the redemption of the world happened in a specific time and place. What the event signified might vary from person to person, but certain things happened and could not be put aside.

We know how these first historians of the Christian faith felt: we have been glued to our television sets, watching important news unfold before our eyes, examining every detail of something momentous. I think of the moon landing, of President Kennedy's assassination. These things were so emotionally powerful for us that we couldn't get enough of them. We are historical people. We must tell our story.

October 30

Nations will stream to your light, and kings to the brightness of your dawning. —*THE THIRD SONG OF ISAIAH,* p. 87

The children of Israel, passing through "the nations" on their way to the promised land, were concerned about the danger of becoming *like* the nations. Many of the pilgrims, poor, frightened, and discouraged, wanted to stop walking and just settle down. It would have been very tempting to do so: just stop and become Amorites or Amalekites or Canaanites. The leadership of Israel had to struggle against this temptation, had to struggle to keep the promise of God alive in people's hearts. That struggle survives in warnings against the nations.

Isaiah is writing much later. Israel has its own city now, and Isaiah ministers in its temple. He looks at the nations differently. They are no longer a threat to our faith, he thinks; God will bring them into the fold, and they will worship God just as we do. Israel has a new relationship to the nations: not to keep apart from them, but to reach out to them.

We at the end of the twentieth century have still *another* relationship to the nations. We cannot see God's activity in terms of winning over whole nations to our way of thinking, as Isaiah could. When I think about nations coming to the light, I think about the justice and mercy that characterize God's community also showing themselves in the world's communities.

October 31

. . . Keep alive their joy in your creation. . . . —PRAYER FOR YOUNG PERSONS, p. 829

Tonight our streets will be full of little ghosts and goblins, and we will open our doors and give them gifts of candy and good things to eat. Our children dress up in costume and play at being scared. But for millions of the world's children, terror is no game.

The child symbolizes the hope and potential of the human race. The child is openhearted and curious. The child's vulnerability has a natural claim on adult protectiveness, no matter what. No matter what.

But there are people who buy and sell children. There are nations in which the juvenile sex industry is a significant factor in their economies. Thousands of children robbed of their youth for no better purpose than to satisfy the perversity and greed of adults: this terrible volume of ravaged innocence cries out for justice, and I am a Christian. I must cry out for justice, too. Whatever has happened to pervert the natural order of things, that causes adults to hurt children instead of protecting them, it is the enemy of all of us. For mark my words: the children of abuse and terrible neglect grow into enraged adults, adults who feel no responsibility toward a society that has felt no responsibility toward them. Evil begets evil and we ignore the suffering of those who cannot protect themselves at a cost, not only of their suffering, but of ours as well.

November 1

Grant us grace so to follow thy blessed saints. . . . —COLLECT
FOR ALL SAINTS' DAY, p. 194

A tall order. Besides the saints in our church calendar, there are hundreds whose holiness of life seemed so exemplary that many feel they *ought* to be canonized.

Different kinds of holiness are valued in different eras. Most of the saints of the early church were martyrs. Most of them also renounced family life and were highly venerated for their celibacy. Many of the saints of the medieval period were kings and queens. Many nineteenth century saints were missionaries. And our own age? Most of the newer figures on the calendar were active participants in the political struggles of their times and places.

In responding to the call to be saints, we join a colorful company, but not a perfect one. The idea that the saints are sinless is a mistaken one. They grow into holiness, like everyone else does, and for some of them it is quite a transformation! Even the process of selecting them to be saints—and the values that govern that process—is not perfect and timeless; it changes from age to age.

So who are they? They are the people whom God loves. We remember those who became translucent enough for us to see God through them.

November 2

. . . for all those whom we love but see no longer. —BURIAL OF
THE DEAD, p. 498

I know a woman who was ordained a priest shortly after her
mother had died. It was a happy day for her, of course, the
culmination of all those years of hard work. But it was also
bittersweet: the mother who had supported and encouraged
her throughout her life would not be in the front row.

At the party after the ordination service, she rose and offered a few remarks about her mother, closing with her regret
that they could not be together on that special day. An older
priest took her aside. "When I was ordained," he told her, "my
father had recently died. Don't think that the dead are not
present with us when we gather like this in the house of God.
Your mother had the best seat in the house this morning!"

The few decades we spend on the earth do not sum up the
totality of our lives in Christ. After death, life is changed, not
ended. The life our departed ones live is not like the life they
left behind; they are fully alive to God now, in a way we will
not understand until we, too, live that life. But the fact that
they are alive to God in a new way does not mean that they
are indifferent to us.

Easy to understand? No, of course not. Death is a great
mystery, and the life beyond the grave is a mystery to us as
well. But it is not a mystery to them. It is a brilliant reality.
They are not missing out on the important moments. They
have the best seat in the house.

November 3

. . . we confess that we have sinned against you . . . by what we have done, and by what we have left undone. —CONFESSION, p. 360

The Catholic priest who founded Covenant House, a shelter for runaway teenagers in New York City, tells a story of the owner of a brothel who sent him a jar full of money that he had collected. It was, he said, from his "girls" and he wanted to give it to the shelter. Knowing that this money was part of the proceeds of the very business that victimized so many of the young people who came to him for help, the priest sent the money back. But as he did so, he was divided in his mind. The sender was surely a sinner, but the impulse was generous, maybe good.

Many of our choices are morally mixed. It is a rare one that is completely clear. We usually wrestle with several sides to a moral question, and we often have lingering doubts long after the decision is made. When we encounter an "unmistakable sinner," then, it is worthwhile for us to remember just how ambiguous a path moral choice can be. The charge to us, to hate the sin but to love the sinner, is a serious challenge. One of the things that makes it so difficult is our reluctance to own the mixture of sin and virtue within our own souls. But if we can do that, we will not *need* the conspicuous sinner as a distraction from our own shortcomings. Then maybe we can love him.

November 4

. . . and though this body be destroyed, yet shall I see God. . . .
—ANTHEM AT THE BURIAL OF THE DEAD, p. 469

We know that the early church, for whom this ancient verse had great meaning, experienced the shock of persecution for their faith. Many died. Try to imagine your parish church holding up under something like that. You would need some encouragement, too.

In their vision, those whose lives had been cut short in cruel ways are central to the eternal joy of the household of God. The dirt and blood of martyrdom is gone; they shine in white robes, untouched and unscarred by any of the horrors that they endured. The blood of the Lamb has cleansed them of their sorrow and pain. I read these words and close my eyes; I can see those shining ones, once in agony and now in perfect joy with God. I see people that I myself have loved and lost amid the throng, people to whom I ministered and who ministered to me, even in the midst of their own pain. I picture all this very concretely. I open my eyes and feel them fill with tears at the goodness of God.

There are those who think that the idea of heaven detracts from our imperative to seek justice here on the earth. Not me. The sight of God's abundant goodness in my mind's eye is too vivid to ignore; I am spurred on to greater love by the promise of that joy for those whose joy on earth is in short supply. It tells me that we are not alone in our ministry of reconciling; God's own self is with us in this work.

November 5

. . . that with calm expectancy I may make room for your power to possess me . . . —PRAYER FOR TRUST IN GOD, p. 461

The idea of trusting in God is a foreign concept to many people. The notion of self-sacrifice has fallen on evil days, in which selfishness has become something of a virtue in the eyes of many Americans. Although we are assured, over and over, of the robustness of our economy, this is nonetheless an era of defensiveness, a time of hoarding. The generations of immigrants' children and grandchildren have forgotten whence they came. "Perhaps there will not be enough," the merchants of fear whisper in our ears. "We'd better not let any more of The Others in." A selfishness unworthy of the grandchildren of pioneers is abroad in our land, a selfishness that will, if we are not careful, rob us of the gifts of diversity and talent that have made us the great nation we are.

When we are possessed by a spirit of fear we are unable to trust in God. Trust does not content itself with the discouraging vision of present scarcity, a forlorn focus on what is. Trust in God looks forward to what might be, and asks for the strength to reach for it.

November 6 ❧

. . . that he may be strengthened in his weakness . . . —PRAYER *FOR STRENGTH AND CONFIDENCE,* p. 459

My physical therapist tells me, when I complain about what he's doing to my knee three times a week, that every session we have together is making my injured muscles stronger, and that it is only by getting stronger that I can put the pain in that knee behind me. "Things aren't going to stay the same," he says, "hang in there." He knows how the human body works: some pain and effort now will produce strength and freedom from pain later on. He assures me that, if I do these stretches and flexes faithfully even when it hurts to do them, I'm going to be better than I was when I started working with him. And, indeed, I can see that I already am. I still wish like anything I hadn't hurt my knee, but I can see that I'm getting better. Little by little, I am becoming again what God intended me to be in giving me the gift of life and strength.

Glory through pain. Glory that makes us forget all about what we have suffered.

This, after all, is what God does. In large things and in small things, God always holds out to us the opportunity to grab hold of good in the midst of evil. Always. There is great evil in the world. But there is always the chance to experience good out of it. Is suffering good? Of course not. Suffering is bad. Evil is evil. But good is always possible in its wake.

November 7

I lift up my eyes to the hills. . . . —PSALM 121:1, p. 779

There was a man named Zacchaeus. He had at least two strikes against him: he was short enough of stature that people remarked upon it, and he was a tax collector for the Roman government, a most unpopular job that probably did not dispose him to be openhearted. One wonders, then, what might have prompted this jaded, disappointed little man to (of all things) *climb a tree*, as we are told in Scripture he did, in order to get a better look at Jesus when he passed by. Surely it was not religious zeal—surely it was mere curiosity. Nothing more laudable than curiosity caused him to look outside himself at Jesus. But what a reward was his when he saw those eyes looking straight up at him! Jesus invited himself over to Zacchaeus's place for dinner. That must have surprised a lot of people.

Here is what this story tells us: Jesus is available to anybody. He does not require goodness on our part in order for the relationship to begin. He does not, even, require purity of heart or of motive.

This is good news. Do we have sins that we cannot seem to budge at all? Do we have sins from which we don't even *want* to be freed, if the truth were known? Of course we do. But do these things cause Christ to avert his gaze from us? Never. It will be with his help that they are dislodged from our discouraged souls.

November 8

. . . we remember before you all poor and neglected persons whom it would be easy for us to forget. . . . —PRAYER FOR THE POOR AND NEGLECTED, p. 826

Three hundred young people were at a diocesan conference. They had slept in dormitories and stayed up half the night, thrown each other into the lake and done all the things young people do when they're together in large groups.

The keynote speaker was from the Church in Haiti. He was there to tell American youth about what life was like in that desperately poor nation. He spoke of Haiti's many orphans, of the difficulty hospitals have in handling the volume of indigent cases, of the explosive political situation. These American kids had to listen hard to understand him, for English was not his native tongue, but they were quiet and attentive. He got a standing ovation when he finished, whoops and yells and whistles from his appreciative audience of young Americans.

Later, after dinner, it was time for games. One of the games was an egg toss: you toss a raw egg back and forth, hoping not to be the one in whose hand it breaks. The Haitian priest excused himself. To his American colleagues, he quietly explained why he could not participate: he could not watch an egg broken for fun when his own young people sometimes went hungry.

In a few weeks it will be Thanksgiving Day in America. We have so much. It is easy to forget that others have so little.

November 9

Wash me through and through from my wickedness and cleanse me from my sin. —PSALM 51:2, p. 656

My wife and I have five children. You can imagine how much laundry there was when they were little. I can see it still: the little shirts and dungarees and dresses dancing in the wind on the clothesline. In some of the places where we lived, water was hard to come by and therefore precious, and the laundry project was long, involved, and primitive, I suppose, compared with the ease with which we accomplish it now.

Still there was a sense of a job well done when the washing was finished. Clothing that four little boys and a girl had climbed and slid and crawled in until it was dirty came down off the line clean again, ready to be worn again, fresh and nice-looking again.

I used to look at the neat piles of clean clothing and think about souls. Dirty and stained like old undershirts, anything but lovely to look at, they can be washed as white as snow again in the forgiveness Christ offers. You don't wash clothes that are clean; you wash dirty clothes. Jesus comes among us not only to congratulate us on our virtues but to help us with our weaknesses.

November 10

I know that my Redeemer liveth. . . . —BURIAL OF THE DEAD,
p. 469

I know of a Methodist minister who, when he was about to
die, sat straight up in bed and, looking out beyond the people
who were with him, said to someone they could not see, "I
always knew you'd come for me!" Then he lay back on his
pillow and died. This faithful servant of God, who had served
rural churches and lived in poverty for most of his life, had
always known that his Redeemer lived. And, at the end, his
patient life of hard work and prayer was rewarded with the
sight of his Savior coming to take him home.

Our faith often falters. Sometimes, we don't know *what*
we know for sure. We just keep on behaving as if we believed
when sometimes we're not at all sure we do, waiting for the
faith within us to quicken into life again. I believe that most
long lives of faith have these dry periods, times when we
cannot feel sure of anything and are tormented by doubt. But
these times pass, for while we may not always be sure about
God, *God* is *always* sure about us.

When we hear stories such as this one about the old minister who saw his Savior coming for him, we feel a little
envious. That man, we feel sure, never had the kind of doubts
we have. But I'll bet he did. Face-to-face with his Redeemer at
last, though, he no longer remembered his dry periods. Neither will we.

November 11

We give thee thanks for all thy servants who have laid down their lives in the service of our country. —PRAYER AT THE BURIAL OF THE DEAD, p. 488

Today is Veterans Day in the United States. A group of merchant mariners meets to commemorate their fellow seafarers who did not return from the Second World War. More than six thousand merchant mariners gave their lives in the war, a higher percentage of war dead than any other branch of the service except the marines.

A husky, gray-headed man went to sea at sixteen; he was too impatient to be a part of the war effort to wait until the other services would take him at seventeen. Another man tells of his time on a hospital ship; after fifty years, he can still barely speak of the suffering he saw. Several participated in the convoys that journeyed through the icy North Atlantic to supply the Russian ports of Murmansk and Archangel; the Russian government has given them medals.

The teenaged grandson of one of the men is at the meeting; he wears his grandfather's old uniform. He is a little embarrassed. The men look at his slim build in the clothes they once wore and remember. They bow their heads while the chaplain prays for the repose of those who did not return, deprived of life in the vigor of their youth. They have slept at the bottom of the sea for more than fifty years. Yet they are not forgotten by their comrades.

November 12

O heavenly Father, who hast filled the world with beauty . . .
—*PRAYER FOR JOY IN GOD'S CREATION,* p. 814

Patti and I love to go to the mountains when we have some time off. One evening it was my job to hunt for dry wood for a fire. I poked around in the woods and found an armful, and was walking through the meadow toward the house when I looked up and saw a large buck and doe grazing. They were not ten yards from me. They did not run away when they saw me. They just stood and looked at me. They were the most beautiful sight I have ever seen. For a moment, it was as if only the deer and I were alive in the whole world, and the whole world's aching beauty was concentrated in the look that passed between me and them.

We stood and looked at each other for a long time. I don't know how long it was. Then she lifted her head and sniffed the wind, and they both bounded off. I resumed my walk back to the house, so excited about the deer I couldn't wait to tell Patti. The sight of those deer, the perfection of their grace and beauty, the wisdom and peace that I saw in their direct gaze, their harmonious partnering of each other seemed, in one wordless moment, to sum up the care of God for the whole complex universe.

November 13

O God, our times are in your hand. . . . —*PRAYER FOR A BIRTHDAY,* p. 830

You often see an article in a supermarket tabloid that purports to foretell the end of the world by looking at the prevalence of contemporary political and natural disasters. The writer has concluded that things couldn't possibly get any worse than they are, so this must be the terrible time foretold. The appointed date and day comes and goes. The world wags on. The tabloids go back to their stories of space aliens and movie stars.

Our god is a god revealed in history. This way of knowing God, which we inherited from the Jews, was a novelty in the ancient world in which it arose. Other belief systems of the time did not look toward the end of things, as we did. Our times and our places were full of meaning—not just to us, but to God.

We sometimes want to conjure with this truth, to read the divine tea leaves so that we may know the meaning of our times to God. Particularly in times of rapid change—like these times—we want some inside information.

To hang in there in uncertain times is hard. Can we trust our God? When the future is uncertain, all we have is the record of the past to guide us. We can trust God in the uncharted future because God has been trustworthy in our sacred past.

November 14

Eternal God, in whose perfect kingdom no sword is drawn but the sword of righteousness, no strength known but the strength of love . . . —PRAYER FOR PEACE, p. 815

Last year I traveled to Central America, where I met people from churches, and people from the governments, and I talked with people about the years they have lived with civil wars. The countryside in Central America is beautiful. Traditionally, the people there have supported themselves by farming, and they are good at it. The terrain is rough in many places, and the villages are remote, but left alone the people know how to use their land lovingly and wisely. Sadly, in recent years the sword has been more active there than the plowshare. Over and over, men, women, and children told me that they want to be at peace. They are content with the rhythms of the land. All they want is to husband the land and enjoy its gracious fruit. Since visiting with them, I have become more intentional in my prayers for them, and my prayers for them have grown to occupy a bigger part of my prayer time.

For me, the people of Central America have become symbols of the integrity of the land. God intends us to cultivate it and use it, not to lay waste to it. Yet we continue to make and use swords, things that destroy life, rather than plowshares, things that help life to spring forth from the earth.

November 15

. . . we thy servants, who now live by faith . . . —COLLECT AT
THE PRAYERS, p. 395

It is a happy fact that it is springtime when we observe the
Feast of the Resurrection in our part of the world. In some
places the weather doesn't change much from season to season,
but here in New York, where I live now, this time of year can
be gray and dreary. People hurry through the streets cursing
the rain, and it's hard to tell *what* we believe. Resurrection?
Never happened!

But we believe. At least we say we do. Who can help
feeling the new life that pulses through the springtime? What
we need is a way to feel that way now in the year's twilight.
What we need is a faith that will sustain us when all evidence
is to the contrary.

I think of the women who went out to the tomb that first
Easter Sunday. What was their evidence of the Resurrection?
Not much. Just that the teacher whom they loved had promised to be with them always. Did they believe it as they walked
along? We don't know. But they went anyway. We are not
told what they felt. We only know what they *did*.

Do we always feel our faith running briskly through our
hearts? Maybe not. But like those holy women, we can keep
right on walking and trusting in our God, and God will reward
our trust.

November 16

Will you love her, comfort her, honor and keep her, in sickness and in health; and, forsaking all others, be faithful to her as long as you both shall live? —*CELEBRATION AND BLESSING OF A MARRIAGE,* p. 424

Once the Pharisees were trying to trap Jesus by asking him about a woman whose seven husbands had each died. Whose wife was she in heaven?

I know of a man whose wife died after a long and anguishing illness. He had been a loyal and devoted husband, and after she was gone, he was a shadow of himself, going through the motions of life like a ghost. This went on for five long years, and his family watched him become sadder and weaker until they feared he would die himself.

Then he met another lady, and overnight everything changed. Before long, they were married, and today they live a happy, productive, loving life together. They both feel that this is the best time of their long lives, and they both loved their first spouses completely and exclusively.

So whose spouses are they in the afterlife? When you meet people like that, you realize that such questions are silly. The husband and the wife who have died are alive to a reality we cannot grasp. We have the law to govern our arrangements in this world. We will not need it in the next.

November 17

. . . and when our mortal body lies in death, there is prepared for us a dwelling place eternal in the heavens. —PREFACE FOR
THE COMMEMORATION OF THE DEAD, p. 382

Those of us who have lost someone we loved know the emptiness and hopelessness that can sweep over us in the first months of mourning. The loss carries such pain with it that we wonder if we can go on in this life ourselves, and sometimes we even wish for death to come and take us, too. We find ourselves fascinated in a painful way with the moment of death our loved one experienced, reliving it again and again in our mind, wanting to go back to it. Hating it when we do.

For those who mourn, the lost one is frozen in the moment of death, and for a while that's all we see. But that's not really true. He is not frozen there on his deathbed. That is really over. He has passed through death to the other side. We may be stuck on that terrible moment, but he is not. After a while, we come to glimpse this now and then, and the glimpse comforts us. Life goes on, for them as well as for us. It remains painful to miss them so. But they live still.

November 18

. . . we your unworthy servants give you humble thanks. . . .
—*THE GENERAL THANKSGIVING,* p. 125

Soon, people all over the United States will pause to give thanks to God for the blessings they enjoy, remembering the Pilgrims' first feast. Many of the Pilgrims did not make it. They died of fever, or on the long voyage across the sea, or they starved to death. One wonders at the hardships they endured. Did their spirits ever fail them? Did they sometimes lash out at their leaders, like the people in the crowd did at Jesus on the cross? "He saved others; let him save himself." The Bible is full of such failures of nerve; remember the murmuring of the Hebrews as Moses led them through the wilderness? The way of the cross is always a hard way. It is no wonder that our hearts fail us sometimes.

But what *is* a wonder is how often they don't. People may come close to giving up without doing so. We may come close to the bottom, only to be lifted up by God's grace, empowered to keep on walking, keep on working, keep on fighting.

In only a little more than a month, we will see the year come to a close. For some of us, it has been a banner year. For others, it was all we could do to keep putting one foot in front of the other. But we made it! For that we give thanks.

November 19

FEAST OF ELIZABETH OF HUNGARY

. . . to become partakers of their joy . . . —COLLECT OF A SAINT,
p. 199

Elizabeth of Hungary, whose feast falls today, was born a
princess and destined for an advantageous marriage, one that
would further the plans of her royal father, who alone had the
right to decide who would be the lucky man. That is why, at
the tender age of fourteen, she married the prince of a nearby
state. At twenty, she was a widow. She spent the rest of her
life (all four years of it) enduring separation from her children, undergoing physical abuse and hard work by serving the
poor in a strict monastic life.

One wonders if poor Elizabeth had much of what we
would call happiness in life. Most of us would see Elizabeth as
an abnormal person if she lived her life that way today. There
is a sanctity for each age, it seems, and we must look carefully
before critiquing the standards of one age according to those
of our own. What seems like a sad life to us seemed to the
people of the Middle Ages to be an inspiring and heroic one.
They looked at Elizabeth and saw the intensity of her devotion to God shine forth in her service to God's poor. While we
may pity Elizabeth's situation and lack of choices, we can
understand *that* part: a love of God that outweighs all else in a
person. It was rare then. It still is.

November 20

. . . your faithful servants bless you. . . . —PREFACE FOR A
SAINT, p. 381

In many Asian homes, a shrine to the family's ancestors occupies a corner. It is kept fresh and pretty: candles, flowers, maybe a small offering of rice. The first missionaries to Asia thought this display of ancestor veneration detracted from the worship of the one God. I don't know why. Christianity has venerated the saints for many centuries. We pray for the dead at our Eucharists as if they were still alive, because we believe they *are* still alive. The practice of ancestor veneration is not a version of polytheism, but a statement about the enduring love of the community of the human family. The gospel message of Jesus' victory over death on our behalf only confirmed and strengthened the people of Asia in their conviction that family members who had died lived still.

Can we really believe that the God whose creative love swept through the universe, making this beautiful earth and millions of other worlds and stars and galaxies, is limited in the scope of his divine love to our three score and ten years? That our deaths are as resoundingly final to God as they are to those who mourn? I think not. The gospel message is not that death ceases to be a part of our experience—people still die—but that the loving power of God overcomes death's meaning, flooding it with the enduring goodness of life.

November 21

Show them that your ways give more life than the ways of the world, and that following you is better than chasing after selfish goals. —PRAYER FOR YOUNG PERSONS, p. 829

To a great extent we have become a people that literally worships money and power. We live in a moral climate that encourages people to climb, claw, shove, and do whatever else they have to do to get to the top. I think we have sold ourselves on the idea that winning is "the only thing," as the football coach Vince Lombardi used to snarl to his teams. Of course, we slap people on the wrist when we find out that they have behaved this way, but all the while we celebrate the successes of people whose ends have justified their means. And we walk around the poor in our midst; they are in our way.

The church has a responsibility to work on influencing the moral climate. I've given my life to this effort, and so have many others. What can we do to make things better? We can resolve to live our lives as if God were our judge—God *is* our judge! We can reflect theologically upon our lives and our moral choices. We can pray to discern God's will for us—as individuals and as God's community. And we can remember that God loves the arrogant and the greedy, too. Although we must not adopt their values, we can pray for them. And we can cultivate humility and self-knowledge: sometimes "they" will be us!

November 22

Jesus told Pilate his kingdom was not of this world. Then he went to his death, a death that joined him with the lowest of criminals, dressed in mock kingly robes, a crown of thorns pressed cruelly into his forehead.

The one through whom all things came to be—standing in the midst of a jeering circle of soldiers. That humiliation must have appeared total to those who witnessed it. But the shame of it is suffused with a nobility beyond any we know because it was endured out of love for the human race.

The Feast of Christ the King was quite late in its appearance on the Christian calendar after the first World War. It was intended to be a feast day of earnest prayer for peace among all nations under the kingship of Christ. How right that seems! Human sinfulness has so often expressed its shameful self in the hatred of nation for nation, and this has so often been acted out by kings at war with kings. Yet *this* king, who rejected the power of earthly kingship, will bury those hatreds forever in the graceful government of love. And *this* king, whose last earthly crown was of thorns, is crowned in peace and glory to rule lovingly over the universe.

November 23

For health and strength to work . . . —A LITANY OF THANKSGIVING, p. 837

Most of us started working when we were adolescents, and most of us have not stopped working since. People need to work in order to feel completely human. Those who feel useless wonder, deep within themselves, if the world would miss them at all should they disappear. Those who work need never wonder, for their contribution to the world is clearly visible, valuable to the world and to God.

Friends who have retired have told me that it is a strange feeling at first. They may have planned for their leisure for many years, but the shock of no longer having a world of work in terms of which to define themselves draws them up short. As the months pass, they adjust. They stop thinking of things in terms of lunch hours and feasibility and start thinking of them in terms of personal satisfaction and fulfillment. They also find that work does not end when paid employment ceases; the chance to direct their own work energies toward service to others without regard to compensation charges them with new energy. Many friends have told me—only half joking—that they work harder now than they did when they were on the payroll, and find a pleasure in it that eluded them before.

November 24

. . . we give you thanks for the fruits of the earth. . . .
—COLLECT FOR THANKSGIVING DAY, p. 246

We sit down at a dinner table loaded with wonderful food. We know we're going to eat too much. If at all possible, family members get together for Thanksgiving dinner, and if at all possible, people have a holiday from work. "I've earned it," they tell each other. "It's been some year!"

And yes, the food on the table is the fruit of our hard work. Somebody had to earn the money to buy that food. I look forward to this holiday for weeks in advance: a day of food and family, love and relaxation. But I cannot help but remember, when my family sits down for our Thanksgiving dinner, the many people who also work hard and do not enjoy the comfortable lifestyle I enjoy. Maybe I earned this good fortune, but so did many who have not received it.

Patti and I have spent the American Thanksgiving holiday in a number of different parts of the world over the years; every time, we have been struck by the immense gulf between what we have and what is the norm throughout most of the world. Our comparatively moderate American lifestyle looks like fabulous wealth when compared with that of the majority of humankind.

The point of reflections like this is not to ruin a wonderful family holiday with guilt. It is only to remind myself of my many blessings, and the gratitude I owe to God for them.

November 25

Almighty God, whose loving hand hath given us all that we possess . . . —PRAYER FOR THE RIGHT USE OF GOD'S GIFTS, p. 827

Christianity has what the world would consider an upside-down view of power. There is no shortage of examples of this: God chose the Hebrews, not Pharaoh; Jesus was born in a stable, not in a palace. That the religious establishment has amassed so much wealth and power does not destroy this truth. Ultimately, God is on the side of the weak and poor, not the strong and rich.

What does that mean for those of us who have been blessed by material prosperity? Is the love of God withheld from us? No, of course not. We are beloved children of God, too. But we have work to do: the strong and rich come close to God, not through our power, but by coming to terms with our ultimate weakness. We will not take our money with us, and we need to learn to separate our souls' worth from that of our stock portfolios.

November 26

Look with compassion on the whole human family. . . .
—PRAYER FOR THE HUMAN FAMILY, p. 815

I have been lucky enough to travel throughout the world and to live in several parts of it. I always prepare ahead of time when I'm going somewhere new, so that I will be aware of some of the history and customs when I arrive.

When I can show a new friend from somewhere far away that I want to know about him and his world, that I want to show respect for the way he does things, I feel wonderful. For instance, I'm not compromising my American heritage in the least when I bow in the Asian fashion; I'm expanding it, honoring the wonderful mixture of people God has made, honoring their uniqueness.

I rejoice in the similarities between peoples just as much as in their differences. In the intimacy between a Japanese mother and her son, I catch a glimpse of my wife stroking the hair of one of our children. In the way a pair of Palestinian children starts to run around while their parents are sitting and talking, I see many a summer evening when my own were little and did the same thing. Just like home.

Nations are made up of people. When I pray for peace, I pray first for the people: the children, the mothers and fathers, the grandparents. If we all knew about the pleasures we could have from honoring the similarities and the differences within the human family, nation would not rise up against nation.

November 27

O ye frost and cold, bless ye the Lord. . . . O all ye green things upon the earth, bless ye the Lord. . . . —BENEDICITE, OMNIA OPERA DOMINI, p. 48

Just as the natural world appears to be going to sleep for the winter, there is a quiet excitement within the awakening bud: as we prepare for winter, spring is coming. Dry leaves swirl in a breeze that grows chillier every day, lifeless brown souvenirs of summer's juicy green. Back into the earth they will go, there to return to the primal elements from which God called them forth. They will empty themselves as they decay back into the soil, and the lives they yield to the earth will enrich it. The new life to come will soak up the remains of their lives and grow strong, and in the spring, the branches will put forth tiny new green leaves.

Death and decay are natural parts of life. Eventually, it will be over for all of us. But we continue to nourish the world, both in ways we choose and ways over which we have no control. The most selfish among us has no choice but to yield his body back to the earth from which it came, entering again into the cycle of biological regeneration that produced him.

And those who transcend the limits of their own self-centeredness in life live on in other ways: in the lives of those whom they have nurtured, in concrete achievement, in blessed memory.

November 28

. . . for thine is the kingdom, and the power, and the glory, forever and ever, Amen. —*THE LORD'S PRAYER,* p. 54

Every so often, I see a story in the newspaper about the end of the world. The time of its demise comes and goes; nothing happens.

We are told frequently in Scripture about the signs that will appear at the end of time. They are usually bad things: wars, animosities, natural disasters. One is never at a loss to discern these things in even a superficial glance at the world around us, for there will always be bad things happening in the world. But we are not told exactly when the end will happen. Why not?

I think it is because we are not built to know. We are built to assume the continuation of the world, not its end. Our loves and our work, our hopes and our dreams, are built upon the assumption that this world has a future. We know that it will also have an end, but our life is not constructed in such a way that we are capable of knowing when that end will be, and our lives would crumble around us if we did know.

The end of time is in the hand of God. Our world, or at least a substantial part of it, is in our hands, put there by a God who requires that we care for it responsibly and well, not as if it were something that would disappear tomorrow.

November 29

Be present in your goodness with your servant. . . . —PRAYER
FOR RECOVERY FROM SICKNESS, p. 458

I know of a woman who was beautiful. She was not vain, but her appearance was important to her, and she took pleasure in it, especially in her luxuriant red hair. She wore it long and never wore a hat.

In her forties, she was stricken with cancer. During the tough treatments she tried to be a source of pleasure and comfort to those she loved, just as she always had. But then one day she awoke to find almost all her hair lying loose on her pillow. The nausea, the exhaustion, the worry—these she had weathered. But the sight of her lovely hair lying there on the pillow was more than she could bear. She went into a deep depression, staying in her room. Not willing to see anyone.

After a few days, she emerged, her head wrapped stylishly in a colorful scarf, and announced to her husband that they were going shopping for hats. And they did; they bought a dozen hats, beautiful ones in different colors. She learned a lot about life before she died—that the goodness of God went beyond the physical survival of the things she held dear, that there was a way of joy beyond the loss of things she thought she couldn't do without. She left a legacy of strength and joy that comforts those who knew her.

November 30

. . . through the waters of baptism you clothed me with the shining garment of his righteousness. . . . —SACRAMENT OF RECONCILIATION, p. 450

Long ago, there were people who could not bring themselves to believe in the divinity of Christ. Why, they asked, would God, who was perfect, condescend to become one with the imperfect? Why would God become less than God? Why should God descend to the human? Better that the human ascend to be like God, and that our oneness with God start with *that* ascent, rather than with a crazy idea like incarnation.

But we believe that God *did* become human. We believe that God became human so that humans could become one with God, and we believe that this was the only way that could happen. Passing through the suffering and inadequacies of human life, God's fullness was not diminished in any way. In fact, the purpose of creation was fulfilled in that action.

I think of the lovely woman, whose story I told yesterday. Shocked and crushed by the loss of her perfection, she was then beautified even more by passing through that loss to a perfection more striking. She felt at first that she was less a woman without her beautiful hair. It turned out that she was much *more*.

December 1 ❧

Therefore we praise you, joining our voices with Angels and Archangels. . . . —*THE HOLY EUCHARIST,* p. 362

We don't become angels when we die. Angels are created beings who have not lived mortal lives. They belong to the world of the spirit, and in Scripture they only visit our world to bring us a message, never to stay and live among us.

Jesus didn't come among us as an angel, someone who had never lived a life like ours. He came among us as one of us, and he died a death like the deaths we die. And then he was raised to sit at the right hand of God, the place of honor and inheritance in an ancient feast. This is what makes the Incarnation the central idea of our faith: God choosing to come among us and live our life, mightily crossing the chasm that separates us from heaven so that we might be lifted up in a resurrection of our own, made possible by Jesus' resurrection.

We know that we could never have lifted ourselves. The best and strongest among us could not reach heaven under their own power. It is grace that empowers us and transforms us, grace that welcomes us into the household of God whether we are weak or strong. It was sublime grace that made the choice to walk in our world so many centuries ago, and it will be grace that carries us to heaven when we are finished here.

December 2

. . . King of kings and Lord of lords . . . —COLLECT FOR
PROPER 29, p. 185

Very soon choral societies the world over will begin their
annual performances of this beloved musical creation. And, of
course, there are any number of recordings of *Messiah*, so that
you can hear it in your home anytime you want to.

But there is one *Messiah* recording that is unlike any other.
It is an arrangement of the overture and fifteen of the most
beloved arias from Handel's masterpiece, envisioned and produced by a group of eminent African American artists. It's
called *Handel's Messiah: A Soulful Celebration*, and it casts
these tunes we have all loved for years and years in new
voices: the self-confident power of African drums; the courageous patience and sorrow of spirituals sung by enslaved
people, punctuated by the cruel rhythm of the lash. The
brashness of honky-tonk, the elegant syncopation of ragtime,
the fulsome joy of gospel, the smooth intelligence of jazz, the
wit and bite of hip-hop—in all of these musical styles and
more, the extraordinary gifts that the African American
musical community has given to the world join hands with
the immortal tunes of a German musician in an English court
two hundred years ago to produce a synthesis that says: *We
are all in this together, the living and the dead.* People who are
just like us and people who are as different from us as they
could possibly be. We do not remain the same when we live in
community. We teach each other. And we are changed.

December 3

How shall I repay the Lord for all the good things he hath done for me? —*THANKSGIVING FOR A CHILD,* p. 443

People who read this book in the morning may have already awakened to the smell of coffee from the kitchen. Or perhaps they have slept late, taking a day off from work, and they woke up to the sound of their children's laughter, wafting in from the living room. Or they may keep the book in the kitchen, next to the toaster, and they may be reading it with one hand while they're stirring oatmeal on the stove with the other. I hope they don't burn themselves.

Other people are waking up this morning in places that aren't their homes: in shelters, in welfare hotels, in subway cars. The idea of a home of one's own seems like heaven to them. They dream of pretty bedrooms for their children, of comfortable chairs, of lamps that work, of hanging plants.

It is customary at this time of the year to give thanks for the goodness of life. It is also customary to remember anew those less fortunate than ourselves. Let us resolve that we will not allow the day to end without making a concrete plan to show that remembrance. Whether it is donations to a charity or a service to someone you know needs help, let us make today the day we give back to God the gift we have received.

December 4

Save me, O God, by your Name. . . . —*PSALM 54:1*, p. 659

It is a commonplace that people call out to God when they are in trouble, and leave God alone, for the most part, when they are not. And it is common for people to let their individual prosperity be the rule by which God's effectiveness is measured, to say things like "How can God be just and powerful if my mother died young?" with a genuine sense of having been personally betrayed by God. We tend to lash out in a spasm of blaming when things go against us, unwilling to face the fact that there is evil in the world and that we are bound to feel the effects of it from time to time.

Jesus *is* the Christ. He *has* saved us. Our sins are forgiven if we will accept the forgiveness. But God has *not* sent us to heaven; we are still here in the same old ambiguous, broken world. He has *not* turned us into angels; we are the same broken people we were. But with our salvation comes the invitation to heal that brokenness, to resolve that ambiguity, to grow into the stature of the one who redeems us.

December 5

May your rest be this day in peace, and your dwelling place in the Paradise of God. —COMMENDATION AT THE TIME OF DEATH, p. 464

The idea of Paradise is a tough one for modern people to swallow. Maybe that's because we can't help thinking about it as if it were a *place*. Maybe Paradise is not a place but a state of *being*. We are flesh and blood, and our minds work on the premises given them by our living in a physical world. But God is spirit. That's why God had to *become* flesh in Jesus. So Paradise, the state of perfect union with God, is a spiritual state, and one that we cannot be expected to understand or describe.

We know we *want* to be in it. So we have imagined it in the only way we have to imagine things: through painting pictures in our minds. The streets are paved with gold. People wear white robes. They have incredible, symbolic animals there, creatures with many eyes. Angels fly there, singing God's praises.

Those imaginings of ours are approximations of something unspeakable and unknowable. But we can know something about Paradise from Jesus' words to the penitent thief on the cross: "Today you will be with me in Paradise." These words tell us that Paradise is open to the penitent and the brokenhearted, that it holds their comfort and their joy, that it is personal, intimate union with God.

December 6

Bless, O Lord, these gifts to our use and us to thy service. . . .
—GRACE AT MEALS, p. 855

By now, my grandchildren are *most* interested in the where-abouts and activities of our version of Saint Nicholas. All the children are, and the television encourages them to become more and more excited about him until they vibrate themselves to sleep on Christmas Eve, to awaken before the sun.

St. Nicholas is joined in folklore all over the world by other beings like him: the Three Kings in Italy and Spain and South America, a rabbit at Eastertime. The unearned gift, given out of love, is a powerful symbol in our culture. It is also the meaning of the Incarnation.

Of course, there is that bit about Santa Claus coming only to good children. That sounds to me like a desperate parental attempt to get some order in the pre-Christmas house during some long-ago December, not like the Incarnation. For in the gift of Christ to the world, God was certainly not rewarding our good behavior! God loved us too much to let us go, and so the Son of God came among us freely, to set us free and heal our sorrows, making it *possible* for us to choose the life in the spirit for which we were intended when we were formed. St. Nicholas is the special protector of the weak and of children. His gifts remind us of the One who protects and loves the whole creation.

December 7

FEAST OF ST. AMBROSE

*We do earnestly repent. . . . —CONFESSION OF SIN AT THE
HOLY EUCHARIST,* p. 331

It was on this day in 1941 that the United States entered the
Second World War. With the attack on Pearl Harbor came an
outpouring of energy and common purpose as the nation
girded for war. The last unanimity we were to have about an
armed conflict carried us to Europe and to the Pacific, and it
would be four long years before we came home.

That unanimity, which filled those of us who were alive
then with so much emotion, had its dark side. Many of us did
not know about the internment of Japanese Americans at the
beginning of American involvement in the war—or if we did,
we somehow forgot. It is only recently that we have allowed
ourselves to remember this shameful policy, and to make
amends for it. We were fearful of our enemy, and we felt
threatened, and so we countenanced something at which we
now look with remorse. To the degree that we can do so from
a distance of over half a century, we make amends. This does
not undo the evil that was done; that is part of history. But it
builds a bridge between sinner and sinned against, and invites
both to walk across and shake hands. It proclaims its fault
honestly and without embroidery or excuse, and it asks forgiveness for them.

December 8 ❧❧❧❧❧❧❧❧❧❧❧❧❧❧

Grant that we may share the divine life of him who humbled himself to share our humanity. . . . —COLLECT FOR THE SECOND SUNDAY AFTER CHRISTMAS DAY, *p.* 162

We got a handful of Christmas cards this morning. Many of them, of course, are religious scenes: beautiful copies of stained glass, of medieval illuminations, of ancient mosaics. But some of them are Victorian—pictures of people riding in a sleigh, or dragging a Christmas tree home through the snow, or singing carols in the light of a gas lamp. This time of year makes many of us long for an earlier time. The present is difficult. We long for the institutions of the past.

But it is not human institutions, even those we sprinkle with silver glitter and send each other on Christmas cards, in which we place our trust. All of them are changing; none of them will remain the same. It is the One who enters into those institutions and sanctifies them, the One who makes them into ways of understanding the divine love. Our trust is in the Lord, the maker of heaven and earth, the Lord of all the centuries and all the people who have lived and those who will live to the end of time. Our trust is in the Lord in whose mighty hand a changing world finds the eternal rock upon which we ground ourselves amid the storms and hardships of life.

But you can't put a picture of *that* on the front of a Christmas card. So we look at pictures of ourselves instead: our Victorian selves, our medieval selves, our ancient selves. God has loved them all and will not abandon our future selves.

December 9

Merciful God, who sent your messengers the prophets to preach repentance . . . —COLLECT FOR THE SECOND SUNDAY OF ADVENT, p. 211

When John the Baptist stood on the bank of the Jordan River, his fiery denunciation of what he saw when he looked around his world was based on what fruit the people bore. Did they bear fruit worthy of repentance, of an honest and accurate understanding of where they stood in relationship to God, or did they not? We hear him call them a brood of vipers, and right away we know what he thought!

We also know what happened to him—you'll recall that his head ended up on a silver platter. Preaching repentance to a society built upon injustice doesn't win us friends. John the Baptist lost his life for that message. It takes courage to stay with it. Accommodation would be so much easier. Yet we know that faith ceases to be faithful if it abandons its call to repentance and settles down to get comfortable. It becomes an easy tool for unjust power to wield. We know this can happen; we have seen it. Faithful to Scripture, alert to the lessons of history, we must remain on our guard so that it will not happen to us. Forgiveness does not mean forgetting. If we forget history, we are doomed to repeat it. When we forgive, it must always be in the honest light of true repentance: honest admission both of where we have sinned and where we have been sinned against. If it hasn't happened in that bright light, it hasn't really happened at all.

December 10

And, that we might live no longer for ourselves . . . —HOLY
EUCHARIST, p. 374

I know of a man who is always doing something to help
someone else. If it snows, he's out shoveling his own walk and
the neighbor's. If he sees someone with a flat tire, he stops
and helps. If someone has a problem, he has a book to lend
that speaks to it. He sometimes agrees to do things he would
rather not do—serve on a boring committee, say—because he
knows that it will be hard to find someone else to do it, and
he doesn't want to make life hard for anyone. People ask him
to do many things like that; he is an easy mark! And people
with something on their minds call him on the telephone—
sometimes several times per night—because they know that
he will always take the time to listen.

His wife sometimes worries about him, but he is happy
doing things for people. He is not conscious of being especially "good," and he can list his faults as someone who knows
them all too well. But his loving attitude toward others seems
to her to cancel out those faults, making them scarcely worth
mentioning. So out he goes into the snow, whistling, to get
his shovel. She watches him from the window, loving the
Christ within him.

December 11

. . . our divisions being healed, we may live in justice and peace. . . . —*PRAYER FOR SOCIAL JUSTICE,* p. 823

In the eleventh chapter of the book of Isaiah, the prophet talks about the Messiah. "He shall not judge by what his eyes see," we are told. Isaiah foretells a glorious time in which many of the canons of conventional wisdom and prudence are overturned in a new order of grace. The bias of judgment will turn toward the poor, instead of toward the rich and powerful as it does now. Natural enmities are turned to friendships, and those things that everyone knows hurt us, will hurt us no more.

"He shall not judge by what his eyes see"? You should believe half of what you see and none of what you hear, the old saying goes. It is usually brought up as advice to be skeptical about unproven allegations. But here in Isaiah it is used to alert us to the dramatic difference between the peaceable kingdom of God and our own angry world. We think the strong always prevail. We think that we know who our enemies are, and that they cannot be our friends. We think we know how the world works, and up to a point, we do.

But God is not a prisoner of how the world works. God is a God who works miracles, and God judges and heals the nations. It is God's reality that is final, not our discouraged one, and so we are given unlikely pairings to imagine—the lion, the wolf, and the lamb, and a little child leading them—as example of just how graceful a healing that God will work among us.

December 12

In you, Lord, is our hope; And we shall never hope in vain.
—*MORNING PRAYER,* p. 98

We know, by the time we reach early adulthood, that the things we have—the house, the car, the clothes—are perishable. We buy insurance for these things simply because they are perishable, so that we can get some money to buy new ones if something should happen to the ones we have. The insurance industry exists because life is unpredictable and perishable. In the twinkling of an eye, everything we have can be taken from us.

You sometimes hear people say something like "I'd rather focus on what I can see" when the talk turns to God. They have a hard time with the whole idea of God. But what is left to them? Trust in things which they know beyond the shadow of a doubt they will someday lose? That's not a good deal. It *insures* heartbreak and deprivation for us. It suggests that the only thing that will never leave us, that we can never lose, is not worthy of our attention and devotion.

Those who have lost everything still have the company of God. Sometimes that is all we have. But we have it more surely than we have anything else we think we have. That is why people are able to survive the incredible things they sometimes endure: God turns out to be the only thing in which we can trust absolutely, and the only thing we can serve absolutely.

December 13

O God, who makest us glad with the yearly remembrance of the birth of thy only Son Jesus Christ . . . —COLLECT FOR CHRISTMAS DAY, p. 160

What will your children remember about Christmas Day, when it finally arrives? The toys they received? As much legwork as you may have put into procuring the hot toy of the season— and I remember what *that* was like—that probably will not be what lasts in their memories. Not as much, I'll bet, as the feeling of their family together, a potpourri of sights and sounds and smells that all mean love to them. Years from now, as adults, they will catch a glimpse of something, hear a snatch of song, smell food cooking . . . and today will return to them in a flood of memory. What kind of people will they be when we who love them are in the past? What will we leave behind that will strengthen them for the challenges they will face, challenges we can't even imagine yet? The most important thing we will leave them is the example we set for them. Let them remember parents and elders who were not afraid to stand up for their beliefs. Let them remember us as people who were not discouraged by minority status or financial reverses. Let them remember that we were people who valued our faith so highly that we were glad to sacrifice for it, whose hope was so lively no power on earth could wreck it. If this is our legacy to them, they will have all they need to live and grow.

December 14

He has cast down the mighty from their thrones, and has lifted up the lowly. —*MAGNIFICAT*, p. 119

In a Middle Eastern family, the younger person always gives place to his older relative. John the Baptist was Jesus' older cousin, according to some sources, and we might expect to find John "pulling rank" on his kinsman. Instead, he announces to his listeners that this man, who ordinarily would occupy a place in the family less honored than that which John enjoys, is in fact greater than John himself.

This is one of many ways in which Scripture and tradition encourage us to question the power arrangements of our world. Look carefully at the people you see; the ones who seem to have the power will not necessarily be the ones who prevail. Look at your own power, they say, and see if you can stand to lay it aside. In a magnificent gesture of humility, John hands over his seniority to Jesus.

Who among us does not enjoy his or her own importance? If we are honest, we must admit that place and honor matter to us. Children in school push and shove to be first in line, and we are not so far removed from that impulse when we are grown. But the Christian understanding of power suggests that it is best unleashed for good by being set aside. It may be that if nothing is beneath us, nothing will be beyond us.

December 15

I will wash my hands in innocence. . . . —PSALM 26:6, p. 616

When we look at the complexity of modern life, we envy anyone who can claim innocence. Life can force us into some pretty ambiguous situations. But some of our complexities—the harmful ones—are not forced on us. They are things upon which *we* insist.

I remember a man who had become involved in a love affair outside his marriage. The logistical arrangements necessary to keep both his marriage and his affair going at the same time became unbearably complex. He became more and more mired in the web of lies he had woven, and the lies became more and more necessary to keep the whole system going.

In the end, he came to see that the system he had built was unworkable, giving more pain than comfort. The bypass he had built to avoid facing directly whatever truths he and his wife needed to examine in their marriage proved to be no solution at all to his pain and loneliness. The straight path was what he needed to walk.

Although perhaps not in such a dramatic way, we all sometimes make life more complex than it should be, because we want to avoid the implications of the straight path. Is there something we're spending more energy avoiding than we would spend facing squarely? If something we are doing isn't working, it may be because we should stop doing it.

December 16

O God . . . in knowledge of whom standeth our eternal life . . .
—*A COLLECT FOR PEACE,* p. 57

One of the people I have admired most in my life was Helen Keller. Blinded and deafened by illness while still a toddler, she lived in a dark and lonely world until a dedicated teacher, Annie Sullivan, broke through Helen's darkness and taught her to communicate. Helen went on to become a figure of courage who inspired millions to overcome their limitations.

Phillips Brooks, the famous Episcopal preacher of the late nineteenth century, was a good friend of Helen Keller. She told him once that she had always known who God was, even when she had no concept of what words were, no name for God. She had *felt* God in her darkness. And later on, when she learned about her faith, she recognized God in what she was told. "Oh, *that's* who God is! Yes, I know."

It was not enough, though, that Helen know only herself and God in the darkness of her mind. God sent her a teacher who would open for her the way to communication with the whole world, so that the love with which God comforted a lonely, isolated little girl would be conveyed through her courage to people everywhere. We are not born knowing how to communicate. By God's grace, we teach each other.

December 17

Our King and Savior now draws near: Come let us adore him.
—INVITATORY ANTIPHON AT MORNING PRAYER, p. 80

It seems to children—I know this because I still remember the feeling myself—that the week between today and Christmas is literally an eternity. Time stops. Little thoughts wander. Wise schoolteachers build in an escape valve for this time, some activities that give explicit license to a child's longing for the Great Day.

Far from being a schoolboy, I am a grandfather now. And yet I must confess that I haven't changed much; I still look forward to great things with so much anticipation that I find it hard to wait for them. After more than thirty Christmasses, Patti and I are not really in the dark about what to expect. We have precious traditions. But when I walk in the door and see that she has put up a familiar decoration, or that she has a mysterious pile of beautifully wrapped packages in the corner, I get that old feeling. Something inside me says, "Oh boy, I can't wait!"

I know what I am really waiting for. I imagine the people of Israel waiting for their redeemer for all those years, so uncertain as to the time and the place and the nature of their deliverance. *O Come, Come Emmanuel. . . .*

December 18

Clothe your ministers with righteousness. . . . —EVENING PRAYER, p. 121

In New York, where I live now, there is tremendous wealth. On Fifth Avenue I see a blouse that would look nice on Patti and turns out to cost more than the monthly rent on our first apartment. As I look at the beautiful blouse and the shoppers, I think of the young couple making their weary way toward Bethlehem. She wears a simple cloak her mother made out of wool she spun herself. He wears an old brown poncholike garment, and they both shiver in the evening chill.

If he loved her as I love Patti—and surely he must have—then he must have felt that nothing was too good for her. That's how I feel. He probably wanted to see her in fine clothing, in lovely silks and soft fabrics imported from far away, things that nobody in Nazareth had. But Joseph was a working man, and this Holy Family would not be settling down in a king's house; they would live in a carpenter's house on what a carpenter earned. Did they sometimes feel a twinge of longing for lovely things? I suppose they did—they were human. But the priorities of the poor set the tone of their lives. And the priorities of the spirit set a holy order upon their house, one that rendered finery unnecessary.

December 19

. . . carry out in tranquillity the plan of salvation. . . .
—COLLECT AT THE EASTER VIGIL, p. 291

When John the Baptist was in prison awaiting execution, he sent a messenger to Jesus with one question: "Are you the one who is to come, or should we expect another?" At the time, John knew himself to be very near death. And so he sent to Jesus, saying, "Tell me my ministry has meant something. Tell me that my death is not in vain. Tell me that you are the one whose coming I preached, that in you the kingdom of God has come among us."

And Jesus' reply is full of love and respect: "Look at what is happening and at the part you have played in it," he says, "and have no doubt that it is really true." The political order did not disappear magically, to be replaced by another one. Earth did not turn into heaven. But the prophetic sight of John the Baptist saw the signs of the kingdom and preached them faithfully, and he lived to see the One who fulfilled them.

I see figures like John the Baptist as people as well as prophets, with very human feelings. I think of this strange young man—brash, impulsive, outrageous in his behavior— and I see young people I have known who were very like him. And I think of him in jail, knowing that he will die. And wanting to know from the one whose authority was everything to him that his life had meant something. Not too much to ask.

December 20

O God, you make us glad by the yearly festival of the birth of your only Son Jesus Christ. . . . —COLLECT FOR CHRISTMAS DAY, p. 212

Christmas is so full of traditions from so many places. Every family has its own. And when people are alone at this time of year, it's those family traditions they think about. They wish they were back home again, doing the Christmas things they used to do, the things they used to get so excited about when they were little. Or maybe they never had any of those things and just wish they had. No matter; they long for them just the same. We all do. People have always longed for home at this time of year.

The most popular Christmas story in the mid–nineteenth century was the same one we all love today: *A Christmas Carol.* When Charles Dickens came to America on a literary tour in the 1850s, people wouldn't let him read anything else. We have not changed; we all know deep in our souls that we need redemption. Like Scrooge, we have turned our backs on good things. We have beheld need and suffering and done nothing, too, and we long for the power to change ourselves, to change the suffering around us. This is not a Christian story, but Christians who read it cannot help recognizing the longing for Christ. The whole creation groans with longing, St. Paul said, and those of us who have been around for a while know it's the truth.

December 21

. . . perfectly and without doubt to believe . . . —COLLECT FOR
THE FEAST OF ST. THOMAS, p. 237

Modern Christians readily identify with Thomas the Doubter. Our culture does not reward a ready trust in things we can see, let alone in those we cannot. The task that Thomas could not perform is hard for us as well.

Or is it? I am not an astrophysicist, yet I trust the two Nobel prizewinners who have detected the presence of gravity waves in the universe. Modern people have to be like that; our technology is so complex that often we cannot even understand what leads to a scientific discovery, let alone duplicate it for ourselves. We rely on each other, then, for our truths.

Our approach to Christian truth follows the same path. We are formed in our belief, at least at the beginning, by the testimony of people we trust. Where there is no trust, belief is not likely to grow. The trust we have in the testimony of others starts us out on the road upon which we are likely to encounter Christ.

Thomas could not bring himself to trust in the testimony of his community, those men and women to whom he was closer than he was to anyone else. But Jesus was not content to leave him standing outside the circle like that. He helped Thomas's unbelief directly. He does the same for us.

December 22

Almighty God, you have given your only-begotten Son to take our nature upon him, and to be born . . . of a pure virgin. . . .
—COLLECT FOR THE FEAST OF THE NATIVITY, p. 213

We know that Joseph was concerned about his future with Mary because they were not yet married when she conceived. We know that he considered divorcing her, as the Jewish law allowed. So Jesus' life began in a difficult and even dangerous situation in that small town in Israel.

This difficulty provides us with what is perhaps the most important ethical lesson we can learn from the Nativity of Our Lord. Not only in his teaching but even in his birth, Jesus showed us that the way of life is a difficult way, and may even collide with the rules of polite society. We can never say that we have fulfilled righteousness because we have followed the rules; Jesus went beyond the rules to the mercy that often lies on the other side of them.

We might object to this idea, saying that the case of the Holy Family was a special case, a case involving a miracle, not like our cases. And so it was. But the purpose of miracles in God's plan is always to show us something about the way God works in the world, to show us the fullness of what God intends for us. None of us is the Blessed Mother or St. Joseph. But by showing us these people in the context of their world, a difficult one as ours is, the Scriptures challenge us to live up to the miracles we see in their pages.

December 23

*If anyone is in Christ, he is a new creation. . . . —NOONDAY
PRAYER,* p. 106

In recent days, of course, I've been focussing in my daily
prayer on the coming of Christ among us. What a surprise it
was to see him come into a poor family! Many in Israel had
hoped for a strong military leader who would liberate them
from their oppression by the Romans—it would not have
been easy for them to see their liberator in the tiny baby born
in a stable to Mary and Joseph. Most people didn't; most
people who were alive in those days passed him right by.
Most of the people who lived and died in the first century did
so without ever knowing about Jesus Christ. We sometimes
tell each other that our age is an age without faith, but there is
a sense in which *every* age has been faithless. Those who
believe have never been in the majority. It has always been
quite possible simply to ignore the spiritual part of life. Not
that much has changed.

   Establish some kind of spiritual discipline in your life,
though, and it's amazing how quickly you become unable to
imagine yourself without it. You begin to see the world through
its lens. The ordinary takes on meaning it didn't have before—
or rather, you begin to see that nothing is really ordinary. A
couple of poor people and their new baby in a barn—or the
hope of the whole human family. Depends on how you look
at it.

December 24

The Gifts of God for the People of God. —*THE HOLY EUCHARIST,* p. 364

I hope you are not shopping for gifts today; the stores will be tense, congested places until late tonight. We are busy people, though. We swore that we would be ready before today, but somehow our good intentions have run out of time. So out the door we go, into the traffic and the taped Christmas carols and the neon.

Let us not go grimly. There is only one reason why we give gifts at this holy season, and that is because of the great gift whose coming we observe tomorrow. Whatever the retailers think, the season does not end then. It begins. And buried within the winter of our hearts is the first green hint of new life. The great drama of our redemption, begun with the first breath of our first parents, is about to quicken its pace. A tiny baby boy, the child of poverty, is about to begin his hand-to-hand battle with Death on our behalf, and he is going to win.

> This little Babe, so few days old
> Is come to rifle Satan's fold.
> All Hell doth at his presence quake,
> Tho' he himself with cold doth shake;
> For in this weak, unarmed wise,
> The gates of Hell he will surprise.
> —*OLD ENGLISH CAROL*

December 25

. . . and receive power to become your children. —PREFACE OF
THE INCARNATION, THE NATIVITY OF OUR LORD p. 378

The centerpiece of our Christmas decorating is a nativity scene.
It began simply: a rough wooden shack with the mother,
father, and their baby. Later came a cow and a donkey. Then
some shepherds and their sheep. And a dog. Three kings and a
page, with camels. Over the years, more and more figures
have found their way to the stable. Friends would give us one,
or one of the children would spy one somewhere and lobby
for its purchase. Our kids loved to arrange the figures in the
creche, to act out the story over and over again, embellishing
it as they went.

It is a motley crowd that assembles each year at the little
stable. A recent visitor to my apartment was startled to see
two blue plastic Smurfs among the faithful. We love the diversity of this odd assortment of worshipers, and we leave the
nativity scene up long after "the season" is over. I smile as I
pass it on my way out the door each morning. There they
are—the people of God welcoming the new birth. They are as
diverse as the Church. They come from everywhere, and they
look different from one another, sometimes in startling ways.
But they are all at the stable for the same reason.

December 26

We give you thanks, O Lord of glory, for the example of the first martyr Stephen, who looked up to heaven and prayed for his persecutors to your Son Jesus Christ, who stands at your right hand. . . . —COLLECT FOR THE FEAST OF ST. STEPHEN, p. 237

Only one day after the celebration of Christ's birth, the Church venerates its first martyr: Stephen, the brave young follower of Christ who set the tone for Christian martyrdom forever by proclaiming his forgiveness of his murderers, just as Jesus himself had done on the cross. Following Jesus, he became like him, and the courage of his death has inspired artists to depict its pathos ever since.

The disciples had not wanted to hear much about Jesus' death while they were following him in his three-year ministry. Whenever he brought it up, they would try to talk him out of it. But Stephen went to his martyrdom filled with the joy of his identification with Christ, and at the end he saw a vision of the heavens opening to welcome him.

Few of us will be called upon to give up our lives for Christ as Stephen did. But all of us are called to live our lives in mindfulness of their ultimate meaning. Tomorrow is promised to none of us—we have only today in which to live, and we cannot know what today will require of us. A life lived in this daily knowledge is a victorious life.

December 27

. . . bring those near to us into his gracious presence. . . .
—COLLECT FOR THE FEAST OF ST. ANDREW, p. 185

Now, as always, in between the feast of the Nativity of our Lord and the turn of the calendar year, we grow introspective about our communal life. Who has died, who has been born, who has moved away—we take stock at this time of year.

On Christmas Eve, by candlelight, we read the old story of that one little community, the Holy Family. We see the cast of characters we remember so well, and our memories go back in time, back to our own families, these families that have in so important a way made us what we are. Through the soft lens of time we see them: our parents, our brothers and sisters, our grandparents. Husbands and wives. Children. Friends.

Nostalgic. Sentimental. But all of us who live in community know that the pastels in which some of us want to remember our families in the past are not really the truth, don't we? Or at least, they're not the whole truth. We did learn about love from our families, to be sure, but in that crucible of our personalities we also learned about jealousy, about rivalry and competition, about disappointment, about loss. These days there is much discussion of the dysfunctional family, but we know that there is a sense in which all families are dysfunctional. We don't just bring the good things into our homes. We bring all of ourselves, the good and the bad, our loves and our hates, our virtues and all of our faults.

December 28

Receive, we beseech thee, into the arms of thy mercy all innocent victims. . . . —*COLLECT FOR THE FEAST OF THE HOLY INNOCENTS, p. 186*

Anyone who has loved a child reacts with great emotion to the idea of *any* child suffering. The innocence and beauty of a little child is the best argument I know for the goodness of creation.

That is why this story of the wicked king who slaughtered the little children touches us so. I know of a woman, now well into her retirement years, who never misses church on this day. She lost her six-year-old son over fifty years ago to diphtheria. I know of another man who lost his son, struck down in the prime of his young manhood by a drunken driver; he never misses, either. Both of these people have accepted their terrible losses, but both know that they will never be the same again. Something irreplaceable has been lost to the world in the death of a child. Something unnatural has occurred.

The slaughter of the innocents—the children of any era, not just first-century Palestine—calls us to embrace all living children and feel responsibility for their care. Their innocence, and the right they have to that innocence, forbids us to think of any child as someone else's problem. Not just precious to their parents, they are precious to the human family. The loss of even one is a slaughter.

December 29

All glorious is the princess as she enters. . . . —*PSALM 45:14,*
p. 648

In my office are pictures and objects that bring to mind the people that I love. Wonderful, funny things from the kids: my old tennis racquet with a hole in the middle of it, *bronzed* (a gift from our youngest). A picture of our daughter's wedding in Hawaii. Pictures of the family when the children were little. Some wonderful lithographs by a Japanese artist whom I know and love.

The largest photograph I have in my office is of Patti on our wedding day. There she is, posed in the middle of yards and yards of lace, holding her flowers. It's a beautiful picture. The odd thing is that she has changed so very little, yet is has been so many years. I cannot imagine where all those years have gone.

Patti was a beautiful bride. Our daughter used to love to look at that picture of her mother, small and young and surrounded by lace, splendidly adorned for our wedding. But her real adornment was not that complicated dress, however magical it was. It was her own rock-bottom goodness and strong sense of self, those things that caused me to love her in the first place. Isaiah calls that adornment "the robe of righteousness." I think that's probably why Patti seems to me not to have changed at all. She's still wearing it.

December 30

For to your faithful people, O Lord, life is changed, not ended. . . . —PREFACE FOR THE COMMEMORATION OF THE DEAD, p. 349

They wear white robes. They stand around the throne of God and sing eternal hymns. They are very different from what they were when we knew them. All of their tears have been dried. Those who have died in pain and sorrow are purified. Their suffering has cleansed them.

To all of us must come the loss of a person we have loved dearly. Perhaps it has already come to you. We pity the dying for their loss of this beautiful earth and the precious gift of life, and we pity ourselves for the new and aching emptiness of our grief. But it really does comfort us to know that the death of the body is simply an event in our larger lives, that the love of God that sustained us through life does not desert us after death, but endures.

Do they really wear white robes? Is there really a throne as it says in the Revelation to John? Such concrete questions miss the point. We don't know anything about what heaven is like. But we do know what it means. Heaven is the family of God coming home at last.

December 31

. . . maker of heaven and earth, of all that is, seen and unseen . . . —THE NICENE CREED, p. 358

The old year is represented in cartoons as an old man. The new one is a chubby toddler, wearing a banner with the year on it across his chest, Miss America–style. As the grandfather of just such a young person, I think the symbolism of this child is perfect. Our new year is completely potential. Nothing has yet been written on it; it is as innocent as a child. Our year begins in the darkness of winter, not in the burgeoning birthing of spring, or the abundance of the harvest season. Our year begins without a physical sign of its newness. The newness of the year exists on our calendars and in our hearts before it shows itself in the weather. What light there is, it is up to us to see.

Jesus came to transform darkness into light. The world into which he came did not show the transformation at first, either. It started in people's hearts before it showed at all. Its reality there produced the physical way in which it showed, and the revelation of it snowballed; people listened and believed and were healed. Others saw the healing and believed and preached. Still others heard the preaching and were healed and empowered. The cycle of new life quickened, and the invisible rapidly became visible.

Whose
Service
is
Perfect
Freedom

COPAL C

ABOUT THE AUTHOR

The Most Rev. Edmond L. Browning was elected 24th Presiding Bishop and Primate of the Episcopal Church at the church's 1985 General Convention while he was serving as Bishop of Hawaii. He was installed in January of 1986 for a term of 12 years.

As Presiding Bishop he is president of the House of Bishops and chief pastor to 2.5 million Episcopalians in the United States, as well as Latin America, the Caribbean, and Asia. The Episcopal Church in the USA is one of 33 autonomous provinces of the 70-million-member worldwide Anglican Communion.

Edmond Lee Browning was born March 11, 1929, in Corpus Christi, Texas, the son of Edmond Lucian Browning and Cora Mae Lee. He attended the University of the South, Sewanee, Tennessee, receiving his B.A. in 1952 and his B.D. in 1954.

In 1953, Browning married Patricia Alline Sparks, also a native of Texas, a fine arts graduate of Stephens College in Missouri, who at that time was a student at George Peabody Teacher's College in Nashville, Tennessee.

Browning was ordained to the diaconate in 1954 and to the priesthood in 1955 by The Rt. Rev. E. H. Jones. He served as assistant at Good Shepherd, Corpus Christi, 1954–56; rector of Redeemer, Eagle Pass, Texas, 1956–59; priest-in-charge of All Souls, Machinato, Okinawa, 1959–63. From 1963 to 1965 Edmond and Patti Browning studied at the Language School in Kobe, Japan, before returning to Okinawa to serve St. Matthew's in Oruku until 1968. He was archdeacon of Okinawa, 1967–68, and on January 5, 1968, he was consecrated Bishop of Okinawa.

In 1971 the Browning family, which by this time included four boys and a girl, left Okinawa for Europe, where Bishop Browning served as bishop-in-charge of the Convocation of American Churches in Europe. In 1974 they returned to the United States when he was appointed Executive for National and World Mission at the Episcopal Church Center in New York. After two years he was elected Bishop of Hawaii, where he served 10 years, until his election as Presiding Bishop.

During his years as Presiding Bishop, Browning has made it a priority to listen to the people of the church to determine how he can strengthen or enable church members in their understanding of their mission. Under Browning's leadership this effort has been continued by the Executive Council.

An International Episcopate

The Presiding Bishop's ministry has included a very strong international dimension since he was first called to Okinawa in 1965. This commitment has deepened through his extensive visitations, including ecumenical conversations and official visits to sister churches of the Anglican Communion throughout the world.

In the last few years Browning has traveled globally, particularly to the partner churches of the Anglican Communion. He has also visited many of the world's trouble spots as an advocate for peace and justice and to witness to the solidarity of the Episcopal Church with those who suffer.

Through his travels he has engaged in wide-ranging conversations and consultations with spiritual and political leaders in an effort to advance mutual understanding and to articulate the position of the church on issues of social justice. As a result of these conversations, Browning has also put before the Episcopal Church the vision of the wider church and the role of the church in the world.

Bishop Browning is currently a member of the General Board of the National Council of Churches of Christ in the United States of America, and a member of the Central Committee of the World Council of Churches. Within the Anglican Communion he has served as a member of the Standing Committee of the Primates and on the three-person team that represents the Episcopal Church on the Anglican Consultative Council.